Pauline Periwinkle
and Progressive Reform in Dallas

NUMBER SEVENTY-THREE:
The Centennial Series
of the Association of Former Students,
Texas A&M University

Pauline Periwinkle

and Progressive Reform in Dallas

■ ■ ■ ■ ■ ■ ■ ■ ■ ■ ■

JACQUELYN MASUR
McELHANEY

Texas A&M University Press
College Station

All columns from the *Dallas Morning News*
reprinted with permission of A. H. Belo Corporation

The paper used in this book meets the minimum requirements
of the American National Standard for Permanence
of Paper for Printed Library Materials, Z39.48-1984.
Binding materials have been chosen for durability.
∞

Library of Congress Cataloging-in-Publication Data

McElhaney, Jacquelyn Masur.
     Pauline Periwinkle and progressive reform in Dallas /
Jacquelyn Masur McElhaney.
          p.   cm. — (Centennial series of the Association of
Former Students, Texas A&M University ; no. 73)
     Includes bibliographical references and index.
     ISBN 0-89096-800-4
     1. Periwinkle, Pauline.   2. Women journalists—Texas—
Biography.   3. Women journalists—Political activities—
Texas—Dallas—History.   4. Progressivism (United States
politics)—Case studies.   5. Dallas (Tex.)—Politics and gov-
ernment.   6. Social action—Texas—Dallas—History.
I. Title.   II. Series.
PN4874.P435M34   1998
070'.92   97-32344
[B]—dc21   CIP

For John,

Scott, & Vicky

with love

Contents

Illustrations

Preface

Writing a biography imposes certain obligations upon an author: to bring to life an individual that few readers have known personally; to place that person in the context of his or her times; to determine how the times affected the person; and, finally, to assess what sort of legacy he or she left. Meeting these obligations is made easier when an author can determine a subject's beliefs, views, or opinions as expressed in letters, diaries, and written reminiscences or through interviews with people who have known the subject. Nineteenth-century subjects who were literate generally left a paper trail that can be found by a diligent searcher with the help of descendants or knowledgeable librarians. Twentieth-century subjects have been less dutiful in permanently recording their innermost thoughts, thanks to the telephone, computer, and fax machine. How different the task will be for the biographers of the twenty-first century, who will find more faxed memos and floppy disks than descriptive handwritten letters and diaries of earlier eras. The emotional connection that an author can sometimes make with a subject when holding a personal letter or diary may prove more elusive.

Doris Kearns Goodwin understood the emotional connection well when she observed: "We rummage through letters, memos, pictures, memories, diaries, and conversations in an attempt to develop our subject's character from youth to manhood to death. Yet, in the end, if we are honest with ourselves, the best we can offer is a partial rendering, a subjective portrait of the subject from a particular angle of vision shaped as much by our own biography—our attitudes, perceptions, and feelings toward the subject—as by the raw material themselves."[1] I now better understand and appreciate Kearns's view of the difficulties in keeping one's feelings from affecting the final product.

In 1985, a chance discovery of one of Isadore Miner Callaway's weekly columns in the *Dallas Morning News* piqued my curiosity. Who was this woman writing at the turn of the century in such a modern voice, pointing out with such wit, clarity, and logic the need for Dallas to become a more liveable, humane place and urging women's clubs to work to accomplish that goal? I wanted to know more about the person with whom I felt an almost instant affinity. Isadore Miner Callaway's optimism and willingness to speak her mind seemed extraordinary. Her words reached across a century to make me laugh aloud at their pungency. Her ability to argue with such intelligence for positions that were either controversial or unthinkable, or both, was remarkable. After years of searching out the facts of her life, I was convinced that she deserved a biography that would demonstrate what a unique woman she had been.

Writing a biography of Pauline Periwinkle, the nom de plume of *Dallas Morning News* journalist Isadore Miner Callaway, did pose problems. Not only did Mrs. Callaway have no children to perpetuate her memory, none of her copious correspondence and other personal papers survived. The reasons for this are unclear, though Isadore's mother, Maria LaMoreaux, alleged the Mr. Callaway had Isadore's trunk containing all her papers and her will burned after her death. As Mrs. LaMoreaux had dealt very unfairly with Isadore's inheritance from her father, Mason, a soldier who died just after the Civil War, and then attempted to claim a share of Isadore's estate, her statements may be suspect.[2] While the clubwomen of Texas memorialized Isadore Miner Callaway with a Periwinkle Day set aside each spring to plant periwinkles, and local Dallas clubwomen started a scholarship fund in her name, she was seldom mentioned in histories of Dallas women and their contributions to the city.

What were the circumstances that produced such a woman? Now, more than a decade later, I have found some answers, though the picture remains incomplete. Some sources of information simply no longer exist, thanks to the loss of her personal papers. A valuable resource for many historians—someone who knew the subject personally—came tantalizingly close. In my case it was one of the nieces Isadore took into her home as a child. By the time I learned that she was still living, however, she could no longer recall any of her past.

Without letters, diaries, or contemporaries to humanize Mrs. Callaway, I returned to the most obvious paper trail, the words that had started my search: her weekly columns for the *Dallas Morning News*. To write of her life without including her columns would be an enormous disservice. Accordingly, this biography contains in a few short chapters all that

I could uncover about her life and what shaped her character and personality. The remainder consists of columns that I believe capture her unique talents and contributions.

Isadore Miner Callaway's writings as Pauline Periwinkle deserve recognition for their role in helping improve women's lives and bring about municipal reforms. Her columns helped drag Dallas, not always willingly, into the twentieth century. But in the decades following her death, the significance of her work gradually faded from the community's collective memory. Consequently, she became just another "active clubwoman" from the past, her picture staring out from a page of the history of the women's clubs. Yet her life and work constitute a remarkable chapter in the history of Dallas and the success of the women's club movement across Texas during the Progressive Era. As the twenty-first century approaches, the time has come to acknowledge the debt.

There are other debts. Historians generally build upon the work of those who go before them, along with the advice of those around them. In my case, there have been several generous individuals who have made my task easier. The first owed my thanks are fellow historians Dr. Elizabeth York Enstam, Dr. Judith McArthur, and Dr. Michael Hazel, who have provided invaluable guidance and encouragement from the beginning. They read multiple chapter drafts with discernment and made immensely helpful suggestions, as well as supplying material about my subject that they encountered doing their own research. Dr. Nancy Baker Jones and Dr. Debbie Cottrell offered advice and encouragement when it was needed. Descendants of relatives of Isadore Sutherland Miner Callaway, especially Mrs. Joel Sutherland Rhoads of Fairfax, Virginia, Mrs. Kathleen Crawford Mayne of Austin, and Anne Tyler Fleming of Dallas, have supplied assorted correspondence, family mementos, and several family stories. Jean Davis of Battle Creek has done yeoman duty on my behalf, combing local records in Michigan libraries and courthouses. Mrs. Gene Crawford of Rockwall supplied letters which give unique insights into Isadore's early years in Dallas.

The assistance of dedicated librarians Marlene Steele in Battle Creek, Michigan; Susan Steinke in Dayton, Ohio; Robert Shaddy, director of the Ward M. Canaday Center at the Carlson Library, and Sandra Bell, University of Toledo; and Sandra Gates of the Missouri Valley Special Collections in the Kansas City Public Library eliminated the need for travel. Dolores Smith, Ann Hurley, and Donna Christian of the Local

History Section of the Toledo Public Library in Ohio; Tanja Rushing of the Sherman Public Library in Texas; Dawn Letson of the Blagg-Huey Library at Texas Woman's University; Cindy Swanson, director, and Elizabeth Edrich in the Women's History and Resource Center of the General Federation of Women's Clubs in Washington, D.C., assisted me with every request. The staff of the Adventist Heritage Center at Andrews University in Berrien Springs, Michigan, and Ms. Helen Whiting at the St. Clair County (Michigan) Family History Group supplied valuable data. The librarians at Southwest Adventist College in Keene, Texas, were quite helpful, while Dorian Ruml of Worcester, Massachusetts, provided valuable insights. The unfailing good will and assistance of Carol Roark, Marvin Stone, Joan Dobson, and Cindy Smolonik at the Texas/Dallas Collection of the Dallas Public Library; Mary Ellen Holt at the Dallas Historical Society; and Dr. Gerald Saxon and Marcelle Hull at the Special Collections Library at the University of Texas at Arlington made my research more productive than it would have been without their interest. Dr. Darwin Payne of Southern Methodist University shared his knowledge of hard to find details of Dallas history. Dr. David Farmer, director of the DeGolyer Library at Southern Methodist University, and his staff were diligent in searching for obscure information. The Southern Methodist University Central University librarians, especially Linda Sellers, have been unfailingly helpful and tolerant of my residency in their microfilm room for nearly a decade. Those members of the Department of History at Southern Methodist University who assisted me in securing materials are also acknowledged with deep gratitude. Finally, to my husband John, who listened to countless drafts of chapters read aloud after dinner, and to Scott and Vicky, who each grew up, finished graduate school, and married before "Mom's book" was finished, my grateful appreciation for your love and support. The assistance of everyone mentioned notwithstanding, I accept responsibility for any errors which may be found in the manuscript.

Introduction

Although the nom de plume "Pauline Periwinkle" might suggest a prim Victorian writer of romantic novels or poetry, Isadore Miner Callaway, the remarkable journalist who used it, did something quite different. Arriving in Dallas in 1893, she went to work for the *Dallas Morning News* and turned her energy and talent to helping organize and promote various women's groups, including the Texas Woman's Press Association, the Texas Equal Rights Association, and the inaugural Woman's Congress held at the State Fair of Texas. She even addressed the men of the Texas Press Association, a first for them, discussing the topic, "What Can Be Done to Improve the Average Woman's and Children's Departments in Newspapers?"[1]

Her interest in improving the *Dallas Morning News*'s offerings to women and children was rewarded in 1896 when she was made the first woman's editor of the *News* and given a page titled "The Woman's Century" to fill once a week. Her first column on April 15, 1896, was bylined "Pauline Periwinkle," a name that would become known in households in Dallas and the rest of Texas for the next twenty years. The columns helped prod Progressive Era women's clubs to become involved in reform efforts in their towns and cities. Pauline Periwinkle's Woman's Century page was the first such woman's page in Texas newspapers for it highlighted the work of women's clubs in civic improvement, although many newspapers had society pages and reporters. Among these were Kate Friend of the *Waco Times Herald* and "Harriott Russell" (Hallie Rienzi Flint) of the *Houston Post*. These writers added their distinctive voices to women's activities and club news reporting, but without the tenure or following of Pauline Periwinkle.[2]

Pauline Periwinkle made it clear from the outset that her readers would no longer be fed a strict diet of social events and fashion advice. Instead, she wrote, "I am a firm believer that good accrues from woman's familiarizing herself with affairs that affect her immediate community first, her state next, and her country ultimately—good both to the woman and the object of her inquiry."[3] She viewed women's clubs as an ideal vehicle for familiarizing women with the conditions in their communities that needed their attention. She encouraged existing clubs to expand their narrow focus as study or literary clubs and become instruments of civic change. At the same time, she urged women to create new clubs and coordinate their efforts through a state and national federation.

As club work took hold in Dallas and the rest of the state, Pauline Periwinkle and the Woman's Century page became a source of information, encouragement, and publicity for a myriad of activities initiated by women. During her twenty years at the *News,* Pauline Periwinkle's columns reported on and actively supported efforts in Dallas to secure a Carnegie Library, kindergartens for public schools, a juvenile court system for the city, parks for children, a local pure food law, police matrons, a garbage tax, and a pure water supply. Statewide efforts for such measures as a pure food and drug law, a women's college, and woman suffrage received her incisive coverage. Other columns would describe efforts by women's clubs in cities across the country, the difficulties endured by working women and children, the desirability of electing women to school boards, and the need for higher education for women. She reported the progress of women in public life throughout the country and the positions of the General Federation of Women's Clubs on issues of national concern. And she occasionally offered humorous assessments of the latest fashion craze or the attitudes of men toward women and vice versa.

Pauline Periwinkle took an active part in some of the organizations she wrote about, but she believed her greatest contribution was her column, noting in 1900 that "printer's ink judicially applied to the club idea is a great lubricator and will make it run further and smoother than anything I know."[4] She was willing to apply that ink liberally, as she wrote in 1909 to the president of the Texas Federation of Women's Clubs: "I will do anything in my line, such as giving publicity and such little pen influence I wield to any good cause you wish furthered." She later remarked that she felt she was more effective "as a sort of silent partner, though not silent when it came to boosting . . . plans and measures."[5]

Pauline Periwinkle brought intelligence and political savvy to her work, and she helped unify Texas women behind the forward-looking women leaders of the Texas Federation of Women's Clubs. In the process, she left a remarkable and valuable resource for those interested in the emergence of Progressive Era reform efforts in Texas. It is difficult to imagine how successful many early reform efforts of Dallas and Texas women's clubs might have been without the advocacy and encouragement her columns provided.[6]

While Isadore Miner Callaway claimed only the ability to publicize the work of others, she was in reality a driving force behind the establishment of the Woman's Congress, the Dallas Federation of Women's Clubs, the Equal Suffrage Club of Dallas, the Dallas Woman's Forum, and the Texas Woman's Press Association.[7] As a longtime acquaintance described her: "she was so modest and unassuming about it all. . . . It mattered not how hard she worked for a result, she never claimed the credit. She planned and organized and worked, and then, when the hardest of the fight was over, she stepped aside to allow others to fill the offices while she stood behind them with encouragement and advice."[8]

Who was this journalist whose work affected so many lives? She was born near Battle Creek, Michigan, in 1863. Her father died from injuries sustained in the Civil War and her mother remarried a short time later. Because her stepfather was, as she described it, "rather inconvenient . . . indeed so much so that I have never lived at home with any peace," she moved in with her Aunt Rose, who lived in St. Clair, Michigan.[9] Her aunt and uncle were Seventh Day Adventists, as her mother and father had been, so Isadore grew up with the teachings of that denomination. A difficult childhood was made more so by her mother's actions: she sold the property Isadore and her brother had inherited from their father and withheld the pension money due them as children of a Civil War veteran. Despite such unfair treatment, Isadore emerged an independent and resourceful adult with a large capacity for empathy and compassion. She was very articulate, as demonstrated when, at age fourteen, she petitioned the probate court for information about her inheritance. Her writing ability would ultimately provide a means to self-sufficiency. Following graduation from high school, she was hired by the Seventh Day Adventist Publishing Association. The publishing house was closely allied with the famous Battle Creek Sanitarium established by Dr. John Harvey Kellogg, whose brother founded the Kellogg Cereal Company.

At the publishing house, Isadore wrote for the *Review and Herald* newspaper and later *Good Health* magazine, which focused on health matters. She also met and married James Miner, a fellow worker, who proved to be an unsupportive and possessive husband. She worked with highly motivated women such as Dr. Kate Lindsay, the first registered woman physician in the first sanitarium in the United States, and Eva Giles, who later edited the monthly publication of the Michigan Federation of Women's Clubs. By 1890, Isadore had become an editor and had taken up causes such as women's rights.

Isadore left Battle Creek, and her husband, in 1891 to work for the *Toledo Commercial* in Toledo, Ohio, but she found her prospects for advancement lagging after two years. She then moved to Dallas, where she went to work for the *Dallas Morning News* in 1893. Her reasons for moving to Dallas are not clear, although her mother and stepfather, from whom she had been estranged, had lived in Dallas for eighteen years. Isadore apparently had forgiven her mother's actions, for they renewed their ties and Isadore moved in next door. She remained a Dallas resident until her death in 1916.

From a late-twentieth-century perspective, many might find certain limitations and shortcomings in Isadore's vision and perspective. For her era, however, many of her views—for instance, supporting charity for the "needy poor" only, arguing that "children of negative heredity and training should early be taught obedience and self-control [since] children born of rebellion and lawlessness are anarchist at birth," and bemoaning the latest literature and motion pictures, which she characterized as "trashy"—reflected the current thinking of many social reformers throughout the nation.[10] Isadore's pseudoscientific characterizations of the Chinese and Negro races and even her support for denying the admission of colored clubs to the General Federation of Women's Clubs, despite the efforts of Jane Addams of Hull House, were not unusual among other reform-minded Texas clubwomen. Her views of "the Negro" were southern and stereotypical ("predominance of emotion in make-up, indifferent to reason"), and she wrote of African Americans so infrequently that it was obvious that their problems were not the focus of her attention.[11] She was no doubt quite forward-looking in advocating reforms for Texas, but she publicly never questioned the attitudes that prevailed in the region toward the minority community. Her private opinions, if ever recorded, did not survive.

Pauline Periwinkle left no diaries or private papers and had no children to perpetuate her memory. No books were written about her, but she left a significant legacy in the form of twenty years of weekly newspaper columns. They were a source of inspiration and encouragement, and a strong assertive voice for a generation of Texas women. There can be no doubt that she emboldened women to speak out and work for change in their communities and their own lives. Nearly a century later, much of what she wrote remains insightful, for a keen understanding of human nature informs her writing. Her commonsense, straightforward observations and sly sense of humor can still educate and entertain the modern reader.

Pauline Periwinkle
and Progressive Reform in Dallas

I

■ ■ ■

Women Journalists
and Reform Movements

A reformer and feminist who was separated from her husband when she arrived in Dallas in 1893, Isadore Sutherland Miner soon went to work at the *Dallas Morning News* as the first woman member of its editorial staff.[1] Mrs. Miner, who divorced James Miner in 1895 and married W. A. Callaway in 1900, wasted no time finding a small coterie of women in Dallas who shared her concern for improving women's lives as well as the community in which they lived. She offered her services as a writer to publicize their efforts and her knowledge of women's club work elsewhere as a guide. "[She] was a feminist, and of the militant kind," wrote Alonzo Wasson, a fellow journalist who joined the *News* in 1896. "The popular reactions among the women were not always of an approving kind. Frequently there were liftings of eyebrows out on South Ervay, where Mrs. Minor [*sic*] spent much of her time in quest of social items," he reported.[2]

There is no way to determine how knowledgeable Dallas women might have been about the work of women reformers and journalists elsewhere in the 1890s. Given the wide circulation of women's magazines and newspapers, many were certain to have been familiar with the writings of Elizabeth Cady Stanton for woman suffrage or to have read the columns and

Isadore Callaway. Courtesy Joel Sutherland Rhoads

books written by popular journalists Jane Cunningham Croly and Sara Willis Parton. But what Dallas women could not have known was how Isadore Miner would become a vocal advocate for reform and prove enormously helpful to them.[3]

When Isadore chose the nom de plume "Pauline Periwinkle," she followed an established tradition of earlier newspaper journalists such as Croly's "Jennie June" and Parton's "Fanny Fern." Even before women used alliterative pen names for their bylines, however, they had been involved in newspaper work. As early as the Revolutionary War era, wives and mothers had helped the men in the family in their print shops, where early newspapers were produced. Margaret Craper of the *Massachusetts Gazette and News Letter* and Mary Katherine Goddard of the *Maryland Journal* were among the earliest women in the country to help publish newspapers.[4]

The job of publishing a newspaper did not mean these women were actually writing news articles or offering commentary about events, although we can assume that some did. For the most part, notions of propriety in the colonies constrained most women from offering opinions in public about almost any subject. Consequently, few women wrote or spoke publicly of their views. Among the notable early exceptions were Puritan religious teacher Anne Hutchinson, poet Anne Bradstreet, and Quaker women, all of whom historian Glenna Matthews includes among "America's first public women."[5]

In the early nineteenth century a few women began to utilize printer's ink to promote their views, since general circulation newspapers either ignored women's activities or subjected them to criticism.[6] Frances Wright, one of the earliest newspaper women, edited the New Harmony *Free Enquirer* in 1828 and advocated that women seek a remedy for the "unjust disabilities to which law and custom subjected [them]." Other publications, such as the *Amulet and Ladies' Literary and Religious Chronicle,* the *Female Advocate,* and the *Friend of Virtue* followed, each edited or staffed by women and exhorting females to work for moral reform.[7] Women devoted to particular causes such as women's rights, abolition, and temperance—including Jane Grey Swisshelm, Lydia Maria Child, and Amelia Bloomer—edited newspapers, and this allowed them to express their unrestrained opinions and sentiments. Response to their publications was seldom positive. Swisshelm described the general reaction to the first edition of her *Saturday Visiter* [*sic*]: "The American eagle swooned and

W. A. Callaway. Courtesy Joel Sutherland Rhoads

fell off his perch" at the audacity of a woman editing a political newspaper, while newspapermen complained, "She is a man, all but the pantaloons."[8]

Four decades later Isadore Miner would mimic the tactics of Swisshelm, who used biblical quotations to turn the tables on those who opposed women stepping outside of their "sphere" of home and family. Swisshelm insisted in 1859 that a woman had the right to "meddle" in politics despite the biblical injunction "Let women keep silence in church." In her view, since women in all branches of the church are expected to sing as loud as they are able, "our sex does not disqualify us for delivering any message we may feel that the Lord has sent by us."[9] In 1897, Isadore observed that those "who are most stringent for woman's separate sphere" and "prone to fling at us all sorts of irrelevant scripture" might consult the biblical verse in 2 Kings 21:13: "And I will wipe Jerusalem as a man wipeth a dish, wiping it and turning it upside down." Her interpretation of the verse was straightforward: "if it means anything at all it means that man is the divinely appointed dishwasher, ordained from the beginning to wrestle with the pots and pans. . . ."[10]

Even before Miner's birth in 1863 other women had channeled their journalistic aspirations into more than two dozen publications designed to promote the home and family. Among the most widely circulated was *Ladies Magazine,* which merged in 1836 with *Godey's Lady's Book,* founded in 1830 and edited by Sarah Josepha Hale for forty years. Others such as *Graham's* and *Peterson's* filled their respective pages with fashion coverage, household advice, and guidance concerning feminine decorum and socially acceptable pursuits.[11] These publications and the women who worked for them purposely kept their distance from the reform journals and their controversial subject matter. Hale advised readers of *Ladies Magazine* of Boston that "this semi-monthly publication [New York *Amulet*] is devoted to the work of checking Infidelity and Intemperance. . . . There may be ladies among us inclined to infidelity and intemperance, and if so we advise them immediately to subscribe."[12] Newspapers such as the *Lowell Offering,* produced by the factory girls of Lowell, Massachusetts, in 1840, and the *Health Journal and Advocate of Physiological Reform,* established in 1840 by Mary Gove Nichols, reflected the unique perspectives of their writers.[13]

A few women found careers writing for newspapers in large cities before the Civil War. Best known of this group was Margaret Fuller, who in 1840 became coeditor with Ralph Waldo Emerson of the literary magazine *The Dial*. In 1844 Horace Greeley hired Fuller to write for his *New York Tribune*. She is believed to be the first woman ever hired as a member of the staff of a major newspaper, although she worked from her home instead of in the offices of the paper. Greeley encouraged Fuller to write for women readers, and she obliged him with articles about literature and the arts. Her interest in broader social issues, however, produced articles about prisons and immigrants' problems.

Committed to expanding women's rights, Fuller wrote *Woman in the Nineteenth Century* in 1845. An outspoken volume for the times, it helped lay the groundwork for the women's rights meeting at Seneca Falls in 1848. In 1846 Fuller went to Italy to report on the battles for unification among the many states for the *Tribune*. The trip bestowed Fuller with the distinction of being the first American woman foreign correspondent. Her career was cut short, however, when she died in a shipwreck as she was returning to the United States.[14]

In the 1850s newspapers began to hire a few women as correspondents to write columns from the nation's capital. These early newspaper columnists often did double duty, working for a Washington paper and also sending copy to other major city newspapers. Sara Clarke Lippincott, the "Grace Greenwood" of a popular series of letters that appeared widely in the 1840s, was one of the first women hired to work for the *National Era* in Washington and send copy to the *Saturday Evening Post* in Philadelphia in 1850. Mary Abigail Dodge wrote for the *National Era* and served as correspondent for the *Congregationalist* in Boston. Outside Washington, the *New York Evening Express* employed Ann S. Stephens as an editorial writer and literary critic.[15]

By midcentury a gradual public acceptance of women who worked for newspapers enabled more women to make public their observations and opinions about the world. Although many chose flowery alliterative pen names such as Fanny Fern, Grace Greenwood, and Minnie Myrtle to conceal their identity, they also chose to write about social problems, especially those faced by women. While some focused their attention on fashion, book reviews, marriage, and family duties, others objected to the constraints society placed on all women and advocated the expansion of women's rights.[16] Jane Grey Swisshelm minced no words in expressing her views about the fate of women:

They plough, harrow, reap, dig, make hay, rake, bind grain, thrash, chop wood, milk, churn, do anything that is hard work, physical labor, and who says anything against it? But let one presume to use her mental powers—let her aspire to turn editor, public speaker, doctor, lawyer—take up any profession or avocation which is deemed honorable and requires talent, and O! bring cologne, get a cambric kerchief and feather fan, unloose his corsets and take off his cravat! What a fainting fit Mr. Propriety has taken! Just to think that "one of the deah creatures"—the heavenly angels, should forsake the sphere—woman's sphere—to mix with the wicked strife of this wicked world![17]

Two other women whose work appeared at this time, Jane Cunningham Croly and Sara Willis Parton, illustrate contrasting viewpoints and styles that women could find in the newspaper. Jane Cunningham Croly, who used the pen name Jennie June, began her career in 1855 at the *New York Herald*. Her early columns consisted of fashion, beauty, and entertainment advice. Later she offered guidance for creating a happy marriage, home, and family, including sewing manuals and a cookbook for young wives who were unable to afford servants. Because she sent duplicate copies of her columns to newspapers in New Orleans, Richmond, Baltimore, and Louisville, she is considered the originator of the syndicated column. She edited *Demorest's Illustrated Magazine of Fashions* for twenty-seven years and published several books.

Croly was married to newspaper editor David Croly, had five children, and enjoyed an active social life. She spent mornings with her family, then went to the office to do her work, often until late at night. Her columns about fashion, marriage, and family life were widely read, but she also wrote of expanding opportunities for women who needed to work. She supported a woman's desire to have a career if there was economic necessity, favoring indoor work such as teaching, medicine, waiting tables, or typesetting. Nevertheless, she remained convinced that "a good wife, good mother and helper in the maintenance of the social order was more important to the race than the practice of any profession." She urged married women, however, to expand their intellectual horizons and become involved in civic affairs.[18]

Her writing style was motherly and practical, with a touch of exasperation, as when she advised young women of marriageable age: "this eternal talk about *beaux* is excessively vulgar, and so stupid as to deprive those who make a habit of it of half the charm which belongs to their youth. It is sickening to see the simpering, and hear the silly twaddle which girls talk *at* a young man if he happens to be in their vicinity."[19] Croly's enormous popularity set the format and tone for the woman's departments of major newspapers in subsequent years.

Despite her popularity as a newspaper columnist, Croly is best remembered for establishing Sorosis, probably the first club for women in the country, in 1869. The founding of Sorosis was the direct result of her being denied the right to attend an 1868 banquet for Charles Dickens sponsored by the New York press because she was a woman, even though she was also a noted journalist. Her interest in seeing the growing number of clubs for women exchange ideas eventually led to the creation of the General Federation of Women's Clubs in 1889. She then wrote the *History of the Woman's Club Movement* in 1898, chronicling the birth and early development of the club movement. Although Croly was not an active worker for suffrage, she did reverse her earlier reluctance to support political equality and came to admire Susan B. Anthony.[20] Jennie June was among the most successful and well-known women journalists of the nineteenth century. She urged women to work hard to become competent in whatever endeavors they attempted, espousing equality of effort to secure equality of pay. Yet most of her career was devoted to observing and upholding the conventions of polite society.

Isadore Miner grew up during Jennie June's greatest popularity and seems to have read and absorbed some of Croly's perspective and style. For example, Croly viewed the woman's club as "the school of the middle-aged woman . . . [which] has put an interest into her life which it had never previously possessed." Miner echoed the sentiment in 1899 when she observed that the "chief aim of the club is to get women to think. When thought is aroused, at once they ask themselves, 'what can I do?' and soon are demanding their part of the world's work."[21] Both columnists satirized the extremes of women's fashion, with Croly's Jennie June taking aim at hoops, crinolines, and bifurcated trousers and Miner's Pauline Periwinkle objecting to the use of Texas horn toads on hat pins. "Another Bug-Eater Doomed by Fashion—Horned Toad to Hobnob with Dead Birds on Hats of Women" trumpeted her column lead.[22]

In contrast to Croly's more conventional stance, Sara Willis Parton, who used the pen name "Fanny Fern," offered a different perspective to her readers, one shaped by the harsh circumstances of her adult life. The child of a proper Boston family who believed in a strict religious upbringing, she had resisted their efforts to make her obedient and pious. Her writing ability was evident even as a schoolgirl at Catharine Beecher's Hartford Female Seminary. Her marriage to Charles Harrington Eldredge was a love match, but it ended after nine years with his death. When Parton failed at supporting herself and her two daughters, she received only minimal and grudging financial support from her father and her husband's family. In desperate economic straits and coerced by her father, she married Samuel Farrington, a widower with two children. A jealous and possessive man, Farrington publicly humiliated her by advertising their separation and her untrustworthiness in a Boston newspaper. They were divorced after four years of a loveless marriage.

The end of Parton's second marriage left her again in need of money, so she submitted satirical sketches to three small Boston magazines for publication. Her writing was unlike any seen from a woman before. She used down-to-earth language to describe what she saw as the absurdities of many social conventions, poked fun at pomposity, and challenged the notions of propriety demanded by society. Readers' enthusiastic response led several newspapers to reprint her work and a publisher to gather them into a collection published in 1853, titled *Fern Leaves from Fanny's Portfolio*. The book became a best-seller and prompted a second collection of her sketches, plus a children's book the next year. Within two years Parton's literary output had produced about $10,000 in royalties and led to a weekly column for the *New York Ledger* for $100 a week. Her financial worries ended, and her career was launched.[23]

Parton's personal experiences left her with a nontraditional view of marriage, which, she maintained, was a poor way for women to secure financial support. Women, she believed, should be economically independent even after marriage, with the same access to jobs at the same salaries as men. Parton cast a satirical eye at male pronouncements about society's expectations for women: "I am sick, in an age which produced a Bronte and a [Barrett] Browning, of the prate of men who assert that every woman should be a perfect housekeeper, *and fail to add,* that every man should be a perfect carpenter."[24] Because Parton had been destitute herself, she defended women who had to work and criticized those whose leisure time was filled with meaningless activity. She harbored few romantic notions, caustically observing: "The way to a man's heart is through his stomach."[25] She urged women to develop the intellectual and financial means to be independent of their husbands' neglect or indifference. Yet she was evenhanded in her advice to both marriage partners to share the responsibility for a smooth marriage.

Her weekly columns lasted twenty-one years, during which she became the highest-paid newspaper writer of her time. Her writing focused on topics considered controversial by most: venereal disease, prostitution, birth control, divorce, prison reform, and women's rights. She helped Croly found Sorosis, wrote eight books for adults and three for children, and never missed a deadline for her weekly column. Because of her interest in child development, she produced columns calling for improvements in education and child-rearing practices. The caustic wit of Parton writing as Fanny Fern proved how effective ridicule could be in confronting opposition. She urged women to be assertive and defy the restraints placed on them by "conservative old ladies of both sexes," to "take your rights, my sisters; don't beg for them!"[26]

Miner was a child growing up in an unstable environment during the years Parton enjoyed widespread readership. Although their childhood experiences differed markedly, Parton and Miner's adult lives had many similarities. Miner suffered the indignities of an unfortunate marriage, yet carved out a career as a writer and editor fully capable of supporting herself. She had no children of her own, yet became a strong advocate for all children. She supported juvenile courts, police matrons, and higher education for women. She urged women to prepare themselves to be self-sufficient, advising them, "Every woman dependent, whether she be married or single, owes it to herself to occasionally take stock of her resources and see whether she could ever earn a dollar, and how, if it became necessary to do so."[27]

Miner cleverly defended women seeking improvements in their communities by illustrating the absurdity of those opposing any sort of progress. As she told her readers: "The Progressive woman can always console herself with the knowledge that people have opposed everything new from time immemorial. The inventor of the umbrella was stigmatized for interrupting the designs of Providence, for when showers fell it was evident God intended man should get wet."[28] Miner's words, like Parton's, could entertain and educate her readers. Her sharp wit and talent for getting to the heart of the matter in any subject she surveyed kept readers returning to her column week after week for two decades.

Parton married a third time, to James Parton, a writer eleven years her junior and devoted to her. She remained an outspoken and controversial journalist and enjoyed great popularity during the nineteenth century. The extent of her contributions to establishing the role of women journalists as social critics in the nineteenth century has only recently been recognized. However, her work promoting economic independence for women, single or married, and urging women to develop their intellectual capabilities and secure political power was carried forward by the women journalists who followed her.[29] In a similar fashion, Miner found happiness and support for her career with her marriage to W. A. Callaway. Her columns about the needs of women reflected many of the sentiments expressed by Parton years earlier.

Both Croly and Parton began their careers before the Civil War. The end of the Civil War brought even more women into journalism. In the Midwest and the South, women established weekly newspapers, wrote for daily papers, and reported as traveling correspondents. In the East, two major suffrage newspapers, Susan B. Anthony's *The Revolution* and Lucy Stone's *The Woman's Journal,* were started.[30] In Washington, D.C., an increasing number of women correspondents cast a jaundiced eye on activities in Congress. Correspondent Mary Clemmer (Ames) observed in her column: "Still the Senate gets drunk. Though women struggle to the van, shutting up grog-shops, striving, with voices full of tears, with these very senators; still they get drunk, and the world is no better than it used to be."[31]

Sara Clarke Lippincott, who wrote a column for the *New York Times* under the name "Grace Greenwood," carried on the tradition of women reporters and columnists who used their writing to expose the need for substantive reform. She candidly admitted that she enjoyed what she was doing:

> *I have been sharply rebuked by my brothers, as an indiscreet sister—"speaking out in meeting," and revealing the secrets of the vestry, the deacons, the elders, and holy men generally. I have been roughly reminded that I was a woman, and told that I ought to be sternly remanded by public opinion to woman's proper sphere, where*

the eternal unbaked pudding and the immemorial unattached shirt-button await my attention. That same sphere is a good one to fall back upon. I can "rastle" with cooking and sewing as well as any of my gentler sisters, but just at present I confess I prefer serving up a spicy hash of Southern Democratic sentiment to concocting a pudding and pricking with my pen "the bubble reputation" of political charlatans to puncturing innocent muslin with my needle. I hear I am accused of "making war on the civil service reform." I deny the charge. I attack only the poor pretense, the idle parade, the misleading semblance of reform. . . . which is to so many political enthusiasts "the substance of things hoped for, and the evidence of things not seen . . ."[32]

The reformer's zeal reflected in Grace Greenwood's writing mirrored the grassroots movement for reform among women that blossomed after the Civil War. Before the war, a number of women had been actively involved in voluntary associations, mainly religious and charitable. Temperance and abolition advocates had begun to speak out, and a small group gathered at Seneca Falls in 1848 publicly called for woman suffrage. Their activities represented a bold departure from the societal constraints imposed by the belief in separate spheres for women (home and family) and men (work and political power). Such restraints meant that public speaking, the traditional method of political discourse and debate, was deemed inappropriate and often subjected women to indignities and condemnation.[33] Yet these early reformers laid the groundwork for the post–Civil War reformers who had found roles during the war as fundraisers, nurses, antislavery advocates, and other positions previously closed to them. As Elizabeth Cady Stanton wrote: "The social and political condition of women was largely changed by our civil war. . . . a desire for their own personal individual liberty intensified. It created a revolution in woman herself."[34]

Those who were disappointed with the denial of suffrage to women after the war banded together and then split to form the National Woman Suffrage Association and the American Woman Suffrage Association. The two groups differed on the most effective means to accomplish a common goal. The "American" attracted more followers with its more conservative state-by-state approach, while the "National" viewed suffrage as the means to achieve equality for women in areas beyond the vote.

Other women considered drunkenness and its caustic effects on the home and family as a pervasive social problem that could be solved by uniting under one banner—that of the Woman's Christian Temperance Union (WCTU). The WCTU spread across the country, enlisting women in record numbers.[35]

In the next two decades other reform-minded women began to establish settlement houses in urban areas, while women's clubs multiplied in cities and towns. Each of these groups had an agenda, and all recognized that success for their programs would require a marshalling of sympathy and support from beyond their membership rolls. Women still had little control over their finances and no political voice. Yet reform-minded women turned the concept of woman's sphere, with its concern for family well-being, into a justification for moving from the home into the public arena to confront situations that had an adverse impact on their families. The appeal to family well-being was designed to overcome the reticence of the more conservative women in the community, as well as male opposition. The clubs' emergence contributed much energy to the Progressive Era of the late nineteenth and early twentieth centuries, when ordinary citizens began to address a variety of health and welfare problems that threatened to overwhelm their communities.[36]

To counter opposition to their activities, this generation of reformers would utilize a widely available means to challenge the status quo and educate readers, one available even to disenfranchised women: the press.[37] "The newspaper is the educator of the public," noted Mary Temple Bayard as she addressed the Congress of Women at the World's Columbian Exposition (better known as the Chicago World's Fair) in 1893, "and men and women who write in newspapers have the best opportunities for creating public opinion." Eventually, these women believed, positive public opinion could influence legislative action on behalf of reform measures.[38]

Women reporters, even as they might help other women challenge society's problems, had to contend with resentment from male journalists. There was widespread reluctance on the part of men to accept women in the newsroom. Although only 75 women journalists were counted in the 1870 census, the women persevered, increasing to 288 in 1880, 600 in 1890, and 2,192 in 1900.[39] Their numbers had grown so large that in 1889 Allan Forman, the editor of *The Journalist,* a publication "devoted to Newspapers, Authors, Artists and Publishers," produced an issue honoring women who had made careers in journalism. The stories were designed, according to Forman, to disabuse "thousands of the case-hardened old fogies of the idea that a newspaper woman in any way interferes with the men or that she is any less a woman because she earns her living by wielding a 'Dixon' instead of sewing on buttons for the 'lords of creation.' "[40]

Forman's 1889 special edition came at a time when women journalists were becoming a larger presence in newspapers, where they could make better salaries than in many other jobs. They had to compete with men for jobs as reporters and, according to Bayard, succeeded "as journalists and not as women." No doubt these women were able writers, but the editor of *The Journalist* saw other attributes. He wrote: "What does it take to be a lady journalist? Hard work, dedication, high ideals, sympathy, perception, a dash of cynicism, faith, hope, charity, a relish for news . . . a buoyancy of nature."[41]

Women reporters recognized that they enjoyed a measure of social freedom not available to other women, for they could come and go as they pleased without regard to the "tiresome conventionalities" imposed by society. The increase in women reporters paralleled the emergence of the woman's department or woman's page in many newspapers. Joseph Pulitzer popularized the concept in the 1890s, modeling it after Edward A. Bok's format for *The Ladies Home Journal*. The presence of a woman's page assured women readers for the paper, a fact that was not lost on advertisers.[42] Certainly, fashion advice, book reviews, and recipes appeared regularly, along with detailed accounts of glittering social events and the travel plans of the well-to-do. Although many women reporters disliked doing society coverage, male editors gave them little choice. Only when they were able to write about matters affecting the larger population did women reporters find their distinctive voice as advocates. This transformation to more substantive subject matter was helped along when the woman's page began to cover the work of clubwomen engaged in addressing the troublesome social issues of the time.[43]

Women journalists for newspapers in small towns and cities were essential partners in the endeavor, as they exposed the wide range of problems in their communities and supplied a public forum for the clubwomen's efforts to correct them. By the 1890s, these journalists were distributed throughout the country, each helping to carry on the work of advocates for reform that began decades earlier. There was Theodora Winton Youmans, who began her "Woman's World" column for the *Waukesha (Wisconsin) Freeman* in 1887. Among her subjects were the progress being made by women in politics and the working conditions of servants, seamstresses, and schoolteachers. Youmans solicited questions and personal experiences from her readers, male and female, and reported the activities of women's clubs as they attempted to influence statewide legislation on suffrage.[44]

There would be others in the next two decades. From the woman's department of the *Atlanta Constitution,* headed by Ismay Dooly, came backing for the Atlanta City Federation of Woman's Clubs and women and children's welfare measures, while Winona Wilcox Payne of the *Cleveland Press* put "punch and irony into the woman's page at a time when it was still smothered in lavender and old lace."[45] Sophie Loeb of the *New York Evening World* wrote about the need for child welfare boards, penny school lunches, cheaper and safer taxis, and public play streets, while Rheta Childe Dorr of the *New York Evening Post* exposed the working conditions of young women in the city.[46]

When Isadore Miner began work for the *Dallas Morning News,* she most certainly knew of the work of many of the women in the newspapers of major cities across the nation. Her hiring suggests that Dallas was somewhat behind the trend, for she was the first full-time woman journalist employed by the *News.*[47] She found society coverage of the *News* in the traditional mode, highlighting parties and travel plans of women in Dallas and the surrounding communities. Activities of church and charitable groups, along with those of study club meetings, were duly reported.[48] Reporting these events would pose no challenge to Miner's ability, for she had paid her career dues and learned her craft in the preceding decade. She began her journalism career in 1884, writing and editing for *The Review and Herald,* a publication of the Seventh Day Adventist Church in Battle Creek, Michigan. She moved in 1889 to the magazine *Good Health,* sponsored by Dr. J. H. Kellogg's Battle Creek Sanitarium. In 1891 Miner moved to Toledo, Ohio, where she worked at the *Toledo Commercial* until she left for Dallas in 1893.

Miner's personal life and work experiences shaped her outlook, making her especially sensitive to the needs of women and children. She had observed the reform work of religious groups, women's clubs, and suffragist organizations in Michigan and Ohio, and she brought that knowledge to a city just beginning to deal with the social problems northern cities had faced decades earlier. In 1896, three years after her arrival at the *News,* Miner helped inaugurate the Woman's Century page, which appeared weekly with her bylined column. She would not emulate the style of Jennie June so much as that of Fanny Fern, using logic and wit to explain her position. The conventions of polite society that masked grave injustices and inequities would be ignored in the name of honest appraisal.

The realistic approach to issues and problems mentioned in her columns was the product of her own life experiences, for her childhood was filled with challenges. Blessed with native intelligence and determination, Miner overcame difficulties that would have defeated many young women. Consequently, her early years provide significant insights into the attitudes and actions of the forthright journalist who lectured, chided, and cajoled her readers to make changes that would benefit them, their families, and their fellow citizens.

2

■ ■ ■

"Tie a Knot in Your Thread"

Sara Isadore Sutherland did not remember her father. Less than five months after her birth on September 25, 1863, Mason Montgomery Sutherland enlisted in Company E, First Regiment of the Michigan Sharp Shooters, to fight in the Civil War. When Sutherland volunteered to serve for "three years or during the war," he left Maria, his wife of three and a half years; his seventeen-month-old son Daniel; and his baby daughter Isadore. Sutherland was one of 3,878 men from Calhoun County, Michigan, who fought in the Civil War. Captured in September, 1864, at the siege of Petersburg, he was interned at Salisbury Prison in North Carolina. He was later released to the military hospital in Annapolis, Maryland, where he died on March 17, 1865. He was buried in the national cemetery at Annapolis.[1]

"Poor Papa. So young to die at 27! And how different our lives might have been had he lived," Isadore wrote to her brother in 1900.[2] Her regret only hints at the difficulties they had experienced after the death of their father. The Civil War shattered what might have been a normal rural childhood. Both her father and her mother, the former Maria Lucy Tripp, were born in New York. The pair had married June 3, 1860, in Oneida, Michigan, located in the lower peninsula midway between Lake

Erie and Lake Michigan, when Mason was twenty-four and Maria was twenty-one. They began farming in the nearby community of Grand Ledge, Michigan, a short while later.[3] Daniel Mason Sutherland, their first child, was born there on September 25, 1861. On the same day, two years later in 1863, Sara Isadore was born in Newton, Calhoun County, near Battle Creek. Her parents had already begun to purchase land and build a secure life.

As might be expected, her father's death brought major changes for Isadore. Her mother, like many young widows at the time, remarried quickly. The wedding to forty-year-old carpenter Franklin Frisbie La-Moreaux took place in May, 1866, in Newton, Michigan. Maria and Franklin LaMoreaux had two children, Eugenia Mae, born in 1867, and Frank Lynn, born in 1873.[4] The LaMoreauxs were Seventh Day Adventists, which meant there was probably a healthy dose of Seventh Day Adventist teachings in their home regarding diet and health practices, including a vegetarian diet, two meals a day, and no drugs or stimulants.[5]

Three months after her remarriage, Mrs. LaMoreaux petitioned the court to allow her new husband to become the legal guardian of her two children, ages two and four, for the purpose of "taking care of the interest of said minors in said real estate." The real estate consisted of several heavily mortgaged parcels of land in surrounding counties. Less than six weeks after his appointment as guardian, Franklin and his wife filed an application for an increase in benefits for pensions that had been granted to minor children of deceased Civil War soldiers.[6] In 1862 Congress had approved pensions that amounted to eight dollars a month per child. In 1866 the amount was increased to ten dollars a month. Widows who remarried were not entitled to receive any pension.[7]

The circumstances of the two Sutherland children were not as comfortable as they should have been, however, because the pensions they were entitled to were regularly collected by their mother, who kept the money and sent the children to live with different aunts. When they did live with their stepfather and mother, Isadore and Daniel were charged board.[8] Maria, who had taught school during her first marriage, reported that she saw to her children's early education but gave no particulars. Isadore must have been a talented student. Among the few surviving mementoes of her childhood is a small book, *Miss Thistledown,* which bears the inscription: "Presented to Isadore Sutherland Coopersville, Michigan for one of four correct solutions of a punctuation exercise for the

Little Folks' Column of the *Detroit Commercial Advertiser* of July 18, 1874. Detroit July 18, 1874."[9]

When the LaMoreauxs moved to Dallas, Texas, in 1875 to recover Maria's health, they initially planned to have Daniel and Isadore "bound out" as servants to other families. Instead, Isadore went to live with her mother's sister Rose Worden and her husband Francis on their farm in China Township, Michigan. China Township, located in eastern Michigan about sixty miles northeast of Detroit, was a small farming community similar to the ones Isadore had lived in earlier. Her brother Daniel grew up on farms near Ithaca and Gladwin, Michigan, one hundred miles west of China.[10]

Although her mother replaced her stepfather as her legal guardian in 1869, Isadore was convinced that neither had been fair or honest with her.[11] Two years after she went to live with her "Auntie Rose," in an attempt to recover part of the money she believed was hers, she wrote a poignant letter to the local probate office in 1877 inquiring: "if there are papers on file . . . stating that my brother and I are to have $600 with interest. I was informed that there were such. I would be very happy if you would advise me what course to pursue. If I have not written and worded this correctly, I hope you will excuse me as I wrote it without aid, as I was advised to do."[12] At the same time the determined fourteen-year-old petitioned the probate judge of Calhoun County, Michigan, to appoint a new guardian for her. Eager to sever her relationship with the LaMoreauxs, Isadore wrote the judge a precise explanation of her situation, noting that

> *I have lived away from home over a year and probably will for years to come. The reasons why I want my guardianship changed are, firstly: that she lives in Texas and I in Mich., which makes it very inconvenient to draw my pension money. Secondly, I have a stepfather, who is rather inconvenient also; indeed so much so that I have never lived at home with any peace. Thirdly: that I do not receive my money regularly; sometimes it is entirely used up in the family, and if I do get any, I find that it has been piece mealed off [sic] until it might just as well not come at all for all the good it does me; for with what remains I have to pay the interest on the place of which there is twenty acres. . . . I might go on to seventeenthly [sic] and each would be sufficient in itself, but I think these*

are enough, I have written to my mother and asked her to resign the guardianship, but she will not and indeed insists upon my returning home which I do not want to do. . . . I have never had the use of the money which was due when I was small, and never will.[13]

The probate court judge granted Isadore's request and appointed Rose Worden her legal guardian in March, 1878.[14] Worden made her sister, Isadore's mother, promise to send Isadore her rightful share of the pension. Isadore later reported that her mother sent the first installment, but after a while it didn't come: "Mother wrote that she didn't receive it. My aunt went to Detroit to the State agent, Samuel Post and was shown the receipts signed by her to the effect that she had rec'd [*sic*] it. When I wrote her this she admitted that she had received it but that our property (the 20 acres near Grand Rapids) which she intended keeping for us until we came of age was needing repairs, taxes to be paid, etc. and she thought that as it was for our benefit our money should settle the bill. Nothing more was done, but about two years after that I accidentally discovered that the property was already disposed of at the time she had written about it."[15]

Despite her financial problems, Isadore enrolled in Battle Creek College in January, 1879, with the help of her Aunt Rose and completed two sessions by June, 1879.[16] Worden, who was a fervent Seventh Day Adventist like Maria Sutherland LaMoreaux, obviously wished her niece to be suitably educated.[17] The college, the first comprehensive educational institution established by the Seventh Day Adventist Church, offered courses at the grammar and secondary school levels. Isadore's age placed her in the secondary level, where she studied subjects such as grammar, arithmetic, botany, U.S. history, and German. The school also offered distinctive Seventh Day Adventist teachings concerning health, such as diet and medical treatment, and often brought Dr. J. H. Kellogg from the nearby Battle Creek Sanitarium to present a lecture on hygiene. The Hesperian, a literary club for women, encouraged its members to develop their skills in debate and public speaking.[18] This environment made a strong impression on the independent-minded Isadore, one that influenced many of her future attitudes and actions.

Seventh Day Adventists had come to the Battle Creek area in 1855, bringing their tradition of Saturday sabbath, belief in the imminent return of Jesus Christ, strong moral character, dietary rules, abstinence from alcohol and tobacco, and industrious work habits.[19] Adventists congregated on one side of the Battle Creek River in an area known as Advent Town (later West End). The institution Isadore attended had been established in 1874. Its educational philosophy included the precepts established by Ellen G. White, an early leader of the denomination. White's educational beliefs focused on a "balanced, practical education which embraced the physical, mental and moral faculties" and recommended practical training in manual and domestic arts and subjects such as physiology and business. This combination was not typical of nineteenth-century education programs. Students at Battle Creek College were required to attend classes, and if they accumulated ten unexcused delinquencies, they were expelled. They were also expected to attend regular Saturday church services and were not to be "strolling about" on the Sabbath. To cover their educational costs, students could work part time at the denomination's well-known Battle Creek Sanitarium just across the street or at its Review and Herald Publishing Company.[20]

Isadore's course work at Battle Creek College in 1879 did not complete her education. She returned to her Aunt Rose's home and enrolled in St. Clair High School. The transcript for her senior year includes courses in geometry, trigonometry, geology, astronomy, general history, spelling, and German, with several 100 averages and no grade lower than 96.[21] At her graduation exercises in June, 1881, the seventeen-year-old recited a poem she had written titled "Tie a Knot in Your Thread." The poem focused on the custom of weavers, who tied a knot in each thread to prevent the stitches from slipping. The lines reflected an understanding of the importance of paying attention to the details of life, of not letting opportunities to do good slip by. Isadore's youthful idealism in the face of the difficulties she had experienced was a testament to her strength of character. The Seventh Day Adventist beliefs imparted by her family and the college had left their mark. Her determination to do what was right despite opposition from many would characterize much of her life's work.

In our every day lives the knot in our threads
Is formed by some small word or deed
Which is mighty tho' small, but whose power is unseen
So we pass them by without heed
But ruin they'll work, and regret they will bring,
If left unspoken, undone

And the efforts we've builded our future upon
will slip from our grasp one by one
Tie a knot in your thread and let that knot be,
A motive that's noble and grand,
A purpose to battle for God and the right,
Though you stand all alone in the land.[22]

After Isadore graduated from high school, her options were limited: she could marry, or she could seek employment in one of the few occupations deemed acceptable for women at the time. Although the University of Michigan had been open to women since 1870, the costs associated with attending it were likely beyond Isadore's limited means. There is no indication that she considered marriage. Nor did the most common careers for women appeal to her. The 1880 census listed 10,462 women in the United States as dressmakers or milliners and 7,374 as educators, while store clerks numbered only 909.[23] We know nothing of Isadore's whereabouts or employment from the time she graduated in 1881 until she went to work in 1883 at the Review and Herald Publishing Company in Battle Creek. The small village of St. Clair, with less than 2,000 inhabitants in 1880, obviously did not offer the same opportunities as Battle Creek, which had 7,000 inhabitants.[24]

Battle Creek had been established in the early 1830s where the Battle Creek flowed into the Kalamazoo River. The abundant water supply provided the power for mills and factories that used local raw materials such as agricultural products and forests. When the Michigan Central Railroad arrived in 1845, it brought settlers to the area and took products to Chicago and Detroit. These factors created a vibrant economy that included flour, woolen, and saw mills, and factories producing furniture and agricultural implements.

The Battle Creek community nurtured a progressive outlook toward slaves and women. Blacks escaping their bondage by way of the Underground Railroad were assisted as they passed through. Drawn by the tolerance of the area, Sojourner Truth, the former slave who was among the most eloquent of the abolitionists, had moved to a community near Battle Creek in 1857 and purchased a home in Battle Creek in 1867. She lived there until her death in 1883.[25] When Lillie Devereux Blake, president of the New York State Woman's Suffrage Association, addressed a full house at the Adventist Tabernacle in 1887, she was "frequently ap-

plauded during [her] delivery and elicited the most pronounced dem-
onstrations of favor from the audience at the close."[26] At Battle Creek
Sanitarium, pioneering doctor Kate Lindsay, one of Michigan's earliest
women medical school graduates, began a career which included the
delivery of more than a thousand babies.[27]

The liberal entrepreneurial spirit of the area also tolerated emigrants
with rather unconventional religious beliefs who migrated from western New York. Notable among these were James and Ellen White, who
found strong local interest in their Seventh Day Adventist teachings
during a visit to Battle Creek in 1855. When local citizens offered a building for the denomination's printing presses, essential to their proselytiz-
ing, the Whites moved their headquarters to Battle Creek. The church
and its publishing efforts flourished. By 1878 they had built a 3,000-seat
"Dime Tabernacle" funded by dime contributions from members world-
wide. That same year the Seventh Day Adventist Publishing Association,
known as the Review and Herald Publishing Company, employed one
hundred workers operating seven power presses to print thousands of
books and periodicals. Monthly circulation numbered more than 40,000,
and the company's catalog listed two hundred publications in English,
thirteen in French, twenty-one in Danish, fifteen in Swedish, thirteen in
German, and one in Dutch. It was considered the largest, most complete
publishing house in Michigan.[28]

The Adventist publishing house was a logical place for Isadore given
her writing ability and Adventist background. The reputation of its publications among the Adventist community certainly would have com-
mended it to her Aunt Rose. Isadore may have worked at the publishing
house while attending Battle Creek College, as many of its students did.
Once hired, she learned to edit and to write clearly and persuasively about
social and health matters that concerned the Seventh Day Adventist
Church. She also honed her talent for poetry and fiction writing. During
her tenure at the publishing company, from 1883 to 1891, Isadore also
wrote for the *Review and Herald,* the company's weekly newspaper, and
for the Sunday school publication *Youth's Instructor.* In early 1889 she
became an associate editor for the monthly magazine *Good Health.*[29]

The journalism and publishing field was hardly overcrowded with
women at the time, but at the publishing house Isadore worked along-
side several women who became important role models. This was possible because the Seventh Day Adventist faith, growing out of the visions

of Ellen G. White, did not frown upon women taking an active role in all aspects of church work and society.[30] Among her coworkers were Eva Bell Giles, the daughter of Goodloe Harper Bell, who had founded Battle Creek College. Giles not only served as an editor of *Good Health* she also edited the monthly magazine of the Michigan Federation of Women's Clubs and worked with the Michigan Woman's Press Association.[31] Isadore was probably introduced to these organizations through Giles, for she displayed a clear familiarity with them in later years when she became involved with their Texas counterparts.

Dr. Kate Lindsay, the first registered woman physician at Battle Creek Sanitarium, helped further Isadore's education about the needs of women and children. Dr. Lindsay graduated from the University of Michigan medical school in 1876, and in 1883 she joined the Battle Creek Sanitarium, where she helped found the Training School for Nurses and served as head of the obstetric, gynecology, and pediatric staff. Prompted by Dr. Lindsay's work, Isadore wrote articles about women and children for *Good Health*.[32]

Emma Shaw, an associate editor of *Good Health* and something of a nonconformist, began her career as a tailoress. In the early 1870s she used an inheritance to purchase a farm near Battle Creek with a childhood friend, Ella Harman. Working without the assistance of any men, they implemented the latest agricultural methods with great success. To make their physical labor easier, they adopted the dress style advocated by Mrs. Bloomer,[33] wearing Turkish trousers under knee-length dresses. During one of the first winters they were farming, the two women wrote some children's stories and submitted them to a Boston publisher, D. Lothrop & Co. The editor was so pleased with their efforts that he asked them to plan and edit a proposed children's magazine titled *Wide Awake*. When the magazine began to enjoy some success, the two sold their farm and moved to Boston in 1875. After Ella married in Boston, Emma returned to Battle Creek in 1880 and went to work at the publishing house. Isadore evidently admired Emma's independent streak, for the two became friends. Emma encouraged Isadore to write poetry and urged her to submit her poems to *Wide Awake*, where they were published.[34]

Ella Eaton Kellogg, the wife of Dr. J. H. Kellogg, was also a member of the editorial staff of *Good Health*. She served the WCTU as national superintendent of the Department of Hygiene and later as associate superintendent of the Department of Social Purity.[35] Author of pamphlets such as "Talks to Girls" and "Studies in Character Building," in 1892 Mrs. Kellogg also wrote a popular book on dietetics titled *Science in the Kitchen*. She found time to work with the Michigan Woman's Press Association as well. Despite her involvement, Mrs. Kellogg and her husband took numerous orphans into their home and raised them.[36] The content of Isadore's articles reflected Mrs. Kellogg's concern for improved hygiene and housekeeping, as well as the development of good character. Years later in Dallas, when Isadore took in her half-sister's two nieces and provided for their educations, she was emulating the actions of Mrs. Kellogg and her own Aunt Rose. At the Review and Herald Publishing Company, Isadore met someone else who left a lasting impression: her first husband, James Weston Miner. Although records indicate that Miner had attended Battle Creek College in 1876, he was not a student there when Isadore attended in 1879. They probably met while working at the *Review and Herald*.[37]

Miner was twenty-seven and employed as an electrotyper in September, 1884, when he married the twenty-year-old Isadore, who was a staff writer. The ceremony was performed by Madison B. Miller, an Adventist minister with whom Miner was boarding at the time. Mrs. Miller was present at the marriage and later reported that the couple lived in her home the next winter and continued to work at the Review and Herald Publishing Company.[38]

Isadore wrote both fiction and nonfiction while working on *Youth's Instructor* and the *Advent Review and Sabbath Herald*. Written for parents as guidance in child rearing, her stories were representative of the philosophy and methods advocated at the time: the need for obedience to loving parents and the unhappy results when children did not behave and mind their parents' directions.[39] In articles Isadore advised parents to rear their children with firm instructions about right and wrong, but she recognized that childhood should be the happiest time of life. In light of her own experiences, this belief was particularly poignant. Despite the years of alienation from her own mother, Isadore admonished her readers: "Never let slip the tender years of susceptibility. Something will leave its impress; let it be the right thing. Somebody will gain the child's confidence; let it be the mother. Priority of possession holds the secret."[40]

Isadore's fiction for female readers consisted of romanticized stories of young women who overcame adversity, made "good" marriages, and lived happily ever after, or who followed their "baser" instincts and eventually suffered from their choices. The simplistic formula that determined the fate of individuals who appeared in these stories mirrored the "trials and triumph" that characterized much of the fiction written by women throughout most of the nineteenth century.[41] The stories were a striking contrast to Isadore's straightforward nonfiction articles, which often appeared on adjacent pages of *Good Health*. With titles such as "Aid for Working-Women," "Co-operative Housekeeping," "Sanitary Care of Clothing," "Physical Culture for Women," "Proper Adaptation of Clothing," "Legislative Influence on Social Sins," "The Study of Higher Mathematics," and "What Girls Should Learn," these articles addressed issues that were widely discussed at the time. As increasing numbers of women entered the workforce, attended college, and began to seek innovative solutions to social problems, Isadore Miner assumed the role of an advocate for improving women's lives.[42]

In March, 1891, Isadore left Battle Creek for a position on the staff of the *Toledo Commercial*.[43] The eight years she spent at the Review and Herald Publishing Company had expanded her horizons and given her the skills to support herself. But she apparently felt the need to leave, for after seven years she had given up on her marriage. Her husband, it appears, had refused to provide any financial or emotional support from the earliest days following their wedding. Depositions given by three witnesses before Isadore's divorce indicate that James Miner was in good health and fully capable of supporting his wife during the years they were married.

In addition, Miner was evidently quite possessive. His antagonism toward Isadore's female friends was hinted at by Myrta Castle, a Battle Creek friend who had moved to Dallas. Myrta wrote to her parents about a suitor who was pursuing Isadore in 1897. Myrta observed that the suitor "likes me well enough to admit me to a relationship Mr. Miner was always jealous of."[44] Isadore testified that Miner's only support and maintenance during the entire marriage consisted of "one dress of the cost and value of $12–$15," and that she had "wholly supported herself during all of that time by her own efforts in a literary way."[45] Her marriage had been nothing like the idealized relationships extolled in popular literature.

Yet Isadore's personal experiences gave her firsthand knowledge of the difficulties many women faced in marriage. They affected her outlook on women's needs and influenced the advice she would later give her readers. Her subsequent insights would often be pointed, with hardly a nod to conventional sensibilities, but they had the unmistakable ring of truth, and her readers recognized and acknowledged this. Psychologists might place much significance on the fact that there had been no strong male figure in Isadore's life. But surrounded by strong women, she managed to emerge from her childhood and first marriage with self-confidence, energy, and a drive to succeed. Isadore spent two years in Toledo, Ohio, where she wrote copy for the *Toledo Commercial* seemingly without a byline.[46] Her growing interest in woman suffrage—a logical progression in her concern for the improvement of women's lives—introduced her to Rosa Segur, who wrote a woman's column for the *Toledo Blade*. Segur had been a founding member of the Toledo Woman Suffrage Association in 1869 and would later be an honorary president of the Ohio Suffragist Association.[47] She must have taken Isadore under her wing and introduced the young journalist to the local suffragist community, although no records have been found of the extent of her involvement. Isadore's life in Toledo left little imprint on the city, but her friendship with Rosa Segur would be of great help in her next move.

As Isadore's second year in Toledo ended and her thirtieth birthday neared, she must have taken stock of her situation. She was separated from her husband with no thought of reconciliation. Her professional advancement was not moving as quickly as she had hoped, for the *Toledo Commercial* had changed hands several times in a short period.[48] Yet she was a well-informed, experienced journalist who understood the power of the press to influence opinion. Isadore would take her talents elsewhere. She does seem to have been appreciated, for at the time of her departure, the *Toledo Commercial* presented her with an engraved gold pocket watch.[49]

The reason for Isadore's move to Dallas, Texas, where her family had lived since 1875, has never been discovered. Perhaps her desire to reestablish family ties overcame the memories of her family's earlier treatment of her. Whatever the factors, the decision would bring Isadore a brighter future and the women of Dallas and Texas a unique advocate.

3

. . .

"An All-Around Woman"

When Isadore arrived in early 1893, Dallas was the largest city in Texas, with a population of more than 38,067. "The Queen of Commerce . . . its motto is progress; its watchword improvement," proclaimed the *Dallas Morning News*. Dallas was described as "a city with 60 miles of cement sidewalks, 40 miles of paved streets, 40 miles of water mains, 45 miles of street railway, the largest grain elevator in Texas, the second largest depot in the world for the sale of agricultural implements . . ."[1] The twenty-nine-year-old journalist went to work for the *News* shortly after her arrival. Exactly how Isadore secured the position is unclear. She did know one employee, James Florer, a printer who was married to Julia Bell Florer, the sister of her friend Eva Bell Giles. But her ten years of writing experience would have been a more substantive recommendation than an employee's endorsement. The *News* management evidently viewed Isadore as highly qualified, for they hired her as "Editor, society, women's and children's departments."[2]

The move to Dallas united Isadore with her family: mother Maria LaMoreaux, stepfather Franklin LaMoreaux, and their two children, Frank Lynn and Eugenia Mae. In 1888 Mae had married John A. Fetterly, now secretary of the Will A. Watkins Music Company. The couple lived at 200 Evergreen, next door to Maria and Franklin. Isadore moved in with the Fetterlys around the time of the birth of their second daughter, Alberta, in February, 1893.[3]

Shortly after Isadore arrived she and her mother began attending various club meetings together. Apparently the ill will that characterized their earlier relationship was gone, but sources do not give any clues to how this happened. Possibly Isadore's years in Ohio left her needing financial help, which her family offered to provide.[4] Some softening of hard feelings must have occurred before she arrived in Dallas, for the Fetterlys had named their first daughter, born in 1889, after her aunt Isadore. Then, in 1890 her brother Daniel Sutherland worked in Dallas briefly as a traveling salesman.[5] Finally, the plight of her stepfather may have dissolved old animosities. In 1893, during a robbery attempt while at his job as a night watchman, LaMoreaux was the victim of an attack that fractured his skull and left him an invalid.[6] With her stepfather incapacitated, Isadore may have felt that she would no longer find him "rather inconvenient" as she had twenty years earlier. Whatever the reason, Isadore and her mother seem to have resolved their past differences and made a fresh start.

Yet Isadore remained loyal to her father's memory, reminding her brother Daniel in a letter: "We are getting old enough to realize all he would have been to us, and it was not his fault that our lives were changed—that he could not live to protect us. Let us give his memory all the love and reverence that would be his due if he were alive. I believe he was a good, just and noble man. Let us try to be like him."[7] She had put the past behind her, as she wrote Daniel: "my work keeps me very busy, and it is such a comfort. I don't get much time to get blue and bitter over the past."[8]

Others helped Isadore feel at home in Dallas. Fannie Segur Foster, the daughter of Isadore's Ohio suffragist mentor Rosa Segur, became Isadore's link to other suffragists in Dallas. Virginia Quitman Goffe, who was working for the *Dallas Daily Times Herald* as educational editor in 1893 and later as society editor, quickly became a friend and confidante as the two women walked along muddy streets and shared streetcar rides to and from social functions they were covering.[9]

Isadore lost little time befriending other working women in Dallas. She used her knowledge of the Michigan Woman's Press Association to write the constitution and bylaws for the Texas Woman's Press Association, which was formed on May 10, 1893.[10] The new group immediately began to organize a statewide meeting of their members during the annual State Fair of Texas in Dallas that October. Isadore provided the publicity for the group's meetings in the *News*.[11] The statewide gathering coincided with the fair's Woman's Day, which was to feature a full complement of women speakers. By the time the fair opened, Woman's Day had become the first meeting of the Texas Woman's Congress.[12]

Isadore addressed the group several times during the October meeting: first, on October 24, about the vocations open to women. On October 25, she led a discussion among her fellow journalists about the business side of the writer's profession. The following day she conducted a panel considering the questions: "What is the best training for journalism? Can it be taught in schools?"[13] When she was not making speeches, she was quite busy, as one woman attested: "Mrs. S.I. Miner of the *Dallas News* proved herself an all-around woman when it came to looking after details, and [*sic*] which when neglected create discomfort. Through her energy and it might also be said ubiquity nothing was overlooked that could add to the comfort and happiness of the visitors."[14]

Isadore's efforts brought rapid recognition, and she was elected secretary of the newly created Board of Directors of the Woman's Congress. The woman's editor of a major newspaper was a clever choice for this post, for her position at the *News* would ensure press coverage. The women were already relying on the paper, according to one observation made after the Woman's Congress: "As the ladies themselves said, the *News* as authority on the subject was a potent factor in keeping them posted on matters of importance constantly arising and many said that all they knew of the movement was what was eagerly looked for in the *News*."[15]

The Woman's Congress galvanized an untapped interest in finding new solutions to problems that affected women and children, just as one visitor had predicted during the meeting: "I think that this woman's congress will have the effect of waking up the women of Texas to an understanding of their influence. Heretofore they have not had an opportunity to know what they could do. . . . I have been simply amazed at the talent and the vim and the snap of our women."[16] Within a month of the fair, the enthusiasm following the Texas Woman's Congress fostered the creation of a local auxiliary in Dallas which called itself the Woman's Council. The members chose Isadore as their secretary, a post she held for three years.[17] That Isadore would be named an officer of the group after less than a year in Dallas reveals the confidence she was able to elicit from a group dedicated to making improvements in women's lives. This was to become a familiar pattern, in which Isadore's knowledge, organizational abilities, and personality made her a valuable asset to any group she was asked to assist.

The Woman's Council brought together a varied group of women: full-time employees such as Fannie Segur Foster, a cashier for the Southwestern Telephone Exchange, and Mrs. Young B. Dowell, a teacher in the East Dallas Public School, as well as women whose positions in the community allowed them leisure time to pursue their interests, such as Mrs. David E. Boice, wife of a lumberyard owner, and Mrs. Joseph Letcher, wife of a surgeon.[18] Their common interest was learning what the most pressing needs of women and children in the community were and how they might be met. This concern was timely, for in 1893 Dallas shared the problems of the nation's depressed economy, despite the activities of the Central Council of Dallas Charity Organizations and the existence of a home for destitute women and children.[19] Among the topics discussed in the first months of 1894 were a free day nursery and kindergarten for the children of working women and the potential for better government if women were allowed to have a voice and vote. The Dallas Woman's Council received prominent coverage on the society page of both the *News* and the *Dallas Daily Times Herald*.[20]

Also receiving coverage was the March 13, 1894, formation of the Dallas Equal Rights Club, a local branch of the Texas Equal Rights Association.[21] Several of its members had helped form the Woman's Council, indicating the growing awareness of the usefulness of woman suffrage in bringing about significant improvements in the community. Isadore focused attention on one aspect of this dynamic when she addressed the Texas Equal Rights Association state meeting in Fort Worth in June, 1894, on the topic, "School Suffrage for Women."[22] She had firsthand experience with school suffrage from her Michigan years: in 1881 that state had allowed women who were parents of school-age children or property owners to vote for local school boards. The Michigan State Suffrage Association had urged women to run for their local school boards. As a result Battle Creek voters elected two women, one of whom—Ann Lapham Graves—was elected president of the city's board.[23]

In 1894 planning for the second Woman's Congress during the State Fair of Texas occupied much of Isadore's free time. As secretary of the Texas Woman's Congress, she used every opportunity to spread the word, even accompanying clubwomen Mary K. Craig and Belle Smith to Denison for a meeting of the XXI Literary Club. There she informed members about the history, organization, and aims of the Texas Woman's Congress and no doubt urged them to send representatives as they had to the first congress.[24] Spreading the word for Isadore meant more than simply appearing before Texas clubs, for she enjoyed a wide circle of contacts outside the state through her earlier positions in Michigan and Ohio. She corresponded with East and West Coast journals "devoted to the significant movements of the day," as well as such magazines as *Arena,* which had expressed interest in the Texas Woman's Congress.[25]

Isadore also wrote to women in leadership positions outside Texas, including Mrs. Robert J. Boylan, the president of the Chicago Woman's Club and vice president of the Illinois Woman's Press Association. Mrs. Boylan responded that she planned to attend the Texas Woman's Congress meeting as an honorary delegate. Isadore's acquaintance with prominent clubwomen such as Mrs. Boylan were another means of demonstrating the potential of club work to the women of Dallas and the rest of the state. Much could be learned from meeting and talking with Boylan about the work of the Chicago Woman's Club. With more than four hundred members, it had supported the founding in Chicago of Hull House, the Legal Aid Society, the Public Art Association, and the Protective Agency for Women and Children.[26]

When the Texas Woman's Congress met at the state fair in November, 1894, a new constitution was adopted, the name of the organization was changed to the State Council of Women of Texas, and Isadore was again named secretary. She was also asked to chair the building committee in its efforts to secure funds for a Woman's Building to be constructed on the fairgrounds.[27] The wealth of knowledge and expertise from her work for women's causes in Michigan and Ohio became invaluable as Isadore worked with the State Council of Women, the forerunner of the Texas Federation of Women's Clubs.

Other, more personal matters also occupied Isadore's attention during this time. Her departure from Battle Creek in 1891 had been, in effect, a separation from her husband. Her marital status, however, was probably not revealed to anyone outside her family, for in polite society divorce conferred a stigma on most women. Nevertheless, something happened to make Isadore go to Michigan and file suit in July, 1894. Although a husband's failure to support his wife was grounds for divorce in Michigan, Isadore had waited three years to start the proceedings. Apparently James Miner had decided to study dentistry at the University of Michigan in the fall of 1894. Michigan law would have made Isadore liable for his debts unless she divorced him and thereby recovered the legal ability to control her earnings. At the age of thirty-one she became a member of a growing class of professional women who found they must manage their lives without a husband in the picture.[28]

Whatever prompted Isadore's decision, she could find a measure of support for divorce among vocal suffragists. Although some did not approve of it, one of the most notable, Elizabeth Cady Stanton, had favored divorce as early as 1860. Susan B. Anthony and Alice Stone Blackwell concurred. In their view, to remain in an unhappy marriage was unacceptable. Their position stood in contrast to the widespread concern for the rising divorce rate in the late nineteenth century. Religious guardians of home and hearth decried divorce as a breakdown in the social order and a threat to domestic tranquility, caused by the growth of secularism and individualism. Scholars of the period claimed that as more women entered the workforce, they were able to abandon bad marriages and support themselves. Others pointed to increased educational levels or the demands of the social purity movement for better treatment of women within marriages as forces raising women's expectations for their marriages. All of these probably contributed to the undisputed fact that by 1890, women were seeking divorces in rapidly increasing numbers.[29] Isadore's decision to proceed with her divorce signaled an eagerness to close an unhappy chapter in her life. She was financially better off than many working women and was gaining recognition for her professional skills.[30]

Even as Isadore was in the midst of her divorce, we have some idea of her view of marriage, thanks to a wedding celebration in Dallas. The occasion honored the New York City marriage of Jeanette Ennis Belo, the daughter of *News* publisher A. H. Belo. Staff members gathered for a sumptuous luncheon followed by speeches from assorted department representatives. While predicting much happiness for the new bride, Isadore offered a personal observation: "I am not a sentimental woman. The necessities that have made the newspaper woman have also robbed her of her sentimentality, which she soon finds an unmarketable stock in trade. So, without thought of being cynical, I will not idealize even now. In real life a woman never marries her ideal. She seldom meets him, and if she does she doesn't like him."[31]

Although written with humorous intent, Isadore's words suggest her disillusionment following an unhappy marriage. Her uncontested divorce was granted in June, 1895, yet for the next two years she listed herself as "Mrs. S. Isadore Miner (widow J.W.)" in the Dallas city directories.[32] Such subterfuge, uncharacteristic of the usually forthright journalist, must have been born of the need to be socially acceptable to the more conservative clubwomen of Dallas, who had already demonstrated a high degree of confidence in Isadore's abilities.

By 1895 Isadore Miner was not only the full-time society writer for the *News,* she also met the demands of activities for the State Council of Women and her position as chairman of the building committee for the Woman's Building. The extensive correspondence and meetings these offices required were accommodated by the *News,* which recognized the value of Isadore's association with women's clubs and the good will the paper would receive from her involvement.

Her responsibilities with the State Council of Women had given her contact with a relatively small number of women who were learning the fundamentals of organized club work from their more experienced counterparts elsewhere in the country. To educate other Texas women who did not have the same opportunities seemed a logical step. Assisting the newly formed women's groups provided the rationale for the woman's editor to put her reformer's Progressive spirit to work. Isadore saw a unique opportunity to bring her readers a new perspective on their abilities to improve their lives and their communities. Women on farms and in small towns had few outlets other than churches for their charitable impulses. And Texas clubwomen in larger communities, like their counterparts in the South, had concentrated almost exclusively on literary topics, except for occasional dalliances with history and current events.

Isadore had a different idea. She had presented her views about what the "woman's department" of a newspaper should include at a 1894 meeting of the Texas Press Association in Fort Worth. Her talk, later published as an article in the *National Printer-Journalist,* was widely praised as "one of the strongest, most thoughtful papers ever given before a press association."[33] In her presentation, she had boldly asserted:

> *Frankly, as a matter of principle, I do not believe in sex in newspapers any more than I believe in sex in [the] brain, and because of that unbelief in sex in [the] brain, gender does not enter into the*

composition of my ideal newspaper. . . . I recognize the conditions that have seemed to make it necessary to treat with [sic] women as if they had no interest in common with their brothers when such interests lay outside the four walls of home; but I also recognize that the public press, as the most potent factor in the education of the people, is largely responsible for the existence of these conditions, and therefore, obligated to make amends. . . . when a good, well stocked cook book can be bought for twenty-five cents, is it not questionable whether or not reputable newspapers can afford to print recipes? . . . Better spare [a wife's] tired eyes the time to read something helpful and refreshing from your own sympathetic mind. . . . Or better still, spare her tired fingers time to take up the unused pen, and enter into the timely discussion that is claiming advocates pro and con among the patrons of your own paper. Nothing excites more live interest and holds the personal attention of your readers better than the opportunity of occasionally appearing in print themselves, to air and exchange individual views. . . . The society column, as a rule, is but a symposium of men and women in their physical capacity, as lay figures to show off elegant apparel—as if they were so many revolving dummies set up in a show window. . . . Why should a woman's brains go by default—God made them!— while the handiwork of her dressmaker receives unstinted and unmerited praise? . . . As to the average Children's Department . . . the story on the Children's page should not merely serve to divert the mind for a few brief moments, but should be the exponent of the best art in literature, the purest culture and the highest ethical standard. . . . Finally, sisters, (and brethren, if to you falls the duty of furnishing woman's and children's copy,) I recommend the words of St. Paul, who seemed to give evidence of a wonderfully comprehensible editorial capacity, when he said, "Whatsoever things are true, whatsoever things are just, whatsoever things are of good report, if there be any praise, think on these things."[34]

A year and a half after her speech, Isadore's vision for a woman's department became a reality. On April 15, 1896, the *Dallas Morning News* published the first bylined column of "Pauline Periwinkle," Isadore's nom de plume. The *Galveston News* premiered her column three days later. Until that time her contributions to the *News* had not been signed.

Women in Dallas and Galveston would soon begin to turn to her column as soon as they picked up the paper.

Her choice of subject matter was decidedly forward-looking. Announcing a new "Woman's Century" page as a weekly feature in the Sunday paper, Pauline Periwinkle wrote to her "dear women centurists": "I am anxious to know what you are going to do with this whole page placed at your disposal."[35] She had no doubts, however, about what she was going to do with her own column: she would use her experiences, her logical approach to problems, and her clever pen to move her women readers "to be up and doing; to live and be no insensate part of this great, wide, wonderful world."[36] She would be engaged in what is known today as "consciousness raising" among the women of Dallas and throughout the state who could read the Woman's Century page and learn how women in other cities were making positive changes in their communities. The spirit of reform and improvement that had already taken hold in eastern and midwestern cities now had a voice in Dallas.

This novel approach to women readers set the *News* apart from other Texas newspapers, which adhered to a very traditional format for their woman's departments. Their focus was much the same as the one Jennie June had offered her female readers decades before: fashion news, home decoration instructions, social activities, and the travel plans of more prominent citizens. The same week the Woman's Century page made its debut in Dallas, the *Houston Post* featured for women a full page of "Spring Time Fancies" with line drawings of shoes and hairstyles, and a page devoted to "In Society's Realm," highlighting "A Brilliant Reception" and "A Pretty Home Wedding."[37] The *Fort Worth Gazette* offered its women readers a "For and about Women" page with sections on "Boudoir Chatter," "Very Gorgeous Gowns," and "To Make Lampshades."[38] Women readers of the *El Paso Daily Times* found no social news except for the list of marriage licenses issued and an article describing local reaction to a touring drama company.[39]

Isadore followed the introduction of the Woman's Century page with a new feature designed for the children of her readers. "For Little Men and Women" probably had its roots in her memories of the *Detroit Commercial Advertiser*'s "Little Folks Column." Introduced on July 21, 1895, the children's page of the *Dallas Morning News* featured poetry and short articles geared to youthful interests. Some were excerpts from publications such as *Harper's Young People* (i.e., "The Great Sails of Racing

Yachts"), and others were submitted by readers (i.e., "The Seven Wonders of the World" by fifteen-year-old Walter H. Butler). Isadore occasionally included poems she had written. A note on the page each week encouraged readers to write letters to the "Cozy Corner" edited by Little Mr. Big Hat. Specific instructions for young letter writers included writing on one side of the paper only, since "Printers never turn their copy."

The readers, who were called "cousins," filled their letters with descriptions of their families and activities along with messages to other "cousins" whose letters had previously appeared in the paper. The *News* enjoyed widespread circulation in Texas, and with the children's page also appearing in the other A. H. Belo publications—the *Galveston News* and the *Semi-Weekly Farm News*—young readers numbered in the thousands. One of the popular sections was Mr. Big Hat's Summer School, which offered a series of weekly lessons during the summer months. These ended in a final examination with prizes for the best papers and diplomas for all who answered at least 60 percent of the questions correctly.[40]

Even with two new features to manage, Isadore's professional activities did not occupy every moment of her time. She had attracted the interest of Dallas bachelors, probably with a combination of keen intelligence, outgoing personality, and distinctive appearance, for she was described years later by a fellow *News* employee as bearing a "remarkable resemblance to Mrs. Roosevelt of twenty-five or thirty years ago."[41] Although her Pauline Periwinkle columns could present an uncompromising critique of the social foibles of the single male, she obviously enjoyed their company, for her personal engagement calendar seemed filled.[42] The extent of her social life was apparent when her friend Myrta Castle moved to Dallas in December, 1896. Adding a postscript to a letter from Myrta to her parents, Isadore described the upcoming week's activities:

> *To begin with, Saturday night we go to the theater, to see Rosabel Morrison (daughter of Lewis Morrison) in "Carmen." Sunday we are invited to dinner on Chestnut Hill and to stay all night. We have an invitation for Christmas dinner and a tandem bike party next week, beside going to my history and literature club, which is very swell (or swollen?). The City Attorney called last night to invite myself and friend to the New Year ball of the Idlewild Club, the most fashionable social organization in Texas. 'Course we'll go. He is sommptions, [sic] too. We (Myrta and I) will give a New*

Year dining, and we are "at home" every Wednesday p.m. and eve. Please call. We will also go see Minnie Maddon [sic] Fiske for Christmas matinee.[43]

A few weeks after their Christmas social whirl, Isadore and Myrta attended the National Editorial Convention in Galveston, followed by a trip to Mexico.[44] Myrta's letters to her parents make it obvious that both she and Isadore enjoyed the attention of several men in Mexico. She wrote that a "Mr. Chase, Isadore's ardent admirer and kinsman," who had lived in Mexico for fifteen years, "wants so very much to get Isadore to live in Mexico with him in a far nearer relationship than one of blood. Now that is *strictly confidential*, [sic] He is a most accomplished and elegant southern gentleman, with generations of culture behind him."[45] Mr. Chase pursued Isadore diligently, for Myrta reported that several days later he and Professor Cormyn took them to Tacubaya, "the Monte Carlo of Mexico," where they "loaded us down at the market with all kinds of eatable and uneatable fruits, and treated us to every drink the Mexican can concoct. They also bought us a few trinkets. It was only by main force that I could keep anywhere near Isadore, with Mr. Chase hawling [sic] her off to whisper in her ears and Mr. Cormyn trying to get me in the opposite direction. When I didn't have the young professor to pilot and amuse me, I might as well have been in Egypt for all Isadore and Mr. Chase knew; they were oblivious to everything but each other."[46] Later in the same letter, Myrta also mentioned "Mr. Byers, Isadore's other would-be attache." She wrote, "he is the gen. manager of a Texas railway and has spent lots of money on us. . . . he's taller than Isadore, and as length and pounds seem to be what she most wants, I don't know what to look for!"[47]

Isadore evidently did not find Mr. Chase as suitable as Myrta did. She told the elder Castles, "I met Mr. Chase on Thursday and he proposed on Monday." Describing him as "dark and lithe as a Spaniard and has had smallpox to boot," Isadore reported that he had been shot on a hunting expedition in the jungles of India and had lost a lung as a result. "How could a man with one lung love a great big woman like me sufficient to compensate me for all the amenities of a civilized life?" she asked Myrta's parents. She felt a stronger attraction to Mr. Byers, whom she described as a "great young Scotch man in Houston, gen'l manager of a whole big railroad, who loves me with his two lungs and more." That he was "tall, fair and thirty-five" made him even more appealing. She made no specific mention of his wealth, but his style of entertainment left little doubt that he was a man of means. He had showered the two women with attention both before and after their trip to Mexico and, according to Isadore, "offered to take me to Japan for our wedding trip." She noted that Mr. Byers was coming to Dallas to visit them that week.[48] What happened to the romance remains a mystery, for no other letters that make any mention of him have been found.

Nor have any letters ever surfaced about William Allen Callaway. Born in Louisiana in 1854, the son of a Baptist minister, Callaway apparently lived in the same boardinghouse as Isadore (160 Holmes Street) before their marriage in July, 1900.[49] He must have overcome Isadore's wariness toward marriage, perhaps because he was nearly ten years older, well established, and willing to let her continue her work—an unusual attribute for most successful men at the time. The announcement of their wedding in Washington, D.C., which appeared in *Beau Monde,* the society newsletter of Dallas, noted that Callaway was "state adjuster of a prominent life insurance company of New York with headquarters in San Antonio." He was in fact a charter member of the Southland Life Insurance Company and served as secretary of the company until his eyesight failed. At that time he became editor of an in-house publication of the Southland Insurance Company and publisher of Callaway's Index, a list of men with more than $100,000 in life insurance.[50] The couple's wedding gifts included a chest of silver from Isadore's employer, A. H. Belo & Co., publisher of the *Dallas Morning News* and the *Galveston News*. Although the couple sailed to Europe for an extended wedding trip, the new Mrs. Callaway sent her weekly column to the *News* from a succession of foreign cities. She maintained her weekly column and her book reviews until her death.[51]

The columns of Pauline Periwinkle represent only part of the active life that Mrs. W. A. Callaway led after her marriage. Her early support for women's clubs and her obvious organizational talent made her a logical candidate for club leadership positions. Her earlier reluctance to assume a higher profile as a clubwoman began to change, although she was selective about the positions she agreed to take. As early as 1901 Isadore turned down an offer to chair the art committee, made by Texas Federation of Women's Clubs (TFWC) President Anna J. Hardwick Pennybacker, because she was suffering a case of blood poisoning.[52] While recuperating in Mineral Wells, Texas, in the spring of 1901, she wrote Mrs. Penny-backer and suggested instead Mrs. [Luther] Clark or Mrs. Anna Raguet Charlton as possible nominees. Because Isadore was also writing for the Music and Art Department of the Sunday *Dallas News,* she offered her assistance "through the *News,* in the furtherance of any art interests that your committee will decide upon."[53]

By January, 1902, Isadore Callaway was back in Dallas, where she entertained a number of friends with an eight-course luncheon at the Oriental Hotel. Among the members of "the old chafing-dish club . . . being brought together for the first time in several years" were several active clubwomen: May Dickson Exall, president, and Eva Whitthorne Trezevant, vice president of the Shakespeare Club; Corinne Kelly Munger, Mrs. John Pope, and Fannie Segur Foster of the Pierian Club; Mrs. W. E. Milligan and Mrs. Luther Clark of the Quaero Club; and Minnie Lee Sims Finley, Grace Simpson Allen, Mrs. C. L. Wakefield, Mrs. T. L. Lawhon, and Minerva Miller.[54] Most had been prominent in Dallas club work from the early days and likely encouraged Isadore to become more involved as a club member, not just as a journalistic supporter. Isadore never mentioned in writing her reasons for becoming a more visible participant in club activities. But she understood the customs of the society in which she lived, and she might well have concluded that her marriage to an affluent businessman conferred a respectability and acceptability she had lacked before.[55]

Although Isadore's membership in the Quaero Club may have been of long standing, her participation in its activities was not noted until 1902.[56] Her first public appearance as a club representative occurred at the November, 1902, meeting of the TFWC, where she took the lead in promoting the cause of restricting child labor. An observer called her presentation there "the most notable action of the convention."[57]

When the Dallas Free Kindergarten Association asked Isadore to serve on its board of directors, she agreed. As a board member in 1902 she wrote a letter requesting from Mrs. Theodore Roosevelt a suitable auction item for the benefit of a kindergarten building fund. The Roosevelt handkerchief netted $121, the largest single amount of the more than $2,500 raised.[58] Later, thanks to her publishing experience, Isadore was able to arrange for the proceeds from the sales of a 1905 volume, *The Legal Status of Women in Texas* by Lawrence Neff, to be conveyed to the Free Kindergarten Association.[59]

In 1903 Mrs. Pennybacker tried again to persuade Isadore to assume a leadership position: president of the Audubon Society. Turning down the presidency in part because of another bout of poor health, Isadore offered instead the name of Dallas clubwoman Mrs. T. J. Carr. She also used the occasion to suggest Mrs. W. Goodrich Jones of Temple for forestry president. Isadore's letter demonstrates a well-developed sensitivity to the value of utilizing personal connections of men and women in winning support for various conservation movements in Texas, as well as her growing personal friendship with one of the state's outstanding clubwomen.

> *Why not suggest . . . the name of Mrs. T. J. Carr, Holmes St., Dallas, for state organizer and president? She is president of Dallas Humane Society, and acquainted with all similarly interested in the state. Her husband is a prominent traveling man, very much interested in bird protection, humane laws, etc., writes a great deal on such subjects for the press, and could help her get members in his travels over the state.*
>
> *Then why not Mrs. W. Goodrich Jones of Temple for Forestry president? Mr. Jones is "pa" of arbor day in Texas, and might help her to "ma" a forestry move. I am always ready to assist any of these worthy "infant industries" with my pen, but cannot in justice to myself undertake to act as their parent. I feel as if I was [sic] in need of nursing, wet or dry, just now myself.*
>
> *Lovingly, Isadore.*[60]

Another reason for Isadore's refusal may have been the illness of her half-sister Eugenia Mae Fetterly, with whom she had lived when she first moved to Dallas. Mae and her husband John had moved to Dayton, Ohio, in 1896. When Mae became ill in 1903, Isadore went to Dayton. Isadore was there when Mae died in September, at age thirty-six, of "malarial-brain fever."[61]

By the end of 1903, Isadore's health improved and she began to play a more active role in club affairs. At the November, 1903, meeting of the TFWC, newly elected president Adella Kelsey Turner of Dallas named Isadore chairman of a committee to work with the World's Fair Commissioners in furnishing the Texas Building at the fair in St. Louis. Six weeks later Isadore headed a group from the Dallas Federation of Women's Clubs in a visit to the Dallas jail and a meeting with Police Commissioner Louis Blaylock to lobby for a police matron.[62]

Life became busier in 1904 when Isadore acquired a family of sorts: her two nieces. Their father, John Fetterly, had married a woman who reportedly treated the girls unkindly. The circumstances were similar enough to Isadore's own childhood experience with her stepfather that she refused to let the girls return home after they spent a summer vacation with her.[63] The nieces, Alberta and Isadore, needed a real home, so the Callaways moved from the boardinghouse at 160 Holmes, where they had lived since their marriage, to a house at 323 Forest Avenue.

When the General Federation of Women's Clubs met in St. Louis in May, 1904, Isadore played a crucial role in the strategy of Texas clubwomen to place one of their own members on the National Board. Named the Texas delegation's representative to the national election committee, Isadore succeeded in having Anna Pennybacker slated as national treasurer.[64] When Isadore returned to the 1906 general federation biennial as a delegate at large from Texas, she was asked to be the national representative for all women in the field of journalism. A short time later, for her work in helping establish juvenile courts in Texas, she was invited to represent Texas at the National Conference of Charities and Corrections in Philadelphia.[65]

Even as Isadore traveled to represent Texas at national meetings, she assumed a higher profile on the local scene. In May, 1906, she presided over the founding meeting of the Dallas Woman's Forum, the first department-style club in Dallas. The Woman's Forum, with Isadore often serving as a delegation member, took the lead in lobbying city officials for numerous improvements, such as the passage of a pure food ordinance.[66] A year later she was named president of the Dallas Federation of Women's Clubs, serving from 1907 to 1909. Her election represented the pinnacle of acceptance by the city's clubwomen. It was a remarkable accomplishment for a woman who knew none of them when she arrived fourteen years earlier, an acknowledged northerner who was husbandless, pro-suffrage, and employed as a full-time journalist.

Isadore's tenure as president of the Dallas federation was notable in many areas. She was the first president to create special committees for each federation project. She urged the city to build the first play park, naming her federation vice president, Olivia Allen Dealey, to head the playground committee.[67] The dedication of Trinity Play Park on Thanksgiving Day, 1909, was the culmination of Isadore's dream. Recognizing the need for pure city water, she appointed Mrs. J. J. Hardin as chairman of a committee on water filtration. The women did their research and then convinced the city to build its first filtration plant. Isadore also brought national suffrage leader Dr. Anna Howard Shaw to Dallas to speak to federation members, and this was apparently the first time the federation had sponsored someone of such stature.[68]

As if the responsibilities of the presidency were not enough, Isadore also served as the state secretary to the General Federation of Women's Clubs in 1907. The next year she was appointed to the Dallas Library Board of Trustees and served as campaign manager for the campaigns of the first two women to serve on the Dallas Board of Education.[69]

All this club activity added to the demands of her weekly column, and Isadore decided to work at home. As she wrote Mrs. Ione [S. J.] Wright in 1909: "Should you have occasion to write me again, don't address care [of] News. My mail often stays there weeks before I get it, while even if you only say 'Dallas' it comes to the house. I rarely go to the office."[70] A few weeks later, Isadore again wrote to Mrs. Wright, the newly elected president of the TFWC. This time she explained her reasons for refusing Mrs. Wright's offer of a state office. Her strong sense of ethical responsibility made it clear that serving at the state level in a policy-making position would represent a conflict of interest with her position as a journalist supporting the efforts of the organization.

My dear friend—

While I appreciate more than I can express the honor you would pay me of being associated with you and those other lovely women on your board, I think I can convince you that I can serve you best off than on. Mrs. Turner paid me the same compliment—hardly would take no for an answer—but I am sure she will approve the statement that I helped her more as a sort of silent partner, though not silent when it came to boosting her plans and measures.

You can readily see that I would be placed in the attitude of publicly praising administrative measures for which I would be supposed to be partially responsible—which always weakens an appeal in the public esteem.[71]

The TFWC president was not the only one seeking to use Isadore's talents. When the Mothers' Clubs of Dallas decided to field the first women candidates for the Dallas Board of Education, Isadore was nominated. She refused because she believed a mother would be a more appropriate candidate. When the two women Board of Education members had completed their first term in 1910 and one of them, Adella Kelsey Turner, announced she would not be a candidate again, a grassroots effort was made to enlist Isadore to run for the spot, but she refused, pleading the need for time to work on projects to which she was already committed.[72]

The projects included creating playgrounds around Dallas and serving as chairman of a committee of the City Plan and Improvement League of the Chamber of Commerce to implement the Kessler Plan for Dallas. The Kessler Plan was a comprehensive city blueprint developed by George E. Kessler, a Kansas City landscape architect, and endorsed by the Chamber of Commerce in 1910. The master plan provided for several major improvements: a belt railroad to circle the city, a central railroad depot to replace the six smaller stations scattered throughout the city, the straightening of the Trinity River and construction of a levee system to prevent flooding, an improvement in street patterns, a civic center of several public buildings, the elimination of all railroad grade crossings in the city, and the removal of the Texas & Pacific tracks down Pacific Avenue. It also called for cleaning up and beautifying the city by eliminating overhead wires and creating a series of parks.[73]

As part of the Chamber of Commerce support, the Parks, Playgrounds, and Social Centers Committee was established "to deal with problems providing for the future needs of Dallas in artistic, healthful and convenient open air places for all classes, particularly to give attention to the needs of the children."[74] Since much of Isadore's time in Dallas had been devoted to such projects, she brought a wealth of experience to the chairmanship.

While her many local activities kept her busy, Isadore remained committed to assisting the TFWC. Her talents were especially useful when Anna Pennybacker decided to run for president of the General Federation of Women's Clubs in 1912. Isadore was named to the Special Committee created by the TFWC to assist Mrs. Pennybacker. Placed in charge of publicity, she created a biographical sketch that was sent to her colleagues who edited woman's pages in major newspapers throughout the

Chamber of Commerce's City Plan and Improvement League, established to implement the Kessler Plan. Pauline Periwinkle on far left of second row. Courtesy Collections of Dallas Historical Society

country. The sketch, with an accompanying photograph, was scheduled to arrive at newspapers in the convention area just before the federation's biennial meeting in June. Isadore apparently did not attend the convention, instead sending her best wishes to Mrs. Pennybacker: "May Heaven prosper you and bring you back in safety with the laurel on your blessed pate."[75] The efforts of the Special Committee were rewarded when Mrs. Pennybacker was elected president at the San Francisco convention in July, 1912.

Following the hectic period of work with the Special Committee, Isadore became involved once again with the suffrage movement. Although the Dallas Equal Rights Club had been established as early as 1894, the group had faded from public view within two years.[76] There were only isolated instances of suffrage activity in Texas after 1894, but the situation was not much better elsewhere. The period between 1896 and 1910 is commonly referred to as "the Doldrums" by suffrage historians, for during that period six state referenda for suffrage were lost.[77] When a major push to reorganize suffragists on a statewide level came in 1913, women in Dallas organized the Equal Suffrage Association in February and named Isadore one of its two vice presidents.[78]

This office was essentially the last public service Isadore was able to render. Failing health curtailed all social activity, including a request two years later from Minnie Fisher Cunningham for Isadore to become a member of the Writer's Bureau for Suffrage she was organizing.[79] Isadore continued working from her home, sending a weekly column and book reviews to the *News* even after being admitted to St. Paul's Sanitarium in June, 1916. Ironically, Pauline Periwinkle's last published item was a review of a book by Helen Knox about one of Texas' outstanding clubwomen: *Mrs. Percy V. Pennybacker, An Appreciation.*[80]

On August 10, 1916, Isadore Callaway died from acute lymphatic leukemia at the age of fifty-two. Her funeral, held at her home on Peabody Avenue, included a uniquely appropriate group of pallbearers: G. B. Dealey, William H. Benners, and Joseph J. Taylor of the *Dallas Morning News;* T. E. Cornelius of the *Semi-Weekly Farm News;* Tom Gooch of the *Dallas Times Herald;* and J. C. McNealus of the *Dallas Democrat.*[81] The tributes that poured into the *News* filled a page, with declarations such as the following: "To enumerate all of Mrs. Callaway's achievements in Dallas it will be necessary to list practically every activity in the city in which the welfare of women and children is involved. But it is not in Dallas alone that her loss will be felt, for she was a pioneer in the cause of woman's advancement throughout the State."[82]

Noted child welfare expert Dr. Henry Curtis viewed Isadore Callway as a national figure, and in his tribute he named her one of the four outstanding women in America, along with Jane Addams, Dr. Anna Howard Shaw, and Carrie Chapman Catt.[83] The Dallas Woman's Forum offered a lasting tribute when it created the Isadore Callaway Memorial Fund with an initial gift of $300. The money was to "establish a Loan Fund to be used for the education of young men or women."[84] The TFWC recognized Isadore's contributions by adopting the third week in May as "Periwinkle Week," during which time members were asked to plant her namesake flower.[85]

An unnamed woman, however, expressed most clearly the impact of the woman's editor of the *Dallas Morning News:* "For over twenty years I have turned first to that page . . . and I voice the opinion of many friends when I say that it has been my kindergarten, my school, my college for there every subject of the day pertaining to the education and enlightenment of women has been clearly, concisely and entertainingly set forth and most of the civic clubs in our town and those for the betterment of humanity all over the State have had their inception because of some suggestion made by Pauline Periwinkle."[86]

4

■ ■ ■

"Verily, We Are Coming On"

At the time of her death, Isadore Callaway had written a weekly Pauline Periwinkle column for twenty years. The columns dealt with a broad spectrum of social and political issues which, Isadore believed, needed attention in Dallas and the rest of the state. These issues were also at the heart of reform efforts throughout the nation in the decades straddling the turn of the century. Historians have offered many reasons for the forces that brought about the Progressive Era, and the reform issues that dominated the nation's political stage at that time. Among them are the anxiety of professional men threatened by a rising business class, a search for order in a time of rapid industrialization, the threats to social stability posed by immigration and urbanization, businessmen's desire to have the help of government in making profits, and decreasing support for the partisan politics of earlier decades.

But the period was also marked by intense civic activity on the part of middle-class women in communities throughout the nation. This activity prompted historian Karen Blair to trace the origins of Progressive Era reform to the early concerns and activities of women seeking to correct societal evils such as illiteracy, intemperance, divorce, child labor, and juvenile crime, which they viewed as threats to the home and family.[1]

The *Dallas Morning News* woman's editor was an unabashed feminist who supported women seeking to improve themselves and their lives.[2] Isadore's bylined columns are exemplary pieces of Progressive Era advocacy in Texas, as well as a source of remarkably intelligent and witty commentary on the period. In a surprisingly modern and unapologetically realistic voice, the columns illustrate how a journalist with the quaint pen name "Pauline Periwinkle" successfully challenged Texas women to envision a better future and bring about significant changes in themselves and their communities.

The clearest illustrations of Isadore's beliefs are found in her columns. The effectiveness of her writing can be measured in part by the events that occurred after she wrote them. What follows are excerpts from Isadore's columns addressing an assortment of concerns. Her words have been placed in the context of the circumstances that prompted them and the activities that followed them. Some columns reported on the work of women's clubs as members learned how to assert themselves and expand their caring instincts beyond their families. Others chronicled the development of a statewide network of clubs that could organize broad-based campaigns for civic improvements, and then promoted those campaigns. Isadore's words bring alive the debates that fueled the Progressive Era and helped move women into the public arena to confront problems and situations that could no longer be ignored. She began by asking for her readers' opinions and views. Immediately after the inaugural issue of the Woman's Century page, Pauline Periwinkle extended an invitation to the literary clubs of Texas to submit their best program papers, along with a history of their club, to her column for publication. The plan of the Woman's Century, she advised her readers, was "to condense in a page each week the bright and beautiful thoughts, the helpful suggestions, the kindly sympathies one for the other of the intelligent sisterhood of a state."[3]

Isadore's invitation came in part from her realization that, in Texas during this time, women's abilities received scant attention. Texas was a fertile field for club organization when she arrived in 1893. Chautauqua circles had been popular in the 1880s, but southern women were reluctant to follow the lead of their eastern sisters in forming women's clubs until late in the decade when "amid sighs aghast and upturned eyes, [they] made bold to change their nomenclature, and women's clubs came into existence in the Lone Star State."[4] Such expressions of reluctance by some reflected the apprehension attached to stepping beyond the clearly defined roles for southern women, roles characterized by femininity, motherhood, and submissiveness. Faced with the changing perception of what constituted "true womanhood," a concept that had shaped women's behavior and expectations earlier in the century, women began to move beyond home and church work. Their involvement with "municipal housekeeping" was a major departure from what most had known and accepted as woman's proper role.[5] Although chapters of the WCTU, societies of the Texas Equal Rights Association, and assorted literary clubs were sprinkled about the state, most women's organizations were concentrated in urban areas and their numbers were only a fraction of the female population.[6]

Despite the enthusiasm evident at the meetings of the Woman's Council at the State Fairs in 1893 to 1896, the organization had only limited success in mobilizing women to become involved in addressing some of the problems facing Texas women.[7] The existence of the group, however, indicated women's interest in a different sort of organization, one that encouraged them to assume expanded roles in their communities.[8] Obviously, women's organizations in the state were lagging behind their contemporaries in the Midwest and New England in matters dear to the heart of Pauline Periwinkle. Whereas clubwomen in Chicago, Louisville, New York, Philadelphia, and Boston were finding success in improving life for children and working women and attacking municipal problems such as garbage and water supply, Texas women's clubs had not focused on these areas.[9]

Constrained in part by the cultural conservatism throughout the region, many women viewed missionary societies as the most acceptable vehicle for doing "good works." The great majority of women's clubs in Texas still confined their activities to the study of literature, art, or music.[10] The few existing suffragist organizations were struggling, and the WCTU had lost memberships after endorsing woman suffrage at the 1888 convention.[11] In Dallas, nevertheless, a group of women had established a Woman's Home for destitute women and children in 1886 and maintained it through donations and fund-raisers. The organizers of the Woman's Home were all members of the Ladies Musicale, whose activities fit the traditional mold. That these women chose to undertake a different sort of endeavor suggests the readiness of some individuals to address the needs of the community in nontraditional ways.[12]

By publicizing the activities of the state's literary clubs for her readers, Pauline Periwinkle wanted to demonstrate the existence of a group of women across the state with the potential to consider matters outside the literary field.[13] By soliciting letters from her readers about their concerns, she offered a sounding board that encouraged lively responses. When her own byline column was added to these other features, the Woman's Century page became a potent means of helping Texas women realize they could become a significant force for improvement in the state. It would, in effect, be the means of introducing the idea of the "New Woman" to many of them.

Although the debate about the activities of the New Woman engaged men and women throughout the nation, the label actually applied to a small segment of the population. Younger women who had chosen to attend college or train for a career in the traditionally male professions of medicine, law, or the ministry were the first group to attract the term. Outspoken advocates of woman suffrage were another. Yet the term could be applied as well to the wives of the emerging middle class who had leisure and resources at their disposal. They were embracing new roles as municipal housekeepers dedicated to making improvements in their communities. Women had begun to assert themselves as higher education became increasingly available to them after the Civil War. As opportunities for work outside the home increased, their horizons broadened beyond the walls of their homes to encompass their communities. Women's clubs, with the ability to organize and coordinate any occasion, were a logical outlet for the energies and enthusiasms of the New Woman.[14] Pauline Periwinkle reinforced this idea repeatedly for her readers.

Finding acceptance for the concept of the New Woman would take time, for although women doing good works were perfectly acceptable in Texas communities, other characteristics were troubling. As one reader wrote, "I am not in sympathy with the new woman when it comes to her wearing bloomers, riding a bicycle and voting, but I do like to see a woman support herself in preference to marrying just for a home, as some do."[15] Pauline Periwinkle began her efforts by pointing out to her readers that "an enlightened womanhood means more for the future than all conceivable legislative reforms."[16] Observing that "a generous education should be the birthright of every daughter of the republic, as well as every son," she favored higher education for women. But she did not limit the concept of education to younger women, pointing out that: "one of the most alluring of the many phases presented by the new woman movement is the promise it holds in store for the middle-aged woman of the future. It remains for this latter day trend of thought to disprove what has long been held, that when a woman marries she incapacitates herself for any future usefullness [*sic*] outside the home, and that if for any reason she be deprived of home shelter in after years, nothing is left in life but a dependency, where she is, mayhaps, simply tolerated."[17]

Instead of dependency, Pauline Periwinkle suggested another option: cultivate the mind and body while the children are at home, so that "when her family no longer requires her constant care" she will have "laid a foundation for a good work to be done."[18] The good work to be done took many forms, as subsequent articles, letters, and columns on the Woman's Century page pointed out. The fourth and, as it turned out, final gathering of the Woman's Council in October, 1896, produced a preview of the areas in which Texas women would be urged to work: "Obtain a state institution for the practical training of girls," "bring together the different clubs of Texas in a general confederation under the council," "urge the appointment of women physicians in lunatic asylums to care for the unfortunate of their own sex," and persuade law officials to secure "competent women to search and care for women wherever they are forcibly detained by law."[19] A "general confederation" of clubs advocated by the Woman's Council proved to be the easiest goal to accomplish, but in a somewhat different format than that envisioned by the council. Instead of organizing within the Woman's Council, eighteen women's clubs answered the invitation of the Waco Women's Club to send delegates in May, 1897, to establish the Texas Federation of Women's Literary Clubs, which affiliated with the national General Federation of Women's Clubs two year later.[20]

A week later (May 24) the Woman's Century page editor announced the birth of the Texas Federation of Women's Literary Clubs, telling her readers of the opportunities that could be anticipated from such an association. With her club experiences before coming to Texas, there can be little doubt that Isadore was a strong promoter of the concept of federation among clubwomen from the time she arrived in Dallas. While her column explained the inclusion of "Literary" in its name, the adjective was dropped when the federation adopted a new constitution in 1899.

Also receiving Isadore's applause was the adoption of "parliamentary usage" as a prerequisite for membership in the Texas federation.[21] Her implicit endorsement of the idea of club federation undoubtedly contributed to the success of the state organization.

> *It is safe to say that there is not a town in Texas that does not hold at least one woman who has long cherished an intangible hope that she now sees realized in the State Federation of Woman's Literary Clubs. The inalienable trait of womankind is sympathy— the longing for sympathy and the quick response to sympathy. In woman the social nature is also strong, and demands for her highest development, association, at least occasional, with those of kindred mind. While this is true of woman wherever she may be found, from a topographical standpoint the need is greater in Texas than in any other state, of some magnet that will draw her forces to a common focus. This consolidation has come to mean the measure by which the culture of the state may be estimated.*

> *As if in open disregard of old traditions, there met at Waco, on the 13th day of the present month, delegates from thirteen of the foremost study clubs of the state, the voting strength being thrice that number. Before adjournment a board of thirteen officers was elected, that will control the interests of the federation until its first annual convention a year later. . . .*

> *A word to amplify the seemingly narrow limitations of "Literary Clubs," as used in the nomenclature of the federation. A more exact expression, if intended to mark the confines of club eligibility, would be found in "Study Clubs," a term that has met with favor among those who have ventured to assert that literature, pure and simple, does not comprise the whole realm of human knowledge, and that science may be quite as vital as Shakespeare as a factor in culture. The name was adopted to serve notification that the object of this particular state organization was to unify those clubs whose pursuits were strictly intellectual, for as pertinently remarked by the president, no organization, of whatever nature, existed that intellectuality did not create, sustain, and carry forward. To clubs, therefore, whose members aim to widen the mental horizon, the federation offers the benefits of contact in exchange for their support.*

■ ■ ■

The objects of the federation, beside those of mutual benefit, which are legion, and have already been fully elaborated, were material- ized in a plan well under advisement, which hopes to bring to Texas and its clubs a series of brilliant lectures and divertisements that have already been found a success in club work in other states. Here- tofore club members living in the smaller towns have been denied much of the means of self-culture found in lectures, reading and like entertainments by competent talent. Not sufficiently strong in- dividually to attract artists to the state, by organization it is hoped the field will prove tempting enough in character of audience and financial returns to secure the best among these popular lecture tourists, etc.

This statewide organization harnessed the energy of its membership to bring about myriad changes in Texas during the next two decades. Pauline Periwinkle had already perceived the potential of the state's literary clubs, and once they had organized she was eager to help them. Her subtle influ- ence can be detected from the report of the first executive board meeting of the state federation. The board's invitation to Irma T. Jones of Michi- gan, a "lecturer of talent on woman's work and a prominent organizer in the national federation," was surely prompted by the columnist, who offered this personal endorsement in her column. "Association for several years in organization work elsewhere with Mrs. Jones," she wrote, "enables the writer to congratulate Texas clubs from personal knowledge."[22]

Several columns on the Woman's Century page were designed to inform readers of the ways effective clubs should operate. Pauline Periwinkle's May 17, 1897 column illustrated the abundance of sociability but lack of in- tellectual content she found in Texas clubs. As Isadore sat through numer- ous club meetings in Dallas, she no doubt compared her knowledge of women's clubs in Michigan and Ohio with what was taking place before her, and then penned these observations. Laced with humor, her critique offered her readers a fresh perspective on their club activities. Her sugges- tion of the need for a state federation was made with the knowledge that just such an organization had recently been established.[23] She chose a clever but effective way to explain why such an organization was necessary.

The womann's [sic] club has been such a splendid factor in the liberal culture of women, that one hesitates respectfully before committing the audacity of even a friendly word of criticism. But the trouble is there has been too much praise—not just praise, but indiscriminate praise. Club women and their papers parallel somewhat Dr. Samuel Johnson's simile of women preachers and their efforts. He said a woman's preaching reminded him of a dog's standing on its hind legs. There was nothing particularly praiseworthy in the feat; he was not even expected to do it well; one was simply astonished that he could do it at all. The fact that women have so quickly emerged from the shallows and asserted themselves—even through such harmless mediums as club papers, has elicited surprise, and this surprise has in too many instances been mistaken as evidence of something intellectually remarkable in the achievement itself. Whereupon has followed a flood of indiscriminate praise that has quite submerged the object aimed at, and removed the flattered individual beyond hope of sensing the deficiencies of inexperienced effort.

There are some things not only bad about these club efforts, but radically bad. The good things are too many to enumerate. That they have from time to time been given abundant recognition in these columns should carry with it the right to call attention to the defects that bar the way to success. These bad features begin at the beginning and stay with us to the close.

If a meeting is set for a certain hour it begins anywhere from a half to three-quarters later. If a paper is limited to ten minutes, it is extended to twenty. If it is confined to the discussion of a certain topic, the writer not only sighs for more worlds to conquer, but proceeds to conquer them. Her valor fails her at the critical moment, however, and she modestly declaims her achievements in a voice audible only to the first three rows of chairs, which have been left vacant by an equally modest audience. One or two numbers on the programme are announced by the president to be greeted by an embarrassing silence. The chagrin of that overburdened soul is doubtless salved by the sigh of relief, apparent if not audible, at the prospective curtailing of the belated programme; but in these days of telegraph and telephone even the distant absentee is not excused from the good form of regrets.

At last everything is worried through, and the tired few on whom the burden has pressed are awarded by hearing between sips of ice and mouthfuls of cake such meaningless encomiums as "Oh, it's all been perfectly charming!" "What a brilliant affair!" "I'm just in love with your club!"—sometimes from those who either could not hear or did not comprehend a word that was said, but were simply impressed with the fact that something was being done and women were doing it. In this way nothing stands on its own merits. It is all of a kind indiscriminately, and therefore will be neither better nor worse so long as lack of distinction prevails.

I do not mean to infer that woman is intentionally insincere. She simply has not learned to distinguish between the dog's standing on his hind legs and his standing on them well. Her release from limitations is in itself so surprising that it is as if she were suddenly confronted by a brick wall, and asked to particularize the bricks. All look alike to her. Some day her sense of value and relative position will become adjusted, but until then we must face the facts. They simply emphasize the need of organized effort all along the line—some educative force, and something tangible to conform to by way of standards.

A standard, to be effective, must be recognized as authority by the many, not the few. The condition of the club movement in Texas calls for the establishment and recognition of such authority as would be vested in the combined wisdom of a state federation. The discipline of such organizations can not fail to be wholesome, and will react to the advantage of local clubs through the representatives present.

These formal conventions give one surprisingly new estimates of the value of rules, of time, of ideas. The little disorders and tardiness incident to the familiar footing of the home members, begin to assume enormity as an offense—stealing, actually stealing valuable time. The chairman aware that eyes are upon her, expects to call the meeting to order at the appointed hour, and does so. The delegate, not feeling quite so free to disturb a convention of strangers, expects to get to the meeting of the season, and does so. She hears a paper on the value of promptness and regularity, in club attendance, and becomes so thoroughly imbued with its importance that she goes home and converts the club sisterhood.

The woman who comes with a twenty-minute paper when she

was instructed to keep it within the bounds of ten, is rapped down at the expiration of her limit by the conscientious chairman. The reader may be inwardly indignant for the moment, but if she has good sense she will get over it, and never repeat the indiscretion. Moreover, a dawning consciousness of the rights of others, including the audience, will begin to pervade her estimate of programmes and the home club will get an airing of her views that will tend to eliminate one of the gravest faults of women's literaries. Programme-makers, themselves, groan over it, too polite to suffer except in secret, and not till some convention gavel imperatively cleaves it in twain, will lesser authorities take heart and declare the club ten minutes to coincide with the ten minutes of the clock.

Nowhere is this long-drawn-out evil made more conspicuous than on special occasions, when the writers seem to be weighed down with the importance of making the effort of their lives. A short, meaty paper, with some snap in its sails, seems like trifling with destiny. This is a serious business and demands plenty of good paper and very little punctuation except well-rounded periods. As a consequence, each paper laps broadly upon the other, while the audience politely languishes through all the stages of expectation, perspiration, desperation and resignation. I say perspiration and desperation advisedly, for the close draped windows and air redolent with the perfume of abundant flowers, distracts one's attention to bodily discomforts, while an ominous tug at the back gives warning that one's best bodice has secretly formed an attachment for the chair, resplendent in a fresh coat of varnish.

Another grief that will succumb to larger association is the disposition to confide to the hearers the awful obstacles that threatened the writer's approach to her subject. After some half dozen women have spent five of their valuable ten minutes in recounting the seeming impossibility of compressing what they have to say germane to the topic in the other five, the advisability of plunging at once into the subject will strike them all about the same moment. The very sameness in expressing the fact will begin to pall on the entire company before number three has well begun, and it is safe to predict that this consumption of time will be in disfavor in every club represented there. Some recognition will then be given to the supposed intelligence of the listener, some little be trusted to their imagination.

The introductory self abasements, especially the kind with rhymed ends, relics of "you'd scarce expect one of my age," will also meet a timely demise. This disposition to commit a jingle can not be suppressed too soon; no one seems invulnerable to its attacks. A labored attempt to consider a list of poets in rhyme was so ridiculous a failure that the venture seemed labeled: "I'm something of a poet myself, you see." If you are mistress of a simple, easy style in prose, be content. Even Longfellow's command of rhyme and cadence would shrink aghast from the task referred to.

A not uncommon triviality indulged at club gatherings is the introduction of personalities, seemingly to bolster one's claim to an audience. It is not the legitimate personality that stamps strong and individual work; it is a catering to a kind of ancestral aristocracy that is very well in its place, but absurdly inconsequent where intellects strike fire. A long line of titled sires won't keep one's poetry from limping, then why should they find mention in connection with the poem? This is an arena in which each contestant must win on individual merit. Otherwise, what is to be done with Paul Lawrence Dunbar, the Afro-American elevator boy, whose poems are warmly approved by William Dean Howells? And what with the Russian peasant poetess whose songs have electrified civilization? Is a cultured civilization less sure of its steel than those of no birth and little equipment?

Contact of association will gradually wear away these excrescences in manners and methods as women begin to deal with subjects more practical, less theoretical. Club federation will throw strong lights on the obscure corners, and reveal the weak places that by united effort can soon be made stanch. Here the field is open to discussion—another great lack in the local club, where food is bolted, never digested. And the topics, too, are less abstract, less literary, one might say, framed to deal with the problems that confront earnest workers, which the local club rarely affects to notice. A club programme under such discipline would be a perfect composite, each part dependent upon and sustaining the other, each equally neces-

sary to the whole—no gaps, no overlappings, no inconsequent frag-
ments and badly matched joinings, but an exquisitely finished
mosaic.

Clearly the woman's editor of the *Dallas Morning News* was leading
Texas women to a broader view of what their roles might be in the new
century. By linking them with their sisters in the women's club movement throughout the nation, Isadore was allowing them to see themselves as a part of a larger group with enormous potential for improving
themselves. She encouraged them to get involved, warned them of the
opposition they might face, armed them with answers for their critics,
and did it with clarity, logic, and wit.

Pauline Periwinkle's column of November 22, 1897, anticipated the
criticism women might expect for becoming involved in club activity. In
it, she cleverly pointed out how earlier efforts to do something new or
different had their share of naysayers. Her words amounted to a pep talk
for women and expressed her conviction that they possessed intelligence
equal to or exceeding that of men, and that as club members they could
be a force for civic improvement.

> *Women, as a rule, are more apt to underestimate than overesti-*
> *mate their influence. Until woman became organized as a sex it*
> *has been impossible to approximate her power as a factor in affairs.*
> *It is a pretty saying, one generally accepted, that "the hand that*
> *rocks the cradle rules the world." Unfortunately, some very capable*
> *hands have no cradle to rock, and some very incapable hands do a*
> *vast deal more rocking than is good. Then, too, there comes a time*
> *when the cradle is empty, and the whilom [sic] occupant refuses*
> *longer to be swayed by mother power. What then? Are women voice-*
> *less except through the nursery oracle, who after all, may not speak*
> *as he was delegated to do, unless he so choose?*
>
> *Women's federated societies answer this question with a stir-*
> *ring No! Within the fold of federation, matron and maid, grand-*
> *mother and sweet-and-twenty count an equal "Aye" in the grand*
> *vote for the best in everything. The woman to whom mothering*
> *days never came, the woman whose mothering days are over, feels*
> *for the first time the force of individualism centered in self—that*
> *she of herself is a factor in the world's progress. And now as the*

federated membership nears the 100,000 mark, she also for the first time begins fully to realize the vast moment of women's influence — not as wives or mothers or sisters, but as women. A woman might be a wife, a mother, a sister — all three — and yet be an uncertain element in the strife for higher things. She might be none of them, and so pass uncounted. But as a federated woman she stands every time as the exponent of all that is best in womanhood in every phase, as a conserver of good homes and good government, for progress in the arts and sciences, for lofty standards in reals and ideals, and for the fatherhood of God, the sisterhood of woman — and the brotherhood of man. Then put her along side 99,999 just like her in 1898 and refute the tremendous influence of enlightened women if you can!

The fatuity of crossing woman's will, once her mind is made up, has frequently been conceded with sorrow. Old-time women have been known to change the route of a railway by seating their ample proportions upon the proposed line, spending the time very comfortably with rocking chair and knitting work, humming good old tunes while the breezes played with their cap frills and disconcerted workmen make themselves useful picking up truant yarn balls. Or armed with their little hatchets they have made very good kindling wood of objectionable telegraph poles that threatened their peace of mind and the appearance of their property.

No matter how good she may be, the ignorant woman has always been and always will be the enemy of progress. The federated woman, from the very fact of her membership is not an ignorant woman. If one such of the old-time women could effectually impede progress, what impetus could be given it by the concentrated force of 100,000 thousand [sic] women expended in the right direction!

What the enlightened woman of the present day needs is not more restraint, but more encouragement; not less opportunities, but less restrictions to make the most of those they already have. It is true that opposition so far has been the whetstone by which the progressive of the sex have polished and sharpened themselves. Those who have determined to do and to know have found a way to take advantage of the old Irishman's advice, "If you can't get one thing, get two," and they have usually come off victorious with their hands full.

The progressive woman can always console herself with the knowledge that people have opposed everything new from time immemorial. The inventor of the umbrella was stigmatized for interrupting the designs of Providence, for when showers fell it was evident God intended man should get wet. The man who brought the balm of anesthetics to a world of sufferers was persecuted, for the design of Providence clearly indicated that a man's limb should ache if it was amputated, and the inventor frustrated that design. . . .

In this country the venerable traditions are used to being disturbed. America was clearly designed to be a disturber of tradition and to leave nobler precedents than she found. The New England "school marm" was once a revolutionary innovation, but she has been abroad in the land ever since and has proved not the least efficient of the great civilizing forces of this country. And so with her intelligent sisters of this later generation. Her opposers may declare her "contrary to nature" and with wise eyes forewarn her of God's intentions toward her, but the next thing will always be—something else. So long as the world "do move" the woman with brains will move with it.

The civic influence of a non-voting but thoroughly organized body is an interesting problem. That such an influence is wielded, one has but to recount the achievements of the federated women's clubs of Chicago, as given by Mrs. Henrotin and reprinted in this issue.[24] Nor is the list exhaustive. There is no town, even in Texas, where women's unfranchised influence might not be productive of public weal.

And right here it may not be inappropriate to conjecture what will doubtless occur to the reader of "Relation of Women and Affairs," that the average club member is about as capacitated to give an intelligent opinion on public questions as the average boy of 21 in proud possession of his first ballot. The woman of 40 who has "seven good financial reasons" in the persons of herself and six children has fully as sound ideas on the money question as her eldest *hopeful who casts his first vote before he has yet contributed a dollar to the common fund. And what does he know about the tariff that she has not already learned by the varying prices of commodities? This does not argue, of course, that the ratio of their information does not change. Froebel never framed a truer axiom that "we learn to do by doing." The boy soon outstrips the woman in knowledge of affairs as he comes in actual contact with them. If women were allowed to do, they would learn just as quickly by the doing. The woman and the emergency are always on a level.*

As well tell a woman that by familiarizing herself with the contents of a cookbook she may become a proficient cook without ever coming in contact with the batter pans and ranges, as to tell a woman that the study of this or that will make her [an] authority on questions of which she has no practical knowledge. The average woman, in clubs or out, is not a calamity howler, neither does she care, at their present low ebb, to dabble in general politics. What she does object to, and that very properly, is the inference that she is barred from the political arena from lack of intelligence alone. The average woman is just as intelligent as the average man, and a whole heap better. Her superior mentality is often proved by the very fact that she doesn't want to vote when she can, and her superior morality by the fact that she does vote sometimes when she doesn't want to, because a patriotic duty is involved.

Having urged her readers to use their "unfranchised influence" for the "public weal," Pauline Periwinkle devoted her next column (November 29, 1897) to the relationship between women's organizations and civic duty. Pointing out inequities in the system of charitable giving, she urged women to reexamine their methods while redefining the whole issue and expanding the notion of what they could do. She was, in effect, setting the groundwork for a Progressive agenda for women's clubs in Dallas and the rest of the state that would mirror the work being done in the Midwest and Northeast.

A reader of Woman's Century, alive to the new thought of the hour, writes that Miss Lyman's article on the civic duty of women's clubs, in last week's budget, was suggestive, but that its practical application needed demonstrating—in Texas. Would I demonstrate it?

The word "civics" is of comparatively new coinage. It is clearly a broadening of the adjective "civil"—a little loosening of its legal phase, a greater impingement on its social meaning. Its definitions read: "I. Ethics, or the doctrine of duties in society. 2. Civil polity, or governmental methods and machinery. 3. Law, in its applications most directly involving the interests of society. 4. Economics, or the principles or laws of wealth and exchange. 5. History of civic development and movement."

From this array of constructions I think the reader who queries the possibility of a relation between women and civics in a state where woman does not enjoy(?) [sic] franchise, may safely conclude her opportunities legion—running the gamut of an actual and active interest in affairs to simple study of doctrines and history. These constructions also prove that, unconsciously maybe, woman already has dabbled in civics in this great state.

Every organization of women for altruistic work has a direct bearing upon civics. Every charitable and aid society, every refuge home, every institution through the purposes of which women forego self-interest—that is civics of a kind pure and simple. And as women progress in the study of the means by which best to advance this work do they progress to higher planes of conception of civic duty.

One feature of this sort of civics might be much improved—that which leaves to woman the burden of sustaining these hosts of benevolent yet public enterprises. Woman has a sufficiently large field to create and encourage public sentiment to a recognition of its duties in such respect, without the obligation of begging from individual door to door to sustain it. The difference between being accosted for your alms directly on the street corner and being solicited for them by charitable promoters lies chiefly in aesthetic compensations, which, the men say, is offset in their case by a businesslike desire to see where the money goes. In addition, every self-respecting woman knows that next to being the veriest beggar herself comes the humiliation of begging for the veriest beggar. I have often heard men remark, after grudging yield of a few dimes to some departing woman whom the burdens of charity had driven on a quest: "I wish there was some law to prevent this sort of thing. I feel like running every time I see a woman. I'd as lief be held up by a hobo as by these petticoated extortionists," etc. I have heard such things and worse, and I have wondered if men realize how apt the proverb "It is more blessed to give than to receive." For, rest assured, the annoyance of the giver is the torture of the recipient.

And why should women forever stand in the attitude of beggars? Take the two classes of dependents—male and female. By far, the larger drain on the public comes through the dependence of vice. When viciousness in man reaches a penal stage the state puts its hand in the public pocket and without so much as by your leave appropriates funds to shelter, clothe and feed him. The property-owning woman is levied on proportionately to the property-owning man to build the penitentiaries, jails and workhouses that are disproportionately occupied by the other sex. Vice in woman rarely goes beyond that bearing the social penalty, and yet, at the mere suggestion of providing refuge and sustenance for unfortunate women incapacitated for a time from earning a livelihood, men suddenly feel themselves overburdened and throw the responsibility onto philanthropic women. Maybe these latter annually pay a pro rata toward the support of public institutions filled only by men; now they must provide privately for those of their own sex needing a public shelter, and if they timidly ask a reciprocity on a man's part they are quite as apt to get a figurative stone as anything more nourishing to their enterprise.

Here is a good civic field for women: Making the public see its civic duty to its unfortunate dependent as well as its criminal dependent. In many cities the institutions of reformatory or charitable nature are as much a part of the city charge as its schools, hospitals, jails, etc. It is unnecessary to say that release from this unseemly scramble after funds and undignified methods of money raising where such civil advancement obtains leaves the woman citizen more leisure for her private club and church concerns, for those more delicate and worthy charities where the left hand must not know the deeds of its fellow, and for the nobler phase of civics. Removed from the degrading attitude of chronic begging her sympathetic nature now forces her to assume, her value as a citizen will accrue to the aesthetic and cultured side of civics. Instead of to its sordid side alone—an extension of influence much needed in Texas. . . .

If work of the character outlined in this article does not satisfy the querist that woman has a part to play in civics everywhere, then give me breath to tell of the training and industrial schools, the co-operative and labor exchange bureaus, the free kindergartens and day nurseries, the sanitary inspection boards, the fresh-air funds, the tree-planting and park-creating societies, etc. that are engaging the attention of energetic and far-seeing women, and making our cities and towns something else than irresponsive brick and mortar.

Pauline Periwinkle continued to prod women to broaden their own and their clubs' horizons. Convinced that they could improve their programs with more initiative, she urged clubwomen to expand the range of their study subjects. Her preference for social issues, not literary subjects, was evident. Her September 19, 1898, column offered a critical but humorous view of how little independent thought and effort club members gave to the club papers. It provides a revealing glimpse of many women unaccustomed to thinking about the issues and arguments that concerned women in northern and eastern cities. Isadore then singled out the programs of the First Literary Club of Tyler as a model for others.

The province of woman's clubs is, ultimately, to teach women to think for themselves to some purpose. If it fails in this, then, and to the same degree, is the club a failure.

While all knowledge in itself is a good thing, still at best it is like water in a well with no way of getting it up if no channels are opened for its application. The reception given the assignment of topics at a club exemplifies this in a manner perfectly familiar to the average club woman. So long as the programme committee sticks to "character sketches" (so-called) or anything in the range of events antediluvian or prehistoric, or of literature from "Chaucer to Bok," so long is everything serene and each woman lugs home her topic with an air of assuredness that would be amusing were it not so extremely pathetic—assuredness, because, you see, she knows exactly where in the encyclopedia to find all in the world she needs to rehearse on the subject. But let any such topic be assigned as "the psychological influence of dress," "the value of art in the public schools," "Is woman's character and influence weakened by a multiplicity of pursuits?" or "Does social life unfit one for serious work or thought?"—in fact, any subject that is not fossilized in books, and the wail will go up: "Oh, don't give me that! I know I can't find a thing about it." If woman is devoting herself to dead poets, foreign languages and abstruse science and a dozen other fads in club study that don't at all matter, and can't waken up to living issues, can't find a thought in her own cranium about problems worth the solving, then is club life, so far as she is concerned, a failure.

Don't misunderstand me; don't think I view irreverently poets who have breathed their last, languages that are not mine, or sciences that are not easily mastered. I value them highly—as implements; nutpicks by which to get at the real meat of life. Their worth lies in their application; in the facility with which they loan themselves to human needs. Possessing them all, we may still share the unhappy fate of one who

> *Was stuffed with erudition*
> *As you stuff a leather cushion*

If I were running a woman's club (joy that I am not!) I believe I should demand at least one paper during the season from each woman on a topic that she couldn't possibly find anything about in encyclopedias or floating literature, or for that matter from her husband. If a lawyer's wife descanted on "The Legal Rights of Women" and the paper bore tell-tale and oft-repeated "aforesaids" and "Whereases," I should promptly fine her. I should even be suspicious of the paper by the doctor's wife, important though it may be to know "The Value of Fruits as Food and Medicine."

Right here let me ask, ought not the club to demand a high sense of honor of its members—a literary conscience, as it were? Ought it to permit its members to present essays torn bodily from their moorings between book covers, or written by male conspirators, no matter how near and dear the relationship? The club does permit it, for the woman who palms off thoughts other than her own need not flatter she deceives her fellow-women; mental cosmetics no more fool the other woman than do the kind applied by the close scrutiny of the hand mirror.

Women are not at all lacking in the machinery with which to think. It has simply not been set in motion properly, and never will be so long as wisdom as found in books alone is resorted to. It is like trying to swim without leaving shore. They hug a library and revel in musty lore, thereby fondly considering themselves "literary," without contributing one iota to the world's thought. Yet they would readily recognize the absurdity of a like body of "artists" who never had touched a brush nor ever expected to touch one. If you really want to swim, strike away from shore, taking care not to get beyond your depth (since drowning isn't swimming). If you really want to prove your right to be a literary club, strike out for yourself (with just as much care for your limitations). You may strangle a little at first, and the sensation is not pleasant nor the sight artistic, but in a short time you can swim most anywhere (figuratively speaking), and in your own little sphere add something to the sum total of the world's thought and life's meaning.

Women think too much of the initiative stage; their vanity can't contemplate strangling in full view of even a circumscribed and sympathetic public. They are too much taken up with the particular costume they are to wear; they are critical about the manner in which they are to take water; the foam they are making splashing about seems a most important part of the proceedings, etc. If a woman, having been given a topic requiring original handling on her part, would sit seriously down and decide upon her points in exactly the same way in which she would decide, "How shall I take the stain out of that front breadth of my blue dress without injuring the color?" and then write it out with the same force and clearness she would write the process of the supposed cleansing in a letter to a friend, she would have added more to the world's stock of literature than if she had rummaged thorough books and pieced together a hodge-podge of other people's sayings. After a time she may aspire to augmenting force and clearness with the artistic embellishments that some very foolishly conceived to be the real gist of literature, when it is in truth but the fringe that decorates the garment, yet does not warm. It is true that a great many recognized writers are using literature as a means of exercising a florid vocabulary or to exhibit their skill at word-juggling; but the sen-

sible club woman will do well to strive after a plain, direct style, whose sole aim shall be to convey ideas. . . .

. . . but about the best thing in the conception of club's beneficence comes from the First Literary Club of Tyler. Its year book contains a gamut of subjects from the all-important, "Should Boys Be Educated in Their Own State?" to "How Far Does Smith County Produce Its Own Food Supply?" Any woman who can belong to that club and dodge an original idea, or rather a continuity of ideas, will have to go armed with an intellectual umbrella warranted deluge proof.

Pauline Periwinkle's enthusiasm for women's clubs was contagious. The first annual convention of the state federation in April, 1898, reported "fifty-five clubs, combining the power for intellectual and moral enlightenment of nearly 1200 women."[25] Approved at the convention was a move to allow the Woman's Century page and its editor to monitor the work of clubs statewide. The federation named Kate Scurry Terrell of Dallas the editor of club news, giving her the responsibility for conveying all club news to newspapers throughout the state. The May 9, 1898, column noted that the "Woman's Century, in particular, will be open to all that is bright, fresh and of general interest to clubdom."

Having seen the Texas federated club movement off to a running start, Pauline Periwinkle did not sit back and quietly observe the activity. She knew that sensitivity and tact were needed to convince her readers to move from their late-nineteenth-century "proper place" as guardians of the home and family and become active municipal housekeepers. She realized that many women in the South had been slower to embrace the new activism.[26] To overcome this widespread reluctance, the Woman's Century page editor pressed her case with simple logic. Her column of June 12, 1899, illustrated her method.

The great obstruction to all progress is lack of thought. The impatient scientist who roused the ire of the sex a few years ago by saying: "Woman stands for embodied conservatism and embodied obstructions" unconsciously did a good deed, for he stirred us to thinking. He but voiced the idea that has been slowly crystallizing in the efforts of club promoters—and that is: The chief aim of the club is to get women to think. When thought is aroused, at once they ask themselves, "what can I do?" and soon are demanding their part of the world's work. The club provides the personal preparation, and the results are countless live factors in the progress of humanity.

When I speak of the "world's work," I do not mean that kind of labor that finds its incentive in the wages given in exchange, but that gratuitous service that to the thoughtless is known as "nobody's business," but which, unperformed, impedes progress in every department of life. Whether so elusive in character as to defy definition other than "molding public sentiment," or taking such practical form as freeing city streets from unsightly billboards and unhealthful conditions, it is all the world's work in which the awakened woman sees duty's beckoning hand. Look at the public endeavors and benefactions that have sprung up in the last decade as the result of woman's thought, and ask if it has not been worth while to enlist the influence of that larger half of humanity in the furtherance of public weal, instead of relegating it exclusively to those things labeled "domestic." The fear that the foundations of the home would become unsettled if the borders of woman's domain were enlarged has proved as childish as the cry of the bogie man.

Now, one of the chief benefits accruing from the mental stir of thinking is to think to some purpose. "It is not good enough to be good; one must be good for something," may be paraphrased: "It is not enough to think; one must think to some end." That woman will get the most developmental exercise for her wits who will find out for herself the application of these various lines of club work to her own community. It stands to reason that any suggestion must be evasively general, and that local needs and conditions must really govern. And much of the value of all this work, so far as the public is concerned, will lie in just that fact—that the community has not been sawed off or stretched out to fit any Procrustean devices, but that those whose interests are wrapped up in the progress of their particular section are suiting procedures to the temper of its people. The wisdom of this is seen in the various ways adopted to advance library sentiment; in the end the work is accomplished, but through widely differing methods, and each community is the stronger from having thought out and carried to success its own ideas.

■ ■ ■

The work of Pauline Periwinkle was widely acknowledged by an official resolution passed at the 1899 state convention of the TFWC. The resolution thanked the Woman's Century page for its "staunch support of and interest in the woman's movement of Texas and all that goes to extend woman's influence for good." That support would continue, as seen by the message Isadore sent in 1901 to Anna Pennybacker, president of the TFWC: "Yours to command so far as I can assist with my pencil."[27]

When the clubwomen convened in Galveston in April, 1899, they adopted a new constitution omitting the word "literary" from the name and voted to unite with the national General Federation of Women's Clubs. They also took a major political stand. The legislature was in session at the time, and under consideration was a bill to establish a State Industrial School for Girls, the same bill for which several local women's groups had been seeking passage. When a resolution pledging federation support for the bill was passed unanimously, the clubwomen served notice that they had come of political age.[28] Pauline Periwinkle endorsed their action in her May 14, 1900, column. She wrote: "The proper way for federations to secure the objects they have in view is to obtain favorable legislation wherever practicable, and thus insure the permanency and support of such enterprises as far, from the nature of their benefits, of State character. Once assured, the federation is free to turn its energies in other channels, to promote other useful measures. To neglect using its influence to obtain proper legislation is to retard the very many measures that must receive due encouragement in this new industrial and intellectual era dawning for Texas. If the hands are too full, some things will be lost in the attempt to grasp all."

Pauline Periwinkle's November 21, 1904, column included a description of how women's clubs in Colorado had approached their legislature. It had been reported by Sarah Platt Decker, president of General Federation of Women's Clubs, who attended the TFWC convention that year.

> On the discussion of how to secure favorable action on the proposed bill for a State library commission, Mrs. Decker recommended the measures adopted by the Colorado club women when interested in legislation. They fairly snowed under their Representatives and Senators with letters of indorsement, until the poor men in despair cry, "Take anything you want—the whole treasury if need be—

only stop this never-ending stream of correspondence." "Nagging isn't a very attractive word," said Mrs. Decker, "nevertheless nagging is just about what occurs when we encounter a case of this kind. Interviewing our legislators has also proved effective. Of course it's lobbying, but it's religious lobbying when the cause is just, as women's causes are."

Thanks to the steady stream of club news from Texas crossing her desk, the Woman's Century page editor was able to monitor the various projects underway.[29] Despite the growing popularity of women's clubs in Texas, many women apparently failed to appreciate the impact their club news might have on the wide readership of the Woman's Century page. Pauline Periwinkle devoted space in her June 4, 1900, column to a lecture on the value of publicity for the advancement of club work. She also served notice that it was the clubs' responsibility to supply newspapers with information in a businesslike fashion.

If the articles come in neatly written and prepared with evident regard to local conditions; if they do not overrun the space allotted, and thus occasion the editor a spasm of regret, knowing how his readers "skip the long pieces"; if the signature is supplied, thus lending a local interest to the matter treated upon, don't you know you will find in that editor an advocate unrivaled, whereas nothing would make him so skeptical of the efficiency of clubs and club women as a carelessly written, scrappy-looking article without end or beginning, unsigned, taking thrice the space he promised, and without the least application to the community in which the paper is published?

Now, printers' ink judicially applied to the club idea is a great lubricator and will make it run further and smoother than anything I know.

Two years later, in her column of November 28, 1904, Pauline Periwinkle recalled for her readers the remarkable changes that had taken place in women's clubs since the founding of the Texas federation.

It almost takes one's breath to contemplate the evolution of the Texas federation. Seven years ago the word "culture" comprehended its broadest meaning, and a book was its symbol. One would imagine that society had no ailment, spiritual or moral, that could not be relieved by a good strong dose of culture, administered in book capsule. Dooley's vision of Carnegie handing out a library to a starving man on his back doorstep, would have served as a pen-portrait of the club idea. Do you remember the "yard of roses," "yard of pansies," et al.—those popular gift lithographs that once cemented the friendship of women for their favorite journal? Well, the papers read at those old-time club occasions were like that—sentimentally rounded periods interspersed with flowery quotations, and set in formal rows, a yard, yes, two or more tiresome yards in length.

Now the federation counts its philanthropies by the scores—libraries and scholarships, kindergartens and civic betterment, music and art for the enjoyment of those unable to supply their own. Aesthetic science, patriotic endeavor, work for home and schools, and for that unfortunate element that has known the influences of neither good homes nor schools. The federation has awakened to the fact that the progress of the world does not depend on the acquirement of a little more culture on the part of a limited number of fairly well-educated women, but on the amount of leavening those women are enabled to impart to the masses.

As for prosy papers and flowery reports, the convention will have none of them. "Cut the papers and give the time to discussion" is the cry. When the presiding officer of the northeastern division presented the work for her division, the federation listened with eager attention to a concise statement of what each club in the district had accomplished, and I could but recall the listless interest once exhibited in the long, rambling reports that evaded the issue in the attempt to achieve literary distinction. And whereas great stress was always laid on the social side of club gatherings, one long instance of where "eatables and wearables" got the best of "thinkables and doables" raised a smile of toleration. Verily, we are coming on.

5

. . .

"The City That Has Not Doffed Its Village Swaddling Clothes"

As Pauline Periwinkle promoted self-confidence and encouraged improvements in club mechanics and participation with her columns, she also began to make pointed observations about civic improvements needed in communities. Across the nation reform efforts attacked many of the ills produced by rapid urban growth and unregulated industries.[1] In Texas the need for public libraries received Pauline Periwinkle's hearty endorsement, and in Dallas, her personal involvement. Her columns about local conditions that offended citizens' eyes, noses, and stomachs were written to galvanize efforts to secure laws for pure food, milk, and water.

The woman's editor was, in effect, encouraging Texas clubwomen to join nationwide efforts to do something about the lack of amenities such as libraries, the condition of city sanitation, and the sale of adulterated food. Pauline Periwinkle reminded readers that because their efforts to find solutions could affect everyone living in an urban setting, including their families, they had an obligation to become involved.

This municipal housekeeping concept had received the endorsement of the General Federation of Women's Clubs several years before.[2] It encouraged women to extend their concerns for their families beyond their homes and supplied a rationale for those who were reluctant to become active in public debate to overcome their hesitancy. For Dallas, municipal housekeeping was an idea whose time had come, and Pauline Periwinkle urged women to acknowledge what women in cities such as New York and Chicago had already discovered: they could protest civic shortcomings and unsanitary conditions and get results.[3]

Dallas was a prime candidate for municipal improvements during the 1890s, for its government was ineffectual and its finances in disarray. The ward system of representation was blamed for the election of council members who were rapidly turned out by voters for mistakes they made because of their lack of governmental or financial experience. The turn-over assured that no political machine could control the city, but it also meant that much owed in taxes went uncollected, for many refused to pay taxes for the inept leadership they perceived was running the city. As a result, many city expenses were curtailed and maintenance of basic amenities such as streets and sewers suffered.

Although civic groups in Dallas urged businessmen to stand for election to help the city, the inadequacies of municipal government were not substantively addressed until citizens voted in 1906 to switch to a commission form of government. This charter change was patterned after a plan developed in Galveston following its disastrous hurricane in 1900, when a system of commissioners, each responsible for one city department, was devised to respond quickly to the emergency. Until the new form of municipal administration took control in Dallas in 1907, it was left to citizens outside the political sphere to generate enough support to loosen city purse strings for improvements.[4]

Pauline Periwinkle used a column with a report on the Self-Culture Club of Palestine program, titled "What May We as a Club Do to Improve Palestine," to describe problems in many communities in 1897. The biting sarcasm of her commentary injected a dose of realism into the often lofty discussion of doing good works:

> *It is too bad that men are excluded from club work of this sort. It would be interesting to hear them enumerate the things they were doing for their town. One can imagine a list like this: Making the sidewalks filthy with accumulations of tobacco juice; idling on street thoroughfares to the risk and rights of pedestrians; allow-*

ing saloons on every attractive corner of business streets, permitting disreputable places along the lines of street car travel, where children riding to and from school will not have to wait for actual contact with evil to get their finer natures blunted, providing no retreat for the horribly deformed or afflicted, but allowing them to depend on street charity; for children, building school houses that are veritable Calcutta black holes for lack of ventilation, light and sewage; allowing the youth of the city to roam the streets unrestrained, and providing no safe entertainment for their leisure in a public library. These and other things are being done for our towns, until it is high time if men are too busy or too indifferent, that earnest women unite in undoing them.[5]

Given an understandable reticence on the part of many women to become involved in the more offensive sorts of problems Pauline Periwinkle mentioned, it is not surprising that the lack of public libraries generated the first activity. In a letter published in Pauline Periwinkle's column two weeks earlier, Ruth Carroll, then president of Dallas's Quaero Club, complained that her club faced the dilemma of acquiring the books needed by members preparing papers for discussion. "[C]an we of enterprising towns 'pull all together' and get up a public library?" Mrs. Carroll asked. Pointing out the demise of an earlier library in Dallas "which flourished until the city 'fell upon evil days' or in other words, got on the wrong side of a boom," she reminded Woman's Century readers that the books had been turned over to the YMCA and could serve as the nucleus of a new library.[6]

Less than a week later the executive board of the newly created Texas Federation of Women's Literary Clubs met in Dallas and discussed public libraries at length.[7] When Pauline Periwinkle determined their interest along with that already expressed by Mrs. Carroll of the Quaero Club, the stage was set. She would suggest that Dallas women's clubs become involved in the endeavor. "What force better fitted to set the ball rolling than woman's capable hands?" she asked in her November 29, 1897, column. But, she warned, the success of the venture required more than simple fund-raising. The essential element in this and any other project was the arousal of public sentiment in favor of the clubs' work. "Half of the effort expended by women in pink teas and their ilk in the futile endeavor for a library, if expended in turning public opinion and funds into this legitimate channel, ought to bring the matter to successful issue," she advised.[8]

Other women added their approval to the Woman's Century page. "A city claiming 50,000 inhabitants, with not a vestige of a library! Surely we should boast no more," wrote Eula Gunter Hardie, the wife of a farmer in Grayson County.[9] "The majority of working girls lunch in town, and there are very few of them who would not only be able, but eagerly willing to pay a monthly subscription fee for the maintenance of such a laudable enterprise," reported Kate Mayers. Mayers was a thirty-year-old widow with two children who lived with her sister and mother. The two sisters were possibly among the "working girls" mentioned in her letter.[10]

Interest in libraries was not confined to Dallas. Shortly before the first annual convention of the Texas Federation of Literary Women's Clubs in March, 1898, Pauline Periwinkle had challenged readers across the state to work for libraries: "Surely no better field for practical demonstration of the value of organized effort among club women could be afforded."[11] Clearly, the Woman's Century editor was laying the groundwork for the state organization's subsequent actions, for she was well aware of the lead that women's clubs were taking in a nationwide library movement. At its April, 1898, meeting in Tyler, Texas federation leaders had little difficulty convincing delegates that the establishment of public libraries should be the first demonstration of what a federation of women's clubs could accomplish. They formalized their intent with a resolution: "That the establishment of public free libraries in Texas be adopted as the work of this federation."

State leaders also revealed their rapidly developing political acumen by inviting an influential public figure, University of Texas President George F. Winston, to speak for the public library. At the meeting Mrs. Edward Rotan, the federation president, announced a plan to meet with Dr. Winston, State Superintendent of Public Instruction Professor J. W. Carlisle, and a committee of clubwomen to devise "a practical working plan whereby the clubs could succeed in establishing libraries."

In her succinct style, Pauline Periwinkle reported to her readers in May, 1898, that "the first annual convention of the federation boiled down into two words, reads 'Public Libraries.' "[12] She also reprinted the federation's resolution of thanks acknowledging the important role the *Dallas Morning News* and its Woman's Century page were playing in the women's movement in Texas: "To the News, more than to any other medium, is due the wonderful diffusion of interest in the woman's movement in Texas. Its sturdy independence, its breadth of policy, its freedom from sensationalism and its facilities for circulations make it a most desirable conveyance for reaching enlightened Texas homes. Above all, the News has never assumed a carping or belittling attitude towards woman's work and endeavor, and its unprejudiced course claims the admiration and gratitude of every woman in the state."[13]

Meanwhile, efforts in Dallas to establish a public library moved forward, and the progress illustrates how Pauline Periwinkle used her experience and professional position to assist clubwomen in reaching their goal. Shortly after the meeting of the state federation, her column reported the success of the Fort Worth Federation of Women's Clubs in securing a "lot for the proposed library building, the stone for a substantial structure and a goodly nest-egg toward the funds necessary to complete it."[14] A week later the Woman's Century page featured an article by University of Texas President Winston on the need for public libraries in Texas. He noted that a state law passed in 1874 provided for the establishment in any incorporated town or city of a free public library to be supported by funds from the municipal revenues.

That same day, June 13, 1898, Pauline Periwinkle's column offered a plan of action: "Produce the sentiment in favor of turning public moneys [sic] into library channels and the supply will equal the demand."[15] She informed readers that the Texas Woman's Press Association had endorsed the library movement and four hundred to five hundred newspaper editors throughout the state had pledged to help.

In the face of the success already enjoyed by Fort Worth clubs, Dallas women went to work. In November, 1898, the City [Dallas] Federation of Women's Clubs[16] had been organized in Dallas, and its members had adopted the public library as their first project. They publicized their intentions in a letter to the *Dallas Morning News* and sent a committee to the Dallas Board of Education to obtain their support. Then they asked for a meeting with several prominent men whose endorsements would help sway public opinion. The group met with delegates from the City Federation of Women's Clubs at the Oriental Hotel.[17] "All believed that the time was ripe for pushing this matter to a successful issue," the *News* reported on March 7, 1899. The women's efforts culminated in a "mass meeting" of about two hundred people on March 30, 1899, at the Commercial Club.[18]

There the Dallas Public Library Association was formed and those present adopted a constitution and elected a nine-member board of directors. Five of the directors were women, including May Dickson Exall, who was chosen president. Mrs. S. Isadore Miner was named acting secretary of the assembled group. She proposed that the library be presented to the public in the newspapers and offered to request interviews on the need for a Dallas public library through the *News*. In her capacity as secretary Isadore sent out 139 requests for interviews with prominent citizens whose support would help the drive for a library. The library association supplied the stationery, the services of a stenographer, and part of the postage. From the replies came the names of a "sympathetic constituency with which the [library association's] directors can at once begin to work."[19] The prolibrary sentiments of that sympathetic constituency were then sprinkled liberally on subsequent issues of the Woman's Century page.[20]

At the same time the women's clubs divided the city into districts and assigned their members to solicit donations.[21] Fund-raising efforts brought nearly $12,000 by midsummer, when Mrs. Exall wrote to Andrew Carnegie asking for funds for a library on city-owned land and maintained with city funds.[22] With his affirmative reply in September, 1899, the Dallas Public Library was assured, and the clubwomen tasted their first success in a citywide endeavor. They had joined the ranks of women in many other states who saw libraries as essential to educating the public and worked to provide them for their communities.[23]

Pauline Periwinkle had demonstrated a unique brand of influence to loosen city purse strings—a special talent that would help bring a wide assortment of improvements to Dallas. Her close ties with the leaders of the TFWC and her contacts in other states were invaluable. Familiarity with the agenda of the General Federation of Women's Clubs allowed her to publicize a need or problem and offer information on what efforts had been successful in other cities. Usually the women's clubs took on the task of implementing solutions, while Pauline Periwinkle supported their efforts in print.[24]

The columnist had no difficulty identifying local problems. In fact, for anyone who looked closely or inhaled deeply, the extent of one problem, pollution in the city, was obvious. Dust from unswept streets whipped up by the wind blew through open windows of businesses and homes. Sections of the forty-two miles of sanitary sewers had to be dug up and cleaned frequently after residents threw a wide array of objects into them. Refuse picked up by the city was hauled to a site that became known as "Lake Diphtheria" as rainwater accumulated in the middle of it. With an ineffective system of garbage disposal, an unreliable water source, and the increasing use of indoor plumbing that emptied waste into the Trinity River, Dallas in the 1890s was a public health nightmare. "Dallas Smells Bad" noted one 1894 newspaper article describing the city's unpleasant odors and their sources and calling for a cleanup.[25] A typhoid fever epidemic in the cotton mill district in 1895 was only one of several epidemics—of smallpox, scarlet fever, and meningitis—during the decade.[26]

Other growing American cities experienced the same sorts of public health problems at the end of the nineteenth century. Major migration to urban areas from the countryside and foreign lands overwhelmed many municipalities before public works projects supplying indoor water and disposing of waste could be completed. As a consequence, filth was considered the worst public health problem in nineteenth-century cities. The solution would not be simple, for as one author has observed, "the average citizen, accustomed to endure nuisances as a humpback carries his deformity, saunters along sublimely indifferent to foul smells, obstructed sidewalks, etc."[27]

To counter public apathy, women's groups in New York, Chicago, and other cities attacked the problems of inadequate garbage collection and street cleaning with reformers' zeal in the early 1880s. Added to this effort was the "City Beautiful" movement of the 1890s, which sought to create or enhance natural beauty in an urban setting. With the Columbian Exposition in Chicago in 1893 as a blueprint for city beautification, Progressive reformers linked civic improvement with aesthetic revival.[28] When the Spanish-American War of 1898 produced an extremely high death rate of American soldiers in camps from typhoid and yellow fever, more Americans awakened to the connection between germ disease and unhealthy living conditions.[29]

Dallas trailed other cities in beginning its cleanup. Several reasons may explain the delay: the emphasis on growth, an official laissez-faire attitude toward intervention on the part of the city, and poor tax collections that caused the city's near financial collapse in the early 1890s. The entire country experienced a financial crisis in 1893 that compounded the problems.[30] Pauline Periwinkle however, was ready to encourage improvements. Thanks to her experience as a writer for the Review and Herald

Publishing Company, she was better informed about methods for improving health and sanitation than many citizens. The Review and Herald publications had emphasized hygiene and healthful sanitary practices, often including advice from doctors on the staff of Battle Creek Sanitarium. In addition, Isadore's contacts among clubwomen in northern and eastern cities informed her of what women's clubs were doing elsewhere. With this background, she took notice of the general situation in Dallas in her December 20, 1897, column: "With the feeling that most effort thus far has been about as telling in effect as Mrs. Partington's broom against encroaching seas, occasionally I feel a call to mount a soap box for pulpit and preach the neglected gospel of the dustpan and the scrubbing brush. It may have been some other noise I heard but the need is crying, whether or not its cry was rightly interpreted. All over the north and east women are engaging through sanitary leagues in mortal combat with their twin enemies—dirt and contagion, yet here in the southland, where warmer suns and moister breezes hasten decay and increase its dangers, thought, if awakened, has given no sign."

The local situation continued to deteriorate until early 1899 when the *News* took an editorial stand and urged that the situation in the city be remedied, noting ". . . especially for the removal of decaying debris from the streets and the sprinkling of the streets to prevent disease-laden dust particles from settling in the lungs of everybody."[31] To focus attention on the problem even more forcefully, the *News,* at the urging of its manager G. B. Dealey, sponsored the creation of the Cleaner Dallas League. The March 7 half-page announcement of an organizing meeting included a prominent invitation: "The ladies are especially invited to attend and lend their aid to this movement." The influence of Pauline Periwinkle seems certain in their inclusion, as well as in the method used by the *News* to galvanize the public behind the league: graphically publicize the problem and quote the opinions of community members.

In the weeks following, the *News* reported among other items that thirty-seven dead hogs had been found in the riverbed. This was followed two days later by the opinion of attorney E. B. Perkins that "Dallas is one of the dirtiest cities in the south and it is time that something was done." City Council Alderman Theodore Beilharz reported that the city was spending $400 a month to keep the city clean, but that the cost the previous summer had been $1,500 a month.[32]

When the Cleaner Dallas League elected its leaders, men composed the entire slate despite the initial invitation to women in the community. Nevertheless, the Dallas Federation of Women's Clubs endorsed the league with a letter offering its assistance: ". . . the women's clubs of this city stand ready to assist in all practicable ways the movement for city sanitation and improvement."[33] Their concern was echoed in clubs across the nation, for among the resolutions passed at the General Federation of Women's Clubs biennial meeting in June, 1900, was a stand to use "greater vigilance in regard to sanitation" and to "forbid the use of small streams as sewers."[34]

The Cleaner Dallas League lost no time in accepting the clubwomen's offer to help. League organizers must have quickly realized that the work necessary to meet its goals would be time consuming and require a coordinated effort. They created a "woman's branch" and named individual clubwomen as "lady ward vice presidents."[35] In a letter notifying each of her election, league president Sam P. Cochran spelled out in detail how she should go about organizing her ward, calling on citizens whose property had not been cleaned up and informing authorities if compliance was not promptly rendered.[36] If the clubwomen recognized that they were being asked to do the most difficult work while the men held all the official positions, they were tactful enough not to mention it publicly.

At the initial meeting attended by the lady ward vice presidents, Cochran received his first taste of the clubwomen's methods. When he questioned the idea of calling public meetings in the wards, remarking that he "never attended a public meeting where the people who took part didn't go home and leave it all to a committee, when the object was to get all interested," Mrs. John H. Shelley, the wife of a traveling salesman, responded immediately: "You have never attended many meetings of woman's clubs, have you, Mr. Cochran? They don't do [it] that way."[37]

The clubwomen's energetic efforts combined with the lobbying efforts of the league before the city council, however, did not magically transform Dallas.[38] Part of the problem was financial, for the city council had reduced annual expenditures after its initial generous commitment of $17,000 to increase trash pickups and street sprinkling. Reports from the city council sanitation committee in 1901 noted that its budget was $5,000 less than the year before. The committee chair also pointed out that much of the problem stemmed from the fact that "while we find many citizens aiding this department as much as possible . . . we regret to say that a great many more are extremely careless or intentionally negligent . . . we frequently find dead animals and fowls as well as all manner of other kinds of filth thrown in the streets and alleys in violation of the ordinances."[39] The annual report of the city's health officer a month later quantified the situation: 728 deaths in the previous year, for a death rate of 12.1 per 1,000.[40] Just how many could be directly attributed to poor sanitation is unknown.

When the city's lack of financial commitment and citizens' indifference became apparent, Pauline Periwinkle used her column of June 9, 1902, to chide her readers. She lectured them about the consequences of their unwillingness to clean up the city, and she questioned their assumptions about risk-taking. Her indignant tone reflected the frustrations many clubwomen must have felt toward less-concerned citizens.

> *Man's audacity in building his home in spots as dangerous as the slopes of Mont Pelee have proved to be [and] have always been a subject for wonder and comment. History affords illustrations of the calm forgetfulness with which the survivors rebuild their dwelling places on the site of most dreadful catastrophes, and the serenity with which their posterity accept the hazardous environments to which they were born. . . .*
>
> *. . . Less than two years have elapsed since the united wrath of wind and wave seemed to predict the doom of Galveston, yet today the city stands as fair and resolute as ever, pulsing with energy and teeming with plans for the future that shall make it rival in security and greatness that other sea-walled city, city of fame—Venice. Unafraid, its people pursue their daily tasks and probably no city in the State receives as many visitors, coming from every part of the world, from every corner of the state, on business or on pleasure bent. The voice of the false prophets and the timid stay-at-home is drowned in the increasing traffic of the port, in the laughter of the bathers on the beach, while only here and there remains a landmark of the storm.*
>
> *Above the hazard of location must be rated the hazard of enterprise. Thousands perish yearly in mines from damp, cave-ins and explosions. Every day the papers chronicle lives lost in the manufacture of explosives, in steamship and railway disasters, in lumber and steel mills, in smelters and factories, and in countless occupa-*

tions that perhaps offer only a living wage. Manufacturing processes that require the constant inhalation of noxious vapors and gases and dangerous dusts have no difficulty in obtaining recruits to fill places left vacant by those who annually pay the penalty exacted by nature. We shudder at the fate of hundreds overtaken by sudden disaster, and forget that more perish every year to hazardous occupations on which the world depends for its progress, well-being and comfort. Life insurance companies recognize this fact, and while they offer financial protection to those living under the shadow of a crater and at the mercy of the sea, it is withdrawn from those who go down into the earth for coal and metals necessary to the world of industry and from others who engage in equally dangerous enterprises.

We who dwell in comfortable homes far removed, as we think, from danger, look in amazement upon the fine audacity of people who are willing to spend their days beneath the curling smoke of a volcano, upon the passiveness of the laborer, who for a scant wage, offers himself as a prey to all the terrors of the mine. We say with a wise shake of the head that nothing would induce us to go here or live there; that we would not trust ourselves to the perils of the deep, to the risk of mountain-climbing, railways, etc. Yet out in the back yard festers a cesspool whose poisonous gases are brought right into the house by defective plumbing. In the alley is an accumulation of filth that every gust of wind brings germ-laden to the nostrils. Dead kittens, chickens, etc. lie for days in our streets, food for the flies that afterwards light on the vegetables and fruit we purchase from the hucksters.

We ride in streetcars and walk on sidewalks where expectoration is permitted, and where the dust, set in motion by traffic and breeze, is laden with the seeds of consumption, typhoid fever and the like. We permit fruit and candy peddlers to expose, uncovered, their wares to the disease-infected dust, and buy, and permit our children to buy, the contaminated stuff. We live in unsanitary houses, our children spend six hours of the day in unsanitary schools, disease and death stare from every corner of the back yard and are met in every turn of the street. With bad ventilation, deficient and insufficient drainage, and abundance of disease germs, we are exposed to risks even greater than those which we swear we would not *undergo. Indeed, more people perish every year from infectious diseases, hence preventable diseases, than from disasters that can not be averted. More people pass years of wretched existence from ill health than from injuries received by accident. . . .*

Science has taught us beyond question that there is death in the bill of the mosquito, in the germ-laden excrement of the fly, in the sputum of the consumptive recklessly befouling public places, in an insufficient and impure water supply, in filth that remains to infect air and water from lack of sewerage. Drive about the streets any day and note the cesspools and vacant lots grown up to uncut weeds where mosquitoes breed and obtain their hypodermic supplies of malaria; the dead rats, cats and chickens that feed the fly today who is to dine with us tomorrow. In the still hours of the night, awaken with the stench that arises from foul outhouse and gutters and breathe a prayer for deliverance from death quite as certain if not as immediate as that which threatens the poor, ignorant Italian peasant and the heathen Celestial. Read with what calmness you can next morning that the budget for sanitary protection has been overdrawn, and then wonder that a mass meeting of citizens is not called to take steps to avert the epidemic of disease sure to follow.

Why the inhabitants of Martinique did not flee of one accord at the first belching of Mont Pelee is one question; why the inhabitants of supposedly progressive cities in the greatest State in the Union will consent to live in disease-breeding surroundings is quite another. The warnings of the scientist who proclaimed the volcano's dangers fell on ears no more indifferent to peril than those who listen to the findings of science concerning food inspection and germ contamination, and whose owners haven't enough gumption to procure an ordinance against spitting on the street and the exposing of eatables for sale upon which this same street filth has blown with the dust. If one had to choose between sudden death by cataclysm of nature and lingering death from tuberculosis contracted by breathing germ-laden dust, food, milk, etc. or typhoid from water and sewage infection, there would be unanimous favor of the former fate. Yet enlightened people are daily making choice of the white plague and the fever route from false economy in sanitary protection.

It may cost money to keep the streets swept and sprinkled; to provide a sanitary force sufficient to inspect every premise in the town and order the uncleanly to clean up; to keep weeds cut and streets and alleys free of garbage and carion; to extend sewerage and drain cesspools; to secure pure and abundant water supply; to secure and enforce ordinances for food and milk inspection; to prohibit the exposure of food for sale on the streets, and expectoration in public conveyances and places. Will it cost any more than funeral expenses, cemetery lots, hospital maintenance, doctors' bills, perhaps years of invalidism and consequent losses to industry? If we are going to court death, let us do it in open, courageous fashion, not by cowardly, niggardly methods. Let us not deplore the foolhardiness of those who choose the perils of fire and water while we supinely await the ravages of diseases because we are too indolent and miserly to keep clean. Better perish on the volcano's slope than die on top of a dunghill.

The sharp words of Pauline Periwinkle had little impact on the politicians at city hall. Financial problems continued to hamper the sanitation department's work. Following a drought and the expenses of cleaning up after the Confederate Reunion of 1902, the sanitation committee reported to the city council in October that they would not have enough money to run the department without "materially crippling" it after November 1. Still, the department had succeeded the previous year in filling up Lake Diphtheria, removing 9,860 yards of garbage from streets and alleys, and cremating 2,291 dead horses, mules, and other animals.[41] Even though many citizens, including a children's auxiliary to the Cleaner Dallas League, had been involved in the effort, little headway was made in ending the city's sanitation problems during the early years of the decade.[42]

Several years later the Dallas Federation of Women's Clubs tried again, organizing a Clean-up Day in March, 1908. This time they were joined by members of the 150,000 Club, a group of businessmen dedicated to growth and progress.[43] Committees were named for each ward and charged with serving notices to all property owners and overseeing the removal of trash. No city funds were provided for the actual work of cleaning up, although the city agreed to provide trash wagons for hauling away the trash from each of the city's ten wards. Dr. H. K. Leake, president of the Health Board, appealed to citizens to do their part in making Dallas "an exceptional example of good health with its attendant blessings of happiness and prosperity."[44]

The Clean-up Day was simply another stopgap measure attempted by concerned citizens. A more permanent solution to the accumulation of garbage would require a significant financial commitment by the city. By 1912 a campaign to pass a garbage tax was under way, with Pauline Periwinkle adding her particular brand of persuasion to the effort. Appealing to her readers' common sense, she noted in her column of March 25, 1912, "so long as a neighboring garbage heap can assail us as effectively as if it were located at our own back door, it is far more economical, even for the large property owner, to pay a sanitary tax rate and get immunity for his money than to pay a monthly dole to the trash man and still be pursued by the germs and noisome odors emanating from the thousands of plague spots that thrive in the city that has not doffed its village swaddling clothes." Heeding their noses—and likely the admonitions of their wives and mothers who had read the words of Pauline Periwinkle—male voters approved the garbage tax 2,666 to 2,115 and laid the foundation for the first modern garbage department in Texas.[45]

Pure water was another troublesome concern in Dallas. City officials worked during the first decade of the twentieth century to end the water shortages that had plagued Dallas as its population increased. In its early years the city had used Browder Springs, located on the bank of Mill Creek south of town, for its water supply. As demand grew, the city had to supplement it with water from Trinity River in the early 1880s. By 1900 the need for an additional water source was critical. City engineers decided in 1901 to dam the mouth of Bachman Creek north of town and create a lake that would serve as a reservoir. In less than a decade the city needed more water, prompting the construction of White Rock Lake and Dam in 1910–11. Dallas expanded its sources for city water, but its purity was still suspect. Numerous institutions such as the Dallas Electric Company, St. Paul's Sanitarium, Sanger Bros., and the Oriental Hotel relied on their own artesian wells for better-quality water.[46]

Clubwomen did not focus their efforts on water purity until 1909, when the Dallas federation began its efforts to secure the construction of a filtration plant. As with other projects, members did research into filtration processes and published their findings to inform citizens and create a demand for improvements.[47] The campaign took four years, but when the plant just west of the site of the pumping station at Turtle Creek was completed, Dallas had water that was softened, clarified, filtered, and chlorinated before being pumped to city homes.[48] After enduring decades of smelly, unfiltered water, a generation of Dallas housewives breathed a sigh of relief.

The mixed results of clubwomen's efforts to improve sanitation and water purity contrasted dramatically with their work toward a pure food ordinance for Dallas. Their concern for protection from adulterated food mirrored nationwide efforts started three decades earlier. Attempts to obtain legislation in Congress had been sidetracked repeatedly by bureaucratic infighting, business interest agendas, and lack of public support. As the problem grew more acute, pure-food congresses were organized, farmers and housewives and groups such as the American Medical Association and the WCTU became involved, and politicians from western agricultural states took up the cause. When Harvey Wiley, a chemist leading efforts to pass a national law, requested the assistance of the General Federation of Women's Clubs in 1903, clubwomen responded with education efforts and publicity campaigns.

In Dallas, General Federation of Women's Clubs tactics and Pauline Periwinkle's columns informed and encouraged clubwomen who set their sights on a law that would improve the condition of food sold on streets and in stores.[49] Not only was blowing dust contaminating food, the sale of adulterated processed food was commonplace. Pauline Periwinkle supplied reports of work being done elsewhere. Her February 15, 1904, column described the efforts of the Chicago Woman's Club:

> *The Chicago Woman's Club is making capital out of the Iroquois theater disaster in securing the enforcement of the city's pure food ordinances, in the violation of which the club has for years been much concerned. The club has issued a circular contrasting the horror and indignation justly aroused by the needless loss of nearly 700 lives through criminal disregard of building ordinances, with the apathy shown toward the enforcement of sanitary ordinances. By the infringement of the pure milk clause alone more than a thousand children die each summer in Chicago, while to the sale of spoiled fruits and vegetables, trade in which moves briskly in the tenement districts, in total disregard of law, is directly traceable diseases that add largely to the mortuary records of certain sections of the city.*

For concerned clubwomen, such flagrant disregard for sanitary ordinances in Chicago was inexcusable. But the situation in Dallas and the rest of the state was even worse, for neither had even a comparable ordinance or law to protect citizens. While the state legislature had passed a pure foods statute in 1883, it was declared unenforceable. The state had never appropriated any money for assuring pure food and drugs after the first year's funding in 1883.[50]

To turn the tide of public opinion in favor of such legislation required a concerted effort. Pauline Periwinkle once again used her pen to help by publicizing the appalling condition of much of the food sold to Texans. Her descriptions came a year before Upton Sinclair's novel *The Jungle*, which exposed conditions in meat-packing plants and set off a public outcry that resulted in the national Meat Inspection Act. Pauline Periwinkle's July 31, 1905, column anticipated Sinclair's book, for it was designed to "turn the stomach" of her readers enough to encourage them to demand action by the legislature.

> *When all appeals to the heart fail, let us by all means appeal to the stomach. Those who have been working for pure food laws in Texas have evidently overlooked the mighty factor of the sensitive stomach in the anxious search for a possible heart. They have told pathetic stories of the babies whose pinched faces and tiny graves were eloquent though mute indictments of milk embalmed by formalin. They have pointed out that the poor men, the man driven by necessity to patronize the cheapest products, was being systematically robbed by rich manufacturers; that the poverty of the poor was being enhanced by a system of cheating that enabled the manufacturer to palm off anywhere from 10 to 50 per cent of non-nutritious adulterants in all such staples as flour, bread, coffee, syrups, jams, spices, baking powders, etc.*
>
> *Little has been accomplished by this means. Few if any cities have official chemists or food inspectors, and graft flourishes accordingly. True, a law has been passed whereby horses and cows and other live stock are protected in getting sufficient nutriment in their feed, by excluding ground corn cobs and hulls, but the human animal must continue to suffer, that greed may be satisfied. And yet the advocates of pure food laws ask no more than do the cattle*

interests. They ask only that the labels on sacks and boxes and packages and bottles that contain alleged foods shall state exactly the ingredients and proportions that go to make up its contents. "Let the label tell" is their slogan. In this way the housekeeper to whom economy is the consideration may have opportunity to figure out whether when she buys 25 cents worth of ground coffee, it is wise to pay 20 cents of it for parched bran, etc., that at most costs 2 cents. Why not give the poor woman, instead of the rich manufacturer, the opportunity to make money by adulterating at home the 5 cents worth of coffee? Dr. Wiley, the Government food expert, says that $375,000,000 is made off the American public every year. Dr. Abbott of the Massachusetts Health Board puts the figures up to $750,000,000. In either what a magnificent sum to save to the plain people yearly, that now goes to distend the already well-filled pockets of the few.

The housewife, naturally, is the one to whom the vital necessity of proper food values chiefly appeals. Alas, she has no way of making her protest score, unless she can touch the men with similar perception. Let her try "the stomach route" of sending her shafts home, since other means have failed. For instance, good housewife, when the head of the house has broken open one of those flaky biscuits for which your cuisine is justly famous, when he is liberally applying to the piping surface a layer of golden butter, suppose you casually remark: "Dear did you read what the recent report of the Pure Food Commission said about the manufacture of butter. It's positively startling. Out of fifty-eight kinds of butter sold in one city not a single one was genuine. They say that most of the butter we buy is renovated. Wait just a minute, I cut the report out of the paper because I knew you'd be so interested. Here it is." (Reads)

"Butter renovating factories have agents in all the large markets who buy up the refuse from the commission men and retailers, take the stale, rancid, dirty and unsuitable butter in various degrees of putrefaction. This refuse is put through a process of boiling, straining, filtering and renovating and is finally churned with sweet milk, giving it a more salable appearance. The effect is only temporary, however, as in a few days the stuff becomes rancid, and the odor it gives off is something frightful. It is usually sold to people having a large trade who will dispose of it quickly, for if it is not

consumed at once, it can not be used at all without being further renovated."

A few readings of this sort, well timed, would be apt to produce effects of some kind or other than "going in one ear and out of the other." He would begin to view with distrust those neat square packages for which we pay a round price, and evince a willingness to "put up" toward paying for a chemical analysis. And if that doesn't fetch him tell him about the London chemist who has discovered how to make a very good "commercial" butter out of ordinary city sewage. If the trust ever gets hold of the invention they will drive every cow into the pens of their fellow plotters, the beef trust, in order to force a monopoly of their revenue-making product.

Milk is, of course, one of the grossest forms of food adulteration, since it affects helpless infancy and childhood. Unlike adults, the young child is limited in diet, and if the milk lacks in nutrition or has been "doctored" to prevent souring the effects are at once seriously manifested. There are some adulterations of adult food that are comparatively harmless. Nevertheless, the purchaser has a right to know what he is buying with his money. Ground white rock, bone dust and starch are cheaper than baking powders, and some of the latter are fully one-third composed of these cheap white dusts.

Then there are the syrups, jams and jellies. The basis of all the cheaper grades of fruit products are the same — apple pulp, gelatine, glucose — flavored and dyed to suit by chemical aids. "But," exclaimed one purchaser of raspberry jam, "I'm sure this is all right, because it's got just lots of seeds in it." The experienced inspector smiled and finally succeeded in convincing her that the seeds were seeds indeed, but extracted from the "head" of timothy grass, and not from a luscious raspberry.

Some of the acid flavors and vinegars are very unwholesome. They are calculated to eat the bottom out of a copper kettle, then what must they do to the sensitive stomach? Pickles and canned peas are oxidized a beautiful early-in-the-spring-green that seems to attract rather than warn by its unnatural hue. Wines and other drinks are also largely composed of deleterious acids. Wood alcohol, aniline dyes, formaldehyde, salicylic acid, even arsenic and strychnine have been found in colored and preserved "sham food."

But probably nothing in common daily use is more subject to

adulteration than our morning beverage. Says a facetious food expert: "A modern Mme. Roland might appropriately exclaim 'O Coffee, what crimes are committed in thy name?'" Even when coffee is pure it is in another respect rarely what it pretends to be. Our Mocha is for the most part the Brazilian peaberry, our Java a product of Bogota. In the whole bean, coffee is difficult of substitution. "All the samples of whole coffee were found to be pure," naively records the latest official food report from Connecticut. But when the bean is ground or pulverized, adulteration is easy. Says the same report: "Chicory was present in all the adulterated samples, and in two cases only was this the only adulterant. In addition to chicory, six of the samples contained imitation coffee, consisting of broken lumps of a brown color, made of wheat flour middlings, and another large pellets made of peanuts and other ingredients." . . .

At the difference in price between coffee and flour, coffee and hulls, coffee and sand, the intelligent consumer can make his own estimate as to whether he is getting his money's worth, to say nothing of the question of preference in the ingredients.

Galvanized by the abuses described in Pauline Periwinkle's column and publicity surrounding the passage of the national Pure Food and Drug Act in 1906, Dallas clubwomen took the lead in working for a law in Texas. Heading the effort were members of the Dallas Woman's Forum, a "department club" established in March, 1906.[51] State Representative William L. Blanton of Gainesville, who introduced the pure food bill in the state legislature early in 1907, recognized the Texas Federation of Women's Clubs as instrumental in arousing public sentiment to secure passage of his bill. "Without your assistance and the assistance of the club ladies, it would have been impossible for me to have passed the bill," he wrote to TFWC President Eliza Sophia Robertson Johnson (known as "Birdie" by all) shortly after the bill had been passed.[52]

By writing letters to all the state senators and representatives in support of the bill, utilizing local clubs to collect information on their communities' situation and then turning the data over to the sponsor of the bill, and investigating other states' laws to see what was most effective, clubwomen provided a textbook example of how to marshal facts and figures to silence critics and win approval for a bill they favored.[53]

Even before the state legislature had passed its bill, a more remarkable event took place in Dallas. The women, after intensive lobbying (which included a head-on battle with local grocers trying to delay enforcement), persuaded the city council to pass the first pure food ordinance in the state. Among the most outspoken of the clubwomen appearing before the city council was Dallas Woman's Forum member Isadore Callaway, who put the matter in stark perspective, reminding them, "if people could rise up in arms against the boll weevil, which was at the time destroying but 10 percent of the cotton crop, they ought certainly to take some interest in the fight against impure food, which was causing the death of one-third of the babies in the country."[54]

The active involvement of Isadore was in contrast to an early reticence to mix her professional and personal activities. She had stepped from her "behind the scenes" role to become a more visible participant in club activities. In fact, she was instrumental in the founding of the Dallas Woman's Forum.[55] Her personal activities and professional obligations had merged flawlessly. Four days after the city council vote, Isadore resumed her voice as Pauline Periwinkle to make a pungent observation about the proceedings in her February 11, 1907, column: "It wouldn't have taken a Congress of Mothers 17 years to pass a Pure Food Law. Men have shut one eye and squinted so hard at commercial interests with the other, that they see little else. The wonder is that doctors and undertakers and tombstone manufacturers don't join the grocers' lobby in defeating measures to injure their trade."

While the Dallas version of the national Pure Food Law was acceptable to clubwomen, the battle for a statewide law did not end with its passage. Flaws in the original version and lack of funding thwarted the intent of its backers, and reformers demanded that a new, stronger law be passed. Pauline Periwinkle joined the chorus, urging clubwomen to assist the newly created TFWC committee to help the state chemist's department in its work. Her column of July 1, 1907, placed the responsibility for significant improvement before Texas women.

The women of Texas have it largely in their own hands whether or not the pure food laws are enforced in this State. They should not be deceived into thinking that because the law has been secured as a State measure, and reinforced by the Federal act, they may relax their energy and vigilance in the matter and look to official authority for security. . . .

Of first importance is safeguarding the milk supply, since plainly our highest duty is the protection of the helpless child, dependent for its very life on the food prescribed by nature. It is a commentary on the selfishness of mankind when such things as beer, whisky [sic] pop and various drinks to which adults resort can be obtained pure, while sublime disregard and carelessness is exhibited as to the source and purity of the milk supply. The extent to which milk has been adulterated, either with water to increase its volume or formaldehyde to keep it "sweet," is eloquently set forth in the language of the milkman when first adequate ordinances are passed for the public's protection.

   Although the purveyors of milk protest against the necessity of such ordinances, they usually retire under the threat that they will have to charge more for milk if the ordinances pass. When pressed for explanation they will say "Well, for one thing, we will have to use a great deal more ice."

   It does not seem to dawn on the one giving this lucid excuse that he thereby stands convicted of having depended on the use of an artificial "sweetner" or else that he has maintained his profits by the admixture of water. A mother told me that her five children were poisoned at the same time by milk from a dealer who gave the above argument against the ordinance, at the same time insisting that the milk was pure. The doctor who treated the children said had there been a trifle more formaldehyde in the milk he would not have vouched for their recovery. People whose consciences permit the use of formaldehyde in any quantity or guise whatever are bound to grow careless in its use. They will toss in too much some day, just as the cook occasionally tosses in too much salt. . . .

We have commercial organizations to publicly agitate building up the town by inviting citizens from the outside. It is just as good civic business to see that the right of our native-born population to mature into citizenship is reserved. Besides, a low death rate is a pretty good argument for the desirability of any place as a resi-

dence. Perhaps the reason why the impression has prevailed that it is hard to raise babies through the teething period in Texas, that they must be taken elsewhere for the first and second summers, has been because little if any attention has been paid to milk protection. Surely, if cities of cooler climates find pasteurized milk plants, municipally operated, a necessity, the cities of the South are in need of this safeguard to infantile health. We are becoming educated to the dangers of milk toxins, to the medium afforded by milk to typhoid and tubercular infection. When that education has advanced a trifle some enterprising citizens or the municipality will erect a pasteurizing plant through which the milk supply will have to pass before it is purveyed.

It is largely the fault of women that there are not more convictions for the infringement of pure food ordinances. "I have made twenty-five arrests," said a City Chemist, "but have secured only five convictions. Women, who are the chief complainants, object to appearing in the court room to testify when the case is tried. Some of them send their cooks or other colored help, but of course if people are not sufficiently interested themselves in the enforcement of the milk ordinances, etc. we can not hope for many convictions. The law will give the offender the benefit of the doubt."

It is sheerest nonsense on the part of sensible women to permit an objection of this sort to stand between them and a vital civic duty. There need be no more publicity in going into a court room than there is in going to church or any other mixed assembly. It is merely because women are not so frequently called upon as witnesses as are men. Perhaps if women went there more some of our court rooms would improve in appearance. "It is positively filthy in our court room, and the crowd is so tough." Dear lady, perhaps you might start a worthy movement by calling attention to these neglected places. Ask your Judge and Chief of Police to provide idle prisoners in jail with scrubbing brushes and soap and set them at work making things clean and tidy and keeping them so. The prisoners themselves would be better for work and exercise, and while being supported by public funds they might make some little return for what society has suffered from their hands. As for the characters that create a court room atmosphere, do they not walk our streets, congest on corners and sidewalks, and perhaps occupy the next seat to

*us in the street car? The thief who snatches at your purse, the
drunken man who lurches along the highway, is a much safer person in the court room under the eye of the law, than when met in
the closer quarters of civic freedom.*

*"I might get my name in the newspaper," pleads another shrink-
ing soul—one of those paradoxical people who scorn "newspaper
notoriety" and yet wax indignant if their name is left out of the
receiving line or off a club program. As well might Florence Night-
ingale, Clara Barton, et al., have foresworn the cause of humanity
because, forsooth, their names might appear in print.*

*The Dallas City Federation has a committee on public health,
the members of which, besides other active work in the interest of
pure food and cleanliness, stand ready to accompany to the courtroom any of their sex whose bill of complaint is sustained by the
City Chemist. Where municipalities find themselves unable to keep
food inspectors on the pay roll to gather in suspicious food samples,
housewives may aid in this essential by themselves sending to the
Chemist questionable food products, and then following up his
findings to the Corporation Court. Just so long as there are no
inspectors, and women refuse to perform this civic duty, unscrupu-
lous dealers will take the risk of disposing of these wares rather than
suffer the financial loss. Where the public has, by the appointment
of a City Chemist, the opportunity of having milk, butter and other
tests made free of individual cost, some appreciation of this service
should be shown by active cooperation. Where there is no municipal officer of this character the citizen would have to pay from $10
to $15 for each food analysis.*

Encouraged by the stand of the state federation and Pauline Periwinkle,
clubwomen across Texas became de facto inspectors, collecting samples
of suspect food and sending reports to the pure food commissioner.
Others started publicity campaigns in their communities designed to
educate both consumers and tradesmen. Especially encouraging to
Pauline Periwinkle was the interest in pure milk and the work to educate
mothers about the need to use it.[56]

While clubwomen worked to overcome the gaps in the law, Pauline
Periwinkle informed her readers of the sorts of problems that remained
in their food supply. Knowing that public opinion had helped carry the

day for the first pure food law in the legislature, she served up descriptions of the abuses that had not been remedied. Her February 1, 1909, column highlighted the annual report of the Dairy and Food Commissioner of Texas:

> *Everybody eats, consequently everybody ought to be interested in foods and their values. The majority of food consumers, however, concern themselves with but one quality—that of taste. If the palate is pleased, no fault is found with the food. So on the intelligent housekeeper rests a double burden. She must please the family palate, and she must see that the food has value. . . .*
>
> *"Cheating" is not too strong a word to apply to food adulterations; sometimes it is not strong enough, for not infrequently more is involved than merely taking one's money without equivalent return, since the adulterant used may be positively injurious, or like water in milk, may lack the nourishment on which life depends. . . .*
>
> *The worst forms of fraud are those perpetrated through the medium of drugs and medicines, even when the ingredients are perfectly harmless. The report points out the danger as follows: "Through the manufacturers' advertisements of their nostrums, the public is induced to diagnose and prescribe for ailments. If such an ailment is an imaginary or hysterical one no harm is done; but if a person is suffering from some organic trouble, and is induced to apply these remedies, harmless in themselves, great harm may come in the delay of proper treatment." Remedies of this character have been analyzed and condemned as "misbranded" by the State Chemist. They are not "illegal" because the manufacturer has complied with the law by filing the formulas with the authorities and secured the right to use the "guaranteed" legend; but they are misbranded when they claim to perform the impossible. Illegal medicines are those which like the blackberry juice sold for that purpose, are found upon analysis to be "artificial" concoctions.*
>
> *With an appropriation commensurate with the importance of the work, and which would permit, as now contemplated, adding inspectors to the force, as in the Health and Live Stock Commission, the Pure Food Commission can protect the public from a lot of imposition and fraud. An inspector for each section of the State is*

needed especially for periodical visits to dairies, meat markets, and manufactories of food products. The State Chemist's time is needed altogether in the laboratory to keep pace with the growing demands for analytical work.

When the legislature passed the new food law in the spring of 1909, several practices were declared illegal. No longer could vendors sell any food stuff that had not been protected from flies and street dust by glass covers. Food could not be colored with any copper compounds, baking powder had to contain at least 10 percent of avoidable carbon dioxide, and any milk was considered adulterated unless sold just as it was drawn from the cow, except for certain "skim milks." Drugs sold under a pharmacopeia name had to conform in strength to the pharmacopeia standard. As Pauline Periwinkle summed it up for her readers: "The new law, as a whole, is a good one—a vast improvement on the original . . ."[57] She had done her part to help clubwomen win one more reform that would make meaningful improvements in the lives of Texans young and old, male and female.

6

∎ ∎ ∎

"The Children of the Present—They Are the Future"

Although she never became a mother, Isadore Callaway had a special concern for children. "I hope you will have children," she wrote her brother shortly after her marriage to W. A. Callaway in the summer of 1900. "I know I should be much happier if I had something all my own, something beside myself to live for."[1] Despite her own childlessness, she made children's needs a recurring topic in her columns. In fact, being childless did not stand in the way of many women who worked for children's welfare during the period.[2] Isadore's columns discussed schoolhouses and the quality of education, the need for kindergartens, and the lack of playgrounds, as well as the most troubled and troubling of children, the juvenile lawbreakers. Children's issues elicited some of her strongest indignation, particularly the general lack of public will to deal with the plight of the neediest and most disadvantaged children in society.

Isadore's empathy was apparent from the creation of a children's page in the *Dallas Morning News* to her ongoing advocacy in her weekly columns for kindergartens, playgrounds, and juvenile courts. She seemed determined to assure children a childhood better than the one she had experienced. The daughter of a teacher and an educated woman in her own right, she knew how valuable a good education would be in the new century.

Her concern reflected the realities of public schooling in Dallas and the rest of the state. An expanding school-age population had brought public school crowding of appalling proportions. The superintendent's report for December, 1899, noted a total of 6,062 students with class sizes of 55–85 students per room in nine different schools. Eighty percent of Dallas children between the ages of ten and fourteen were in school, and their school term lasted nine months, exceeding the national average of 145 days and the Texas average of 101 days.[3] The large increases in school population nationally were magnified in Dallas. Between 1870 and 1900 enrollment increased two and a half times nationally, but in Dallas the increase was seventeen fold between 1878 and 1899, from 338 pupils to 6,062.[4] Overcrowding, short school terms, family finances, and lack of compulsory attendance laws were among the reasons many students left school after only a few years with a poor education.[5]

Kindergartens, Pauline Periwinkle believed, were one way of attacking the problem. She agreed both with Progressive Era reformers who viewed kindergartens as a means of preparing the children of the lower economic classes to attend public schools and with others who endorsed kindergartens as a desirable experience for children of all classes.[6] Her local perspective was based in part on the study of the benefits of kindergarten training made by the Woman's Council in 1894, when the group had lobbied the school board, unsuccessfully, to establish kindergartens in the public schools.[7]

The demise of the Woman's Council didn't dampen the enthusiasm for kindergartens. Between 1895 and 1900 groups of like-minded Dallas women set up three free kindergartens, supported by charitable donations, to serve underprivileged children. They merged to form the Dallas Free Kindergarten Association in 1900 and began a comprehensive free kindergarten program at several sites in the city.[8] When the school graduation season arrived in May, 1900, Pauline Periwinkle's column contained an unusual slant on the annual event. She pointed to the small number of graduates compared to the hundreds of youngsters who entered school for the first time each September. She urged a greater emphasis on schooling for the youngest students as preparation to absorb the material presented in the earlier grades. Her May 28, 1900, column was designed to publicize the need and raise public support for efforts to persuade the Dallas school board to add kindergartens to the public school system.[9] Her words of caution about ignoring the needs of the less fortunate reflect her pragmatic way of looking at problems:

> *When commencement time rolls around, does the appalling disparity between the number who enter the primary department each year and the number who graduate at its close never strike you? Take the cities, for example. Hundreds of children, 7 or 8 years of age, enter the schools each September. The following June, if the graduating class numbers anywhere from fifteen to twenty, it is considered a fine showing.*
>
> *But whoever asks: What has become of the companions of this handful of young people—the hundred or more who matriculated with them ten years ago? Did they leave the ranks of the learners to join the army of workers, or the army of idlers, and when and why? Was it necessity that compelled them to seek contact with the world without that special training that the final years at school is supposed to particularly supply, or was it lack of inclination to further pursue studies that to them were the dead bones of the valley into which no breath of life had been breathed?*
>
> *The graduate is an object of perennial interest, but to me the one who doesn't graduate possesses an interest all his own. If a special fitness for life lurks in graduation, does the lack of it imply that the hundreds who leave school before that happy climax are necessarily hampered in their future efforts? Are the fifteen or twenty alone prepared for and confident of success? Are there any statistics that show the proportionate achievements of graduates and nongraduates?*
>
> *These questions are not asked with any intention of disparagement of a system that turns out less than 5 per cent as a maximum of educated persons—that is, if graduation implies education; they are asked with a desire to know. It naturally occurs to one that a system that is intended for the most general public benefits, and yet that lets go its hold on a large proportion of that public before its aims are fully accomplished, might with profit be open to careful inquiry. If the great majority of children are to be reached only this side of 15, why not expend the greatest efforts on the grades thus*

indicated; that is, if the greatest general good is the real desideratum?

In Texas schools, as far as my knowledge extends, pupils are not admitted until they are at least 7 and frequently 8 years of age. Here is a year or two wasted so far as the influence of the school goes, even under the present system of primary instruction. If we had free kindergartens attached to the public schools, as many States have established with good results, there could easily be gained two years for instruction and influence at a time when the pupil is most susceptible—two years that are now totally barren of systematic effort. These two years would reach the hundreds who enter the schools annually, instead of the fifteen or twenty that annually graduate. Does not a question naturally arise implying a waste of force so far as the greatest public good is concerned, in depriving hundreds of children of two legitimate years of instruction in order that a limited few may acquire a kind of knowledge that can not be classed as essential, since all but fifteen or twenty have to get on without it?

The instruction afforded the last few years of school costs the public more in the way of expensive instructors, appliances, etc., than does any other equal period. And yet this comes at a time when the migration from school life has set in and consequently a much less number enjoys these greater advantages than would if they could be introduced at an earlier period; not the same advantages, of course, but those adapted to the comprehension of the lower grades, whose effect is similar so far as developing the mind and training for future usefulness is concerned.

The earlier application of opportunities would also tend to relieve the cramming process, now menacing the physical and mental well being of the student generation, and whose baneful effects are quite as evident in the primary as in the higher grades. The extension of kindergarten instruction to the masses means the preparation of the childish comprehension. As it is, children struggle on through several grades before any light breaks in upon them. Any idea of practical daily application of the information with which their poor little heads are being stuffed and their parrot-like memories strained, is seldom aroused. You can see this exemplified in their first attacks on grammar. That it has any bearing on their daily conversation is a remote conception. The child who speaks grammatically does so because good English is used in the home, and not because of any rule in the book. He may know every rule by heart and violate all alike, so far as his conception goes into the ultimate purposes of grammar.

The underlying principle of the kindergarten is to adapt all instruction to the comprehension of the child, and then awaken in him a sense of its proper application through "doing" instead of simply learning "to do." One might as well say "I can make good bread," because she can repeat the recipe for bread-making, as to say "I have finished this grade," because all the books have been conned. A child's mind is native soil and it must be prepared for the planting. This is what the kindergarten does. As it is, the teacher is given thirty to fifty little children, fully half of whom receive no assistance from home, and it is about like planting potatoes on a patch of sodded ground to expect satisfactory results. I have talked with many thoughtful parents, and all agree that it is astonishing the amount of facts a child becomes possessed of in the first few grades at school without acquiring any real information. In arithmetic they arrive at the "answers" by a kind of intuition instead of by any reasoning process; indeed, the "answer" is what they are after. It is a species or puzzle, and guessing is as good a way as any.

It is not the teacher's fault; it is the fault of our system. Under present conditions it is impossible for the teacher to give individual attention in the classroom, consequently she is frequently quite as much in the dark as the child, especially if the latter has a good memory and recites well. The child who gets assistance at home, whose parents interest themselves in knowing how much of his school work he comprehends, has a showing for pulling out of the primary slough; but thoughtful parents are not thick as dewberries in June.

Even some thoughtful parents are not broad-gauged when it comes to public schools. They may be able to afford proper advantages in the way of kindergartens and special training for their own children, and they forget that this very fact makes it harder to secure innovations for others at public expense. Especially is this true in the country, where the well-to-do send their children away to school and so are indifferent whether the home school keeps four months or six. The children of the poorer classes suffer, since they are not able, unaided, to keep the schools going.

It is shortsightedness to be indifferent to the welfare and progress of the very children among whom your own must live when they are grown. As you reach out and benefit the young in the community, you improve future conditions for your own children. I was much impressed by the reason a father gave for sending his son to our State university: "If his life is to be lived in Texas then the closer his associations are with Texas people the better he will be fitted to make his way among them and the better grasp he will have on the conditions in the State." No matter how superior one's education may be, he must work on a level with his associates to hope for success. It behooves those who are looking to the future of their children first to assist in building others up to their level and thus lessen the chances of degeneracy.

The subject of kindergartens appeared in several later columns, as the TFWC took up the cause statewide.[10] When the Dallas school board could not be convinced to add kindergartens to the system, the Dallas Free Kindergarten and Industrial Association, as it became known, continued its work. By 1903 it had received enough support to occupy a brick building at Cedar Springs Road and Harwood Street, but it needed additional funds to make it into a full-fledged settlement house patterned after the noted Hull House in Chicago.[11] Pauline Periwinkle described the activities of the association that benefited the neediest Dallas children and urged its support in her January 5, 1903, column. Her words reflected the view widely held by the socially conscious of the era that the poverty-stricken lower classes must be taught the value of work, moral behavior, and hygiene.

The spirit of self-respect and self-help is inculcated in the contact of teachers with children and parents. The work is of course brought close to the classes having the fewest opportunities—the poor "tenter," the cotton mill worker, the foreign so-called "Bohemian" element. The dignity of labor, the work of the hands, in contrast to the degradations of pauperism is kept to the fore. Assistance is frequently necessary, but whenever possible a little work, a small sum of money, must be given in return. One of the methods of effecting this exchange is the "rummage sale" held at the kindergartens every Saturday. Persons interested in the work collect and send to the kindergarten secondhand articles of clothing and furniture. These are repaired and placed on sale for a very small sum— so small, indeed, that where destitution is great, a dime has been known to supply all the deficiencies of the wardrobe. Thus the need is met and self-respect retained, while the receipts assist materially in purchasing the necessary outlays in the industrial departments.

Naturally, the lack of funds and proper equipment is the great drawback. A visitor from a distant city where a fine training school is in operation exclaimed when she saw the plain deal tables and scanty cooking facilities, "Why, we have glass topped tables, and lovely granite ware and gas ranges in our cooking school." But, as one of the teachers happily replied, "Perhaps these children from the abodes of poverty might get discouraged in their attempts to carry out our teachings at home were there so marked a difference in the utensils. Anybody can have a clean wooden table and the few simple dishes we supply in our kindergarten kitchen."

So it is not so much the poverty of what it already has as the need of branching out into other industrial departments that taxes the resources of the association. If that larger, general public was alert to the full meaning of this work for community good, it would see to it that the settlement house with its industrial departments was a paid-up part of that capital—public spirit—that is building a newer, better Dallas.

The Neighborhood House and the Free Kindergarten Association and Industrial Association did receive considerable support from charitable citizens.[12] But the Dallas school board continued to claim that financial difficulties prevented adding kindergartens to the system. When the TFWC gave its official endorsement in 1907 for kindergartens in Texas public schools, it hoped to generate wide support for a bill being introduced in the legislature that would give school districts permission to establish public school kindergartens.[13] An unsuccessful attempt to pass a similar law in 1905 gave the federation added incentive to promote support vigorously this time. The bill passed and became law in 1907, but it lacked the mandatory clauses necessary to force inclusion of kindergartens in public schools. By 1908 only El Paso had kindergartens in the public schools, while Dallas, Fort Worth, San Antonio, Waco, Bonham, and Colorado City had free kindergartens supported by charitable donations.[14] The Dallas school board did not add kindergartens to the system as quickly as Pauline Periwinkle might have wished. Records suggest that a kindergarten was established in one Dallas public school in 1910, but this apparently did not open the door for citywide adoption. Despite the charitable support and interest in the free kindergartens, not until the early 1920s were twenty-nine kindergartens set up in Dallas public schools.[15]

Nevertheless, Pauline Periwinkle continued to remind her readers how valuable free kindergartens could be. Her March 14, 1910, column revealed a sophisticated grasp of childhood development and her view of how education could shape children. She also made a case for education as a means of reducing the threat to the social order created by the unschooled, undisciplined children evident in Dallas and other large cities.[16] While her sociological perspective of the "ignorant, thriftless, vicious homes" has been discredited, it reflected a sentiment shared by middle-class reformers of the period. Her final observation, nonetheless, reflects a commonsense approach to the problems she considers.

> *There is no compulsory education law in Texas. Children 12 years of age who can read: "The cat ate the rat," and write their names may be employed in mines, mills, factories, and stores. Children 14 years of age who can neither read nor write may in like manner be employed. Children of any age, uneducated, unemployed, may run the streets until malicious mischief leads them into crime, and they get their first lessons in wholesome discipline and books within the confines of some correctional institution.*
>
> *Children compelled by necessity to leave school at the tender age of 12 are seldom able to attain the full measure of their capabilities. Through no fault of theirs, they have had but four brief years— less than half—of that training which the State has in its public school system declared essential to the making of desirable citizenship. Add to the dangers of a little learning the dangers of near and absolute illiteracy, and the result is a problem that must be solved ere community or State rises to intellectual, industrial and social efficiency.*

Any means by which the school term may be extended to chil-dren who can not complete the grades; any means by which those from illiterate families may be influenced to secure something of an education, is deserving the earnest consideration and support of those on whom rests the burden of community uplift and progress. This was the viewpoint taken by the State Legislature that made provision for the incorporation of the kindergarten in our public school system. It was not done for the benefit of mothers, neither of the overburdened or the idle classes; it was done solely for the benefit of the child and ultimately of the State. It is true that whatever benefits the child reflects benefit to the home. Picture the conditions of the home of the present without the beneficent offices of the public schools and kindred institutions; though no one now claims that their establishment contemplated invasion or protection of home rights. This narrow conception of paternalism is, happily, rarely to be met. Community of interests is at the foundation of peaceful, prosperous society; the making of good citizenship is a paramount public concern, involving as it does the stability and welfare of com-munity, State and Nation.

When one considers child nature, and the manifestations of nature's plan in his mental development, it is surprising that such scant advantage is taken of a period so keen in observation, so fer-tile in imagination, so tenacious in memory and so susceptible to impression as the period that antedates what is popularly denomi-nated as the scholastic age. If a person acquired knowledge all his life with anything like the rapidity with which he seems fairly to absorb it in earliest childhood, he could become prodigiously learned. The child acquires language, he adjusts himself to the salient facts in nature, he develops a consciousness of right and wrong by which his conduct is governed, he learns to distinguish between individual and social rights and privileges, and so on. In fact, before he enters the schoolroom his character as a future citizen is in many ways determined, and for good or bad, he has learned things that the curriculum does not and can not teach or unteach. Before he enters the schoolroom other forces have predetermined whether he is to be a willing or a sullen student, an apt or a dull one, desirable or undesirable.

■ ■ ■

An undesirable pupil merely from a schoolroom point of view, is the one who takes more than his share of the teacher's time and attention either to instruct or to discipline. He may be dull or fractious or unable to accustom himself to schoolroom routine. He may simply not know how to study, how to get his lessons for himself. In any event, he is undesirable, for he keeps back the pace set for that grade. As the strength of the chain is only that of its weakest link, as the forced march of an army is measured by the weak rather than the strong, so must progress in the schoolroom conform to the slower perceptions rather than to the keenest.

It is a matter of record that 40 per cent of our pupils in the first year primary do not "pass;" that is, they must take this first year of work over again before becoming initiated to school requirements—get into the swing of school work, as it were. It is not too much to say that their backwardness has also had its effect on the sixty who do pass, but who for a year have been made to mark time with the slow steppers. Now, the methods of the kindergarten have been worked out with the training of the powers of observation particularly in view, so that the child who has enjoyed such advantages has a readier grasp of what is expected of him when he is confronted with books instead of objects. The old conception of discipline, that of breaking the will, has given way to the enlightened methods of educating the will; constructive forces have been employed instead of destructive; social conscience involving the rights of others has been trained, so that the child finds his place without friction when self-dependence and self-control are demanded by the schoolroom.

The influence of the kindergarten as a deterrent to illiteracy has long since passed the theoretical stage. That very selfishness that exists among an indifferent parentage that permits the child to pass its waking hours in the street "from under foot" conspires to make acceptable the proffered services of the kindergarten. Intelligent people patronize the kindergarten for one reason; unintelligent for quite another. It makes no difference to the end in view—the good of the child. But the child from an ignorant, thriftless or vicious home comes into a new atmosphere to which its latent susceptibilities respond as they never can after a few more years of hardening influences. Then and then only is the accepted time, when in the

*child himself can be created a craving for better things than he has
known, a desire to go to school, to become a good man, an industrious citizen, and to surround himself in his future home with the
refining indications of his ability and industry.*

*From any point of view the kindergarten is an educational and
social economy. It furnishes a much needed mental equipment for
all classes of children and to a certain class, at least, it furnishes a
character equipment that quite possibly would not be obtained in
any other way. Society must pay at one end or the other. Isn't it
economy to pay for the constructive work of good citizenship rather
than the destructive work of the bad?*

Pauline Periwinkle's publicity for the TFWC's campaign to create public kindergartens represented a subtle change for clubwomen, encouraging them to assume a role in influencing public policy by directing their
maternal instincts toward all children, not just their own. This redirect-
ing of familial sensibilities outward to include the welfare of all children
took place throughout the country as public programs began to replace
private rescue efforts.[17]

In addition to kindergartens, public parks where children could play
received Pauline Periwinkle's enthusiastic endorsement. The innovative
concept of utilizing city parks to diffuse children's antisocial behavior had
been developed in the late nineteenth century in Massachusetts. There
Joseph Lee worked with the Massachusetts Emergency Hygiene Association to devise remedies such as school gardens and playgrounds for
city children who had no place for play. Lee devoted his life to spreading
the philosophy of play and the playground movement, helping make it a
part of the Progressive reform agenda.[18]

In turn-of-the-century Dallas, parks were not viewed as places for
children to play. Real estate promoters had created parks at the end of
the streetcar lines to lure potential buyers "out to the country" for fresh
air or a picnic and—incidentally—to take a look at a lot in their new sub-
divisions.[19] City Park, the only municipal park, was a place to view the
landscaping or hear band music at the pavilion constructed for that purpose.[20] When children tried to use City Park for other activities, they ran
afoul of city ordinances. One specifically prohibited "playing of any form
of ball or cricket, or throwing anything from stones to missiles in Dallas
Parks." Another made it illegal to "lie upon, sit upon, or stand upon, or

go upon the grass, lawn, or turf of the park without permission."[21] Park keepers enforced the prohibitions against children's recreation aggressively, so much so that W. R. Tietze arrested young Tom Blakeney for "fishing in the park" in 1897. When taken before a judge, young Tom had the charges against him dismissed because there was no city ordinance prohibiting fishing in the park.[22]

The city's concept of park usage contributed to the problems created by children with excess energy and little supervision. Throughout the 1890s Dallas wrestled with the same juvenile delinquency issues as other large cities. "Dallas turns out a new crop of juvenile criminals every year," reported Chief of Police J. C. Arnold in 1897.[23] The city council attempted to control the situation by passing a curfew ordinance that year, but it was not successful.[24] Against this backdrop Pauline Periwinkle urged the Dallas Federation of Women's Clubs in June, 1902, to appoint a committee to meet with the park commissioners from the city council about creating parks throughout the city.[25] She then used her column to encourage readers to support the creation of parks for children, especially those who lived in the heart of the city. She observed in her February 2, 1903, column: "The movement for playgrounds in cities means far more than the question of a little fresh air. It means hearty, healthy outdoor play for a class of boys who ought to be thoroughly tired out when night comes, ready to go to bed instead of ready to prowl the street in search of excitement. The majority of the misdemeanors committed by young boys are the result of misplaced energy."

The link between children having no place to play and criminal mischief was obvious to Pauline Periwinkle. She soon embarked on a campaign to make it equally obvious to Dallas citizens. Her August 28, 1903, column linking the availability of parks to the reduction in juvenile delinquency spelled out the benefits for both children and society at large. It illustrated her complete sympathy with the Progressive reform agenda and put her in the company of Jane Addams of Hull House and journalist Jacob Riis, whose crusade against New York slums had exposed the shocking conditions of tenements and their effect upon children.[26]

It is not unnatural that little provision for public parks is made when a town is in its infancy, and fields and woods at its very doors. Few, perhaps, have that gift of prophecy to accurately measure the future growth and needs. It is only when business districts are sol-

idly built up and the residence districts largely extended that the down-town population that seems a necessary evil in all large cities begins to suffer from the lack of forethought in reserving space for public parks. Large interior parks are therefore practically impossible in such sections, as the cost of securing large blocks of improved property would be greater than most municipalities could or would afford. But there are nearly always a few open spaces adjoining closely built up sections that are yet available, which would contribute far more to city values as parks than they could possibly do if occupied by buildings.

It is no longer a debated question as to the need of these large open spaces in the heart of a city. A moment's reflection furnishes the conviction that the welfare and development of the city depends quite as much on that element whose life must be passed close to the heart throbs of commerce as on those who at 6 o'clock can seek the cool and quiet of suburban homes. On the health and morals of this element the city's reputation rests to like extent. Large, open areas liberally scattered throughout the overcrowded districts contribute immensely to the health, morals and legitimate pleasures of the poor, and no city can learn the lessons too quickly to curtail public expense and danger. The experiences of New York and other great cities furnishes [sic] convincing proof that public parks, however small, must be provided, and that delays in this respect are costly. . . .

As feeders to real estate and street car values the suburban parks and outdoor recreation features have few equals. They are essential in the spreading out and rapid growth of a city. At the same time, in those districts where the poor congregate parks should be just as accessible as schoolhouses and churches. The people who most need the physical and moral benefit of outdoor pleasures have not the dimes wherewith to transport themselves and families to a suburban resort. Each section of the crowded residence quarters should have its own little playground, and a point should be made of employing a band for at least one evening each week in the small as well as the large parks. The moral value of providing innocent amusements in those districts where even pleasures have a vicious tendency can not be overestimated or safely ignored. If but one band can be afforded by a municipality, let its efforts be directed toward entertaining the poor, for few homes of the better class are not provided with musical facilities.

When we get the small parks in every down town district, we shall have the key to much juvenile delinquency. So says Jacob Riis, that Moses of the people of the slums. "It is better to have parks and playgrounds than jails and iron bars." A score of years ago the Earl of Meath observed that "crime—children's crime—in our large cities is to a great extent a question of athletics," of giving them the chance to play that belongs to childhood. In crowded districts the children have no other playground than the streets. "There are so many boys in the precinct" was the way the Captain of a New York East Side precinct put it to Mayor Strong's Small Parks committee, "and there is no place for them to play, so they take to the street. Storekeepers complain, arrests are more frequent than before. They used to have vacant lots; now they are being built upon, more houses, more people, more boys—more trouble."

. . . When these little down town parks are established, let it be understood that they are intended for the innocent enjoyment of the children of the vicinity, and not as playgrounds for the police. Don't plant "keep-off-the-grass" signs and establish a blue-coated guardian of the law to see that the little feet, already wearied of pavements, do not yield to the temptation of pressing nature's enticing carpet. With tall buildings shutting out the sky, and the municipality interdicting the grass, God's poor have a hard time of it. If flowers and ornamental shrubs, [sic] and it is found necessary to protect them, it might be well if some person up in orthography were permitted to paint the signs. In one park not far away the word "allowed" appears with one "l" in every instance, while other directions for the guidance of the public are fearfully and wonderfully constructed. If a public park is to be a public educator the effect of a rose bush guarded by sign boards of outlandish appearance may not be quite as intended. . . .

More than half of the population of this country is now in the cities, and unfortunately the indications are that this proportion *will be much greater. Clearly, in the matter of parks municipalities can not afford to be niggardly. Public parks have special functions to perform which are as clearly defined as those of our public schools, public libraries, public baths and other branches of municipal government that are considered essential to the welfare of the whole people.*

Subsequent columns continued to relate the availability of parks to the potential to reduce juvenile delinquency.[27] On February 17, 1908, Pauline Periwinkle announced the creation of the Playground Association of America and described the success of playgrounds in England and Germany.

> *The best solution of our juvenile problems lies in filling the needs of barren human lives. . . . Under the caption "Why Some Boys Are Bad," Justice Julius M. Thayer of the Children's Court of Manhattan classifies the greater proportion of offenders as "mischievous delinquencies," and adds: "Very many children are arraigned because they engage in playing shinner, football, baseball and other innocent games on public thoroughfares, or building bonfires on the asphalt or other pavements. These acts are, of course, innocent in themselves, but are prohibited in the interest of the safety of life, limb or property in our crowded streets. In many cases the Judges find that the children do not know why these acts are prohibited. The child, of course, must play and until the playgrounds of the city catch up with the needs of the child population children must necessarily use the streets and play those games or their variations which have been known to all children for all time. A fine or commitment to a reformatory is rarely imposed in such cases but the Judge presiding takes great pains to point out why the game innocent in itself, must not be playing in the streets, and the parent is also instructed. With the result that very few boys offend twice in this particular. . . ."*

> *Every right-thinking person must agree that the highest interest of the child and society demand the prevention of juvenile crime. The question of so "forming" the child's character that it will not need "reforming" is, after all, the rational, vital one. Students of child*

nature know and those that stop to weigh the matter will admit its reasonableness, that play is even more of a factor in molding a child's character than work is in making of the man's because in the child the mind is at its most impressionable period. To no other form of preventing juvenile delinquency is so much attention being paid at present as to the child's recreations. "Where does the child put in his idle hours?" "Where does the man put in his idle hours?" The answer to either of these queries will give the key to the character of child or adult. It is no wonder then that the subject of playgrounds is uppermost in the schemes of child betterment formulated by leaders in the juvenile movement. As illustration of this fact is to be noted in the recent organization in Washington of the "Playground Association of America." It has now come to be recognized that convenient provision for exercise in the open air is indispensable if we are to preserve health of body and mind, especially as regards children, whose development into healthy and useful members of the community depends largely upon the way in which their physical needs are met. England and Germany have laid stress on this phase of child development and correction for decades. Both these countries enjoy Government commissions that promote the establishment of playgrounds. In the last four years Germany has equipped 400 playgrounds. No sooner is a young citizen of the German Empire born into the world than he is taken care of, if need be, at some public creche, or as we call it, day nursery. As soon as he can make free use of his limbs he goes into the kindergarten. From there he goes to school, where he has playgrounds and skating rinks in midwinter, and is taken on country excursions in summer—all this at public expense. In short, municipalities make every effort to supply their coming citizens with bodily strength as well as mental cultivation. As the result, there is less juvenile crime in Germany than any other Nation.

These columns promoting playgrounds set the stage for the work of the Dallas Federation of Women's Clubs. In 1907 the federation established a playgrounds committee headed by Olivia Allen Dealey, wife of the publisher of the *Dallas Morning News*. The committee initiated a citywide fundraising activity to pay for children's needs, including playgrounds. The resulting "Tag Day" on February 29, 1908, saw an army of clubwomen selling tags with the words "To Help the Children of Dallas, I'm Tagged." The federation also brought Lee F. Hammer of the National Playgrounds Association to Dallas to advise them. Additional money for the playground fund was raised by a lecture by Williams Jennings Bryan. By 1909, Isadore Callaway had assumed the role of chair of the playground committee. With public support demonstrated by Tag Day sales, the committee convinced the city to purchase a 300-square-foot piece of property at the corner of Corinth Street and Cockrell Avenue in the cotton mill district. Using federation funds, the committee provided the salaries for a playground supervisor and assistant to oversee Dallas's first municipal playground, named Trinity Play Park and dedicated Thanksgiving Day, 1909.[28]

The successful campaign for a play park in Dallas demonstrated that the public could be educated to recognize a link between children having no place to play and criminal mischief. But Pauline Periwinkle understood that playgrounds were not the final answer to juvenile delinquency. For young people who had already broken the law, other measures were necessary. Pauline Periwinkle joined ranks with other Progressive Era reformers who believed that juvenile delinquents should be rehabilitated in a home setting, if possible. A probation officer could monitor and educate the offender (and his or her parents) so that the offender need not be dispatched to a reformatory, a method that was being rejected by forward thinkers. Probation was believed to be cheaper and more effective, and the practice embodied reformers' heightened awareness of the emotional ties binding all families.

The emergence of social scientists who looked on delinquency as a social disease provided the philosophical underpinnings for the treatment of delinquents. The framework for implementing such a strategy was the juvenile court headed by a sympathetic judge.[29] Pauline Periwinkle used her column to promote several innovations taking place elsewhere in the treatment of juvenile lawbreakers. Her March 2, 1903, column described the probationary court for youthful offenders in New York City, while her December 14, 1903, column discussed a special school for delinquent children in Chicago. An incident in the state involving two six-year-olds jailed for theft of thread allowed her to focus on the need for local reform. On February 2, 1903, she wrote:

> But little children do not need reformatories; what they need is
> a home, in the highest and best sense of that word. . . . Many of the

county farms and poorhouses in Texas have children as inmates who have no other recourse as shelter.

While cases that call for the arrest of children of six are fortunately rare, they emphasize the need of State paternalism for children of the class from which these come, and of the lack in Texas of just the kind of home their peculiar situation demands. . . . If there is any right on earth that a child is born to it is an "even start" with the balance of humanity. What it chooses to make of its opportunities is a matter entirely foreign to this phase of the question. No one has a right to predestine a child to viciousness and crime because of accident of birth and position. . . . No nobler work claims the attention of the women of this State than that which they have undertaken in behalf of children, and the class that needs protection instead of punishment will not appeal to them in vain.

Not surprisingly, Adella Kelsey Turner, president of the Dallas Federation of Women's Clubs, as well as of the TFWC from 1903 to 1905, shared Pauline Periwinkle's sentiments.[30] Clubwomen across the nation had taken an interest in juvenile justice. The Woman's Club of Chicago had successfully lobbied the Illinois legislature for the passage of a Juvenile Court Act in 1899.[31] Mrs. Turner named Isadore Callaway to serve as Texas delegate to the national election committee at the 1904 General Federation of Women's Clubs biennial meeting in St. Louis. The likeminded reformers had ample opportunity to develop a strategy for a juvenile court during this period. Mrs. Turner appointed two committees of delegates to attend the meeting that May to "interview club women from other States concerning the operation of juvenile courts" and "visit the police department of St. Louis and ascertain facts concerning the police matronship of that city."[32]

As president of the DFWC, Mrs. Turner appointed a local committee to investigate the city jail. The appalling conditions the committee found became the rationale for the federation to come out strongly for a juvenile court law. Mrs. J. C. Weaver, who succeeded Mrs. Turner as president of the DFWC, paid a personal visit to Denver to see its juvenile court firsthand and bring back a comprehensive plan of its operation.[33] At the annual convention of the TFWC in November, 1904, reports from local civics committees described work under way to install police matrons in city jails across the state.[34]

For her part, Pauline Periwinkle continued to educate her readers about the purpose of juvenile courts and their operation. Her first column in 1904 described the work of Denver's juvenile court, where, she noted pointedly, "women, the natural custodians of children, have a voice in the making of laws and the enforcing of public sentiment."[35] Women could vote in Colorado. The DFWC brought Judge Ben Lindsay of Colorado (whose creation of the juvenile court system there served as a model for the entire country) to Dallas in 1904 to tell citizens about the work of juvenile courts.[36] In her May 16, 1904, column, Pauline Periwinkle described the juvenile court system and suggested an industrial training school for juvenile offenders:

> The next Legislature of Texas is to be asked to provide for the establishment of juvenile courts in the cities where their need is felt. Whether this court will have county or municipal jurisdiction is a matter still under advisement, but it will be maintained wholly apart from the Police and County Courts, and its procedures will not be regarded as criminal in character. That is, incorrigible or delinquent youths whose conduct is inimical to public welfare will not be branded as criminals because their misdemeanors have brought them before the probation officers and judges of the juvenile courts. . . .
>
> While it is the purpose of the juvenile court to see to it that the child is taken care of in his own home, that the parents fulfill their duty to the child as well as the child fulfill his duty to the parents, it is essential that there be an institution available to which boys who have not the proper home surroundings can be sent. To save the boy it is frequently necessary to remove him from the environments that have contributed to his downfall. He must be supplied with a good home and trained teachers, and must be taught a useful trade. An industrial school, if disassociated with any penal sentiment, would prove a splendid adjunct to the juvenile court.

As the women's clubs gathered data about jail conditions and heard speakers extol the juvenile court concept, Pauline Periwinkle used her column to answer its critics.[37] Her February 6, 1905, column was designed to meet objections and offer a logical argument for the proposed legislation. In all likelihood copies of the column found their way to the desks of legislators contemplating the bill, for the clubwomen were working for its passage. As the column demonstrates, Pauline Periwinkle subscribed to the then current theory of moral defectiveness as a trait of the lower classes. She was not alone in her sentiments, for Progressive Era reformers perceived the socialization of American's children as key to their vision of a future society without vice, crime, or poverty.[38] Yet Pauline Periwinkle was at her most logical, articulate, and impassioned when she took up a cause that would ultimately help children, theory notwithstanding.

If the members of the Twenty-Ninth Legislature do not pass the Juvenile Court bill, it will be because they do not fully comprehend either the nature or the necessity of juvenile courts in cities that have attained the size of many Texas municipalities. Those who have to wrestle with the problems of city life—police, Corporation Court Judges, Mayors—will tell you that the most perplexing cases they have to deal with are those involving juveniles who have willfully or mischievously gone astray. Of course the strong arm of the law can seize the youthful culprit and put him in jail and punish him in one of several ways; but unfortunately that does not settle the problem. On the contrary, it complicates it. The real question is, whether it is better to seize a child who has started wrong, start him right and keep him right until he grows into a good citizen, or whether the State is justified in letting that child go wrong until he is of an age that the law must take cognizance of his wrongdoing, brand him as a criminal and deal with him as one. Which answer will our legislators choose to give us? If they are parents themselves, if they have one atom of pity and sympathy for the helpless waifs of humanity who are worse than parentless, dependent on the public for their chance to be honest citizens, they will surely make the chance possible. If our legislators are doubtful of the expediency of juvenile courts, it may be well to remind them that since the first one was established by the laws of Illinois in 1899, fifteen other States, (including the District of Columbia) have joined the march of progress in the noble work of saving delinquent children through juvenile courts. Need Texas fear to tread, when New York, Pennsylvania, Missouri, Colorado, Wisconsin, New Jersey, Indiana, Maryland, Kansas, Connecticut, Minnesota, Louisiana and Ohio have tested the trail blazed by Illinois and found that it leads straight and true? Fifteen States and the Nation's capital now enjoy this beneficent law and are experiencing its effective work in dealing with children. Not a single one of these States has asked to go back to the old way, and with each year other States are adopting the new method. Is not that the best proof of all?

What are some of the objections raised by those who are not acquainted with the operations of juvenile courts? We read in the press such words as "paternalism," "expense," "too many laws already," "too many court officials," "not needed in Texas," etc. Yet there is nothing so much needed by wayward children as that one thing—wise paternalism. It is because they lack it that they are wayward, ninety-nine times out of the proverbial hundred. Do the good fathers of Texas—the fathers who are so wise in their own homes that their neighbors choose them as their representatives at Austin—do they realize that the children for whom we ask State paternalism are largely worse than orphans? Very callous indeed is the heart that is not touched by the sad plight of little children deprived by death of their natural parents. The State and the Church and society at large join hands in creating a paternalism that will care for them in orphanages or good adopted homes. How much worse the plight of the child with unnatural parents, vicious parents, weak and degraded parents, for the State says, "Hands off!" He must be left in contact with crime until he commits crime himself before you can touch him. The Church and society want to help, but are driven from the door by those whom the State decides are the "proper" guardians, simply because they are responsible for his birth. Not until the child is recruited to the vicious, until he is behind bars, are the reformatory influences accepted for him, in most instances too late.

Why does the State build special homes and schools for the deaf and dumb and for the blind? Why does it compel parents to send their afflicted children to these schools unless they can afford to have private instruction at home? Because the State knows that ultimately the defective individual becomes a burden on the public unless he is trained and educated to industrious citizenship in spite of his affliction. There is no cry of paternalism raised when the State is taxed for the support of such special institutions. Sociologists will tell you that the children of a certain stratum of society are to alarming degree defectives. True they can see and hear and talk and possess other normal faculties. But they lack the sense of right and wrong. They are moral defectives—the very worst kind of defective, because being supplied with other faculties, they can mingle freely in the world, working harm and spreading their contaminating influence. If they were crippled or blind or dumb there would be some limitation, at least, for their activities. The State makes no provision, however, for training moral defectives for good citizenship, although it is just as certain that this class, by their depredations and subsequent punishment, cost the State far more than all its lame and halt, blind and dumb. Compare the cost of criminal prosecutions and the maintenance of jails and penitentiaries and their functionaries with the cost of those institutions that care for the afflicted children, and the appalling discrepancy speaks for itself.

Then there are our public schools. No thought about the bugaboo of paternalism in that magnificent system devised for sustaining America's great watchwords—Freedom and Equality. The State has declared that its people are born to certain inalienable rights and on that declaration it has builded a system designed to give every boy and girl an equal chance for securing the boon. A liberal education, declares the State, is the surest, safest avenue to successful citizenship, therefore the State wisely provides and compels the child's education. Now, the juvenile court is really nothing but a school for moral training. The judge is the teacher and those whose parents neglect such training in the home are brought to him for lessons. He talks with his wayward pupils, finds out why they have had no schooling, of this particular character, explains the lessons they must learn and practice, and bidding them to return on certain regular lesson days, lets them go for the time to note the effect. The parents or guardians are then visited by the probation officer and given admonition and advice. Experience has shown that in the majority of cases home co-operation is secured and the defective is discharged "cured." The occasional stubborn cases are sent to a regular school established for this kind of defection, with equally good results. Call it paternalism, if you please, if it results in good *citizenship, in emptying jails and penitentiaries, in preserving life and property and good order, what's in the name?*

The matter of expense has already been touched upon in inviting comparison of what the State is doing to help unfortunate children and what it is expending in catching them in crime and punishing them for it when they have attained to the law of responsibility—latitudinous by nature, but rigid in legal application. It must be remembered in this connection that the State does not take into consideration the damages, either material or moral, inflicted upon society by depredatory conduct. It must also be considered that the appointment of a judge for the juvenile court does not necessarily add to the judiciary. The judge deemed most fitted by his associate judges for the position is placed in control of this court. The expense of a probation officer is reckoned as the expense of a policeman, and from what the chiefs of police of Texas say it takes a good man's time to keep up with a tithe among the mischief and meanness going on among delinquent youngsters in all the sizable Texas cities. Every daily paper records the wear and tear on the fire department caused by boys pulling out alarm boxes "for fun;" for the stoning of windows in vacant property and the disappearance of plumbing and everything movable inside; of the driving of horses hitched on the street by the owner, and the looting of carriage robes and whips; of junk shops kept supplied with brasses and kindred plunder by the boy arab. In railroad centers the roads have to engage special men to watch cars from being broken open, brasses from being stolen, and keep boys from endangering life and limb by hopping cars and stealing rides. All this costs money, and doesn't do one bit of good toward remedying the evil that grows greater every year.

But on this question of expense can we not take a higher ground than that expressed in the query, "what will it cost?" Surely every case involving a boy or a girl is more important than any cases involving dollars and cents, no matter what the amount may be. Think of it fathers and mothers. Would you reckon the worth of your own sons and daughters in dollars and cents? Are you not making financial sacrifices every day in the fond hope that your son and your daughter may be a credit to their parentage, respected members of society and nobler citizens of the State because of your self-denial and wise expenditure? And do you ever reckon what it has cost you when you think of them as educated, cultured men and women?

To those whose mental habit it is to think, "Yes, Charlie has a pretty good education: anyway, it cost me $2,018.79," the following impressive figures are presented, taken from the statistics of Colorado. The enterprising Juvenile Court Judge of Denver went over the police records and the records of the Criminal Court, figured up court costs, jury fees, jailer's fees, mileage, attorney for defense, keep in jail and at reformatory, and the total sum was $1,036.76. This was the cost by the old system, and the boy was not yet saved, in fact, was regarded by society as a criminal. An exactly similar case was chosen from the new system, and it cost the State of Colorado just $11.99 to make a good boy of a reckless little street tough and place him in the navy of the United States as a promising youth and useful citizen—the stuff from which heroes are made!

Not all legislators are from the large cities and possibly have never been personally impressed with the conditions that exist there. They are fortunate, indeed, if even as a visitor they have never been in the interior of a city prison or holdover, and never brought into remote proximity with its usual occupants. Our city officials confess that when new to office holding and its duties their first visits result in wakeful nights. By degrees they accustom themselves to sickening sights and conditions, without lowering of moral tone. What must be the results on impressionable childhood? The officials themselves take this into humane consideration, and rather than force hardened criminal association on youth that otherwise might be reclaimed, they fail to make arrests except for very grave offenses. This encourages the boy to further depredation, to the aggravation of the public. The police of every large Texas city will tell you that they are kept constantly between these two fires in the desire to save the boy. Nevertheless, some thoughtless person from a small adjoining town, in ignorance of conditions, will wire the city police to meet a certain train and arrest two runaway boys, perhaps.

Their country parents think it will be a salutary lesson to let them remain a few days in jail before claiming them. Consequently, there will be several young boys in jail as to whose welfare the city police have no option. I know this is so because I have seen with mine own eyes at one time three little boys, the oldest not more than 12, curled up in the grated window of a city prison, courting uncomfortable sleep in an atmosphere reeking with tobacco and liquor fumes, and with the odor of uncleanly negroes and whites, sleeping off debauches. There were no beds, not even a pallet, [and] to lie on the floor meant to lie in a reek of expectoration, vomit and disinfectants. This is a plain, unvarnished representation of the material surroundings in which respectable parents left three innocent country-bred boys who were guilty of probably nothing more heinous than tiring of cotton-chopping and a desire to ride on the cars and see the town.

As to the moral conditions, I can tell nothing. After reading the following report of similar circumstances investigated by Judge Lindsey of Denver, I would not even like to guess:

"The jail was not abolished, for children under 16, without work and a fight. When the fight was on a Police Commissioner said the boys lied to me about the corruption in the jail. I sent for the Governor of the State, the Mayor of Denver, the District Attorney and the President of the Council, the police board and a dozen ministers of the gospel to listen to the story that the boys and I could tell them. They came. I sent 'Mickey' to the street for the boys and for three hours they heard a story of filth and depravity from boys 9 to 15 years of age, that was so horrible and revolting that it did seem hard to believe, yet it was so convincing that the Governor rose up and declared that anyone who said the boys lied, lied himself. In three days our bill was passed and the jail for little children in Denver was down and out forever. Thousands of boys had been locked up there all day and night in the past. What happened can be imagined, but they never told, because no one cared."

I wish space permitted to quote more of Judge Lindsey's report. I wish, farther, that every Texas legislator had that informing pamphlet, "The Problem of the Children and How the State of Colorado Cares for Them." Texas is more fortunate to begin with than

*Colorado, for all the Police Commissioners, police and Mayors I've
ever met are doing all they can to give publicity to these conditions
in hope of stirring up action, instead of trying to hush things up.
But so long as even well-meaning parents remain ignorant of these
things and indifferent parents know but do not care, to whom can
we look, except to the State, for that paternalism that will save the
unfortunate children of Texas?*

The efforts of Texas clubwomen and Pauline Periwinkle to secure a
juvenile court bill from the Texas legislature in 1905 ended in failure. The
bill, introduced by Senator A. B. Davidson of Dewitt County and Representative Curtis Hancock of Dallas, seemed headed for passage after it
survived its second reading and advanced to a third and final reading in
the House only three days before the end of the session. In the frantic
push to pass several other bills that had provoked extended filibustering
by opponents, Representative Hancock succeeded in having the juvenile
court bill called up for consideration only ten minutes before the speaker
adjourned the House of Representatives, leaving the bill on the brink of
a final vote.[39] The clubwomen were obviously disappointed, but the columnist was irate. When Pauline Periwinkle's April 24, 1905, column appeared, she gave the legislators a tongue-lashing the likes of which they
had probably never seen in print, especially from a woman. With it, she
served notice that the clubwomen intended to press for a juvenile court
law with renewed energy.

*There are more ways than one of achieving fame. The name of
Torregiano is remembered for the sole reason that he broke the nose
of his fellow-student, Michelangelo, in a fit of jealous rage because
the latter dared outrank him in the studio. The member of the
lower house who "talked to death" the juvenile court bill may also
rest his claim to distinction on that one dubious exploit, at least in
the opinion of the women of his state who asked the passage of this
measure. In the meantime, relief being denied for treating the boy
on any middle ground between innocence and crime, the courts
will have no option except to turn loose or convict all delinquents
brought under their jurisdiction. Many a mischievous boy, arrested for misdemeanor, has been encouraged to enter a career of
crime under the mistaken belief that the Judge dismissed the case*

*because the offense was not punishable. On the contrary, fearing
the effect of conviction, of attaching a stigma to the reputation of
thoughtless, impressionable youth, the Judge turns the boy loose,
hoping that his reform will be effected outside a penal institution
rather than inside amid doubtful associates. In many instances
such procedure merely encourages the boy to further infractions of
the law, until he wears out the patience of the court, the sympathy
of his friends, and some desperate deed lands him at last in the
penitentiary. The probation system of dealing with delinquent
youths might have checked the boy at the outset. It gave the Judge
power to suspend sentence on good behavior, to keep the boy under
surveillance after he left the courtroom, and if he was homeless or
his home was unfit, to place him where the influences would make
for his reformation and good citizen.*

*With hundreds of boys in every Texas city being hauled into
court as recreants each year, with crime frightfully on the increase,
with the assurance by criminologists that our prisons are largely filled
by men under 25 years of age—nothing is being done to save the boy.
The very house that killed the bill framed to protect the boy passed
one to protect goats and squirrels. Texas is way behind the procession
of States that have cast aside the hide-bound, medieval method of
treating wayward children as criminals. We boast of our empire of
wealth, of the fact that it outclasses all other sections in the variety
and quantity of its productions, and content with material prosperity, we give little if any concern to the more important development—
that of character and good citizenship. The right uses of wealth are
the benefits of humanity. Until we direct the prosperity of the State
to the upbuilding of its people we have little of which to boast.*

Not content to wait until the next legislative session to begin lobbying efforts again for a juvenile court bill, Pauline Periwinkle continued
to remind her readers what was at stake. Her June 19, 1905, column took
issue with the claim of one man that women were "the power behind
the throne." Her response was to call such a notion "twaddle" as she
pointed out:

*It is this "power behind the throne" that the women of Texas
had in such large abundance when they wanted to pass a juvenile*

court bill; but it is the brute force that prevails after all, and permits some bully in office to parade little boys on the streets of our cities with chains about their necks, on the way to penitentiaries. We have many humane Judges and county officials in Texas who are guided by conditions and principle in conforming our laws to the needs of juvenile offenders. Nevertheless, when the latter leave the court room, they may be at the mercy of creatures of low instincts, of contractors who take the job, at so much per head, of landing the convict in the reformatory. If he can chain a string of them together, he saves the expense of extra guards. If he can march them through the streets, he saves transportation. By the laws of Texas he is compelled to show no consideration for the effect on the public or the good of the youth. He is the "bully in office," whose brute power, according to the English view, upholds the fabric of society and must be recognized to the exclusion of the loftiest sentiment and patriotism of which woman is capable. Let every good woman in the State reread this news item from Waco, and regret that she has not the brute force necessary to cast a vote for decency in the fulfillment of public duty:

"Waco, Tex. June 15—A short time ago an officer passed down one of the main streets of Waco with two boys chained together, taking them to the reformatory at Gatesville, one of the boys looking to be not more than 10 years old. Yesterday two other boys were noted in custody of an officer chained together in similar fashion. The two boys who were chained together a short time ago, or the fact that they were so chained, was chronicled in the newspapers and led to an investigation by authorities in charge of this matter and who said that officers had no right to thus chain the boys, and that it was contrary to the regulations. It would seem, however, that the matter has not yet been settled as it was repeated yesterday."

The TFWC renewed its commitment to passage of a juvenile court bill after its initial failure. At the federation's eighth annual convention in Austin in November, 1905, the President's Evening program included a "practical talk upon Juvenile Courts by Judge G. P. Webb of Sherman and an address by Mrs. Harry Churchill, President, Colorado State Federation of Women's Clubs."[40] Clubwomen across the state were mobilized to action.

Pauline Periwinkle helped generate renewed enthusiasm with her column. She demonstrated her knowledge of the political process and her ability as a political strategist in her column of July 16, 1906:

The convention that is to decide who are to be our Democratic nominees for the executive and legislative offices of the State (and in Texas this is practically equivalent to an election), is but a few weeks distant. Are the women who are interested in the success of the juvenile court bill, who realize the vital need of some better, more humane way of dealing with the erring but irresponsible child, awake to the opportunity afforded of placing these candidates on record? If you ask these candidates now, it will be far easier to gain their attention than when they are firm in their seats, engrossed in political measures and surrounded by the usual horde armed with the axes they wish ground. The cry of the helpless is difficult to hear amid the clamor that reigns in legislative halls when the Senate and the House are in session, as the interested women found to their sorrow in their efforts to secure favorable action before the last Legislature.

At all the recent district meetings of club women stress was laid on the urgency of this movement for juvenile courts. State and county associations of Judges, State associations of police and Sheriffs, in fact all our public officials whose duties include meting justice to youthful offenders, have placed themselves on record in favor of juvenile courts. They have opened the eyes of the public to crimes committed against childhood in the name of the law, and have spurred the women on to agitate this needed reform. But of what use is this agitation, this change in public sentiment, unless the men who are to be empowered with legislation and its enforcement are in harmony with the demand and alive to the fact that there is something more in officeholding than being successful in the great game of politics?

Few have displayed the conscience and courage to come out in their "platform" with the measures for which they stand and advocate this service to humanity. Commercial interests, economic retrenchment, taxes, labor, et al., divide attention, but scant words for public betterment, except as measured in figures or other mate-

rial form. "The interests of the people" is a specious phrase when the people themselves, the kind of citizenship, the character that is to shape the welfare of the State in the future, is not considered. At the same time, there are few measures now prominently agitated in the politics of the present campaign that would not be affected more or less by the establishment of juvenile courts. Take the burning question of economics, for example. One of the most expensive luxuries to any State is its penitentiaries. Reduce the number of criminals, and you not only reduce public expense, but you replace bad citizenship with good, add honest labor to industrial valuations, save society from costly depredations, decrease the naturally heavy expenses of courts and jails and police, and therefore directly affect the tax funds.

Invite your candidates for the Senate and House and the chief executive offices to declare themselves. Ask for an expression before the primaries, and the battle is half won. Then ask the man who, according to chivalric traditions, represents you by vote to cast his ballot for the candidate who pledges his support for juvenile courts, and the victory is wholly assured. . . .

Now the question is, what are our Texas candidates willing to do for the children. They are to the front with all kinds of promises to protect the rights of the voters of the present. The voters of the future have rights that they are now deprived of by those unjust laws that hold to criminal accountability children who could be, by rational measures, converted into good citizens. Who will see that the children get their rights?

With the Thirtieth Legislature, the clubwomen finally saw their years of work pay off. A juvenile court bill was adopted, along with laws defining dependent and delinquent children. A short time later, the local federation used part of the funds raised from Tag Day to pay the salary of a probation officer, W. G. Leeman. A year or so later, the city and county assumed all responsibility for the program and for Leeman's salary.[41]

Throughout the long fight for juvenile courts, Pauline Periwinkle's informative, outspoken advocacy had galvanized her readers. Her columns were logical and sensible, and were designed to overcome the objections and animosity confronting clubwomen. She was not reticent or deferential in expressing her opinions, yet her superiors at the *Dallas*

Morning News supported her every step of the way.[42] As she noted succinctly in 1910: "What is the future? Who represent it? The children of the present—they are the future. To reckon without them . . . [would be] like pulling off futurity races without having given thought to the colts."[43]

7

"An Enlightened Womanhood Means More for the Future"

From her earliest columns, Pauline Periwinkle made the status of women her ongoing crusade. With a fervor born of personal experience, she wrote persuasively about such concerns as the need for women's higher education, for working women to receive fairer wages and be able to serve on school boards, and for a change in attitudes toward marriage and divorce. "A brilliant writer and thinker," recalled G. B. Dealey, publisher of the *Dallas Morning News,* "her messages made both men and women sit up and think. She was one of the first, if not, indeed, the very first, to broach the then delicate subject of woman suffrage in Texas."[1] No doubt Pauline Periwinkle's crusade to expand women's opportunities and rights was controversial in some quarters, but she was fearless and tireless in her efforts.

Among Pauline Periwinkle's earliest concerns was securing an industrial arts education for women. At the time Texas women could attend a number of institutions, both coed and all-women, but none offered a course of study featuring training in trades and professions similar to that available at Texas Agricultural and Mechanical College. Sharing Pauline Periwinkle's views were fellow members of the Woman's Council who had discussed a state industrial school for girls at the October, 1895, meeting. The council voted "in favor of fostering a sentiment looking to the establishment by the state of an industrial school for girls."[2] Shortly after the April, 1896, inauguration of the Woman's Century page, Pauline Periwinkle added her voice to those advocating higher education of women as "an imperative need of the time."

The women's college movement had its roots in the post–Civil War era, when many young women began to move beyond the seminaries and normal school educations that had been almost their only option. Their reasons for wanting a college education reflected the changes taking place in society: as more women received public high school educations, the demand for teachers increased, more diverse employment opportunities arose, and the woman suffrage movement encouraged women to seek improvements in their status. For some, college offered a means to escape the demands of their families and establish a measure of independence, while other families recognized that a college education was a good investment in their daughters' futures.[3] The response of colleges to demands that they admit women was not overwhelmingly positive. Although the University of Michigan admitted women in 1870, in other states it took the agitation of women to force open the doors to their state universities. All-women's colleges, beginning with the 1865 opening of Vassar College, provided another opportunity for women's college ambitions. The new women's colleges—Smith College (1875), Wellesley College (1875), Bryn Mawr College (1885), and Mount Holyoke College (upgraded from a seminary in 1888)—had higher admission and academic standards than earlier women's institutions and offered courses of study similar to those at men's colleges. With the rise in educational opportunities, college enrollment for women grew accordingly. In 1897–98, 22,297 women were undergraduates or graduate students nationwide.[4]

In her column of June 7, 1896, Pauline Periwinkle urged her readers to support higher education for young women. While her advocacy was rooted in the concept of "the hand that rocks the cradle," for that era in Texas she was voicing a bold demand on behalf of all women.

Whatever can be said in favor of the higher education of the boy can be said for the higher education of the girl, and more; for it is not the character of the government that speeds or stays the progress of civilization, that crowns with luster or stamps with infamy the name of a nation in the history of nations, so much as it is the character of the women of that nation. Men may make the laws and mold the government; men alone may engage in the history making of their time, but back of all that, it is the character of their wives and mothers that make or unmake them.

Enlightenment is the natural enemy of every form of viciousness and degradation, and an enlightened womanhood means more for the future than all conceivable legislative reforms. . . .

The noblest result of social evolution is the growth of the civilized home. Such a home only a wise, cultivated and high-minded woman can make. To furnish such women is one of the noblest missions of higher education, and no young woman capable of becoming such should be condemned to a lower destiny. It is not alone for the preparation of capable girls for usefulness; higher education may prepare even dull girls for better things than they would have otherwise found possible. Four of the best and most susceptible years of one's life spent in the company of noble thoughts and high ideals can not fail to leave their impress, and a generous education should be the birthright of every daughter of the republic, as well as every son.

When the Woman's Council met again later in 1896, they heard Mrs. S. E. Buchanan of Dallas give a paper titled "The Establishment of a State Industrial School for Girls."[5] Two weeks after the talk, Pauline Periwinkle reported that at the meeting President Ellen Lawson Dabbs had pointed out that "the state fund which went to support the Agricultural and Mechanical college at Bryan was a heritage of the girls as well as of the boys of Texas, and there was no law of privilege by which boys could be given professions and trades at the state's expense and the girls excluded."

When Dr. Dabbs suggested that the legislature be petitioned to add suitable departments to the school at Bryan to cover the requirements of women, however, she was voted down by the majority. According to Pauline Periwinkle, "The idea of a woman's annex did not find favor with the majority, while the co-educational movement was strongly upheld; several present, however, were inclined to a separate institution." Ultimately, a "unanimous pledge of the Council's members" had been given to secure a separate school. The columnist offered space in the *News* for "brief comments that will awaken an interest in, and assist in furthering, this noble enterprize [*sic*]."[6]

It was a formidable task. Efforts had been under way since 1889 to secure a bill favoring an industrial arts college for women. An 1891 bill had passed the Senate but failed in the House.[7] In 1899 V. W. Grubbs of Greenville introduced a bill providing for a women's college with an expanded curriculum of studies not usually found in an industrial college.[8] Even though the Grubbs industrial school bill was referred to the committee on education and "favorably acted upon by its members," other legislators offered spirited resistance. To answer some of their objections and point out the inherent unfairness to women in the existing situation, Pauline Periwinkle devoted her May 22, 1899, column to the status of the Grubbs bill.

> The "Grubbs industrial school bill" as the bill authorizing a state school of useful arts for girls is known, is again before the house, having passed its third reading in the senate, and been referred back. It returned shorn of appropriation, barring $1000 to cover the expense of locating it, and hampered with various amendments, one of which provides for its being an "annex" to the agricultural and mechanical college at Bryan. Some of its promoters contend that this feature will practically cut the school off from large bonuses that might be offered by various Texas cities that are rivals for the location of the school, and whose citizens have pledged valuable sites and financial assistance.
>
> Whatever the outcome may be, two facts are self-evident: 1. a non-voting citizenship is powerless to press its claim to a fair share of public appropriation. 2. a non-voting citizenship will always be regarded as an "annex." Its only hope is through the election to office of such men only as view their power as a means of dispensing public good instead of dividing "political pie."
>
> Aside from the political interpretation of this statement, there is another phase of the injustice done women along financial and industrial lines. It would be interesting to compute from the tax records the amount yearly accruing to the state and community from taxes paid on properties owned by women. Much of this goes to keep up penitentiaries, jails and reformatory institutions in which

women are almost unknown as inmates; to pay high salaried offices which women never fill, and to sustain enterprises in which women have no voice and reap no benefits.

Suppose the taxes paid by women were, in recognition of our forefathers' protest against taxation without representation, set aside for the support of women's institutions and such other enterprises for her welfare that are general in their benefit to her sex. If women would have the handling of what they pay out to support institutions wholly designed for men, I venture to assert that they would not have to be petitioning legislatures to establish a paltry few designed for women.

If I were a sculptor and were given an order to depict the American woman in her most characteristic attitude, I would choose for my pose the attitude of begging. Church, schools, libraries, charities—whenever the question of finances comes up, it is a foregone conclusion that the project must be sustained by the proceeds of woman's begging. Her own disinterested motive is the only redeeming feature of the custom imposed. It is revolting to her finer nature, and it is only because her sympathy outweighs all personal feeling that she accepts the office of Philanthropic Beggar to the Public. It is not right, but present conditions afford no remedy. So I suppose if the girls' industrial school finally receives the sanction of the legislature, even minus appropriation, that honorable body will repair from the scene of its labors warmed with the glow of magnanimity toward its voteless and purseless "annex" who may now proceed to beg for funds wherewith to establish a much-needed institution for the dependent of their sex.

It is interesting, to say nothing of amusing, to dissect some of the reasons given for the "noes" that followed the consideration of the bill in the senate. Said one: "I vote 'no' on house bill 323 (Grubbs industrial school bill) because I am opposed to educating white girls in Texas of the poorer classes, to fit them for making 'servants' to the aristocratic classes." Does not the honorable senator know that every atom of humanity is a "servant?" Even he himself, if he does his duty, is a servant of the people, including the "aristocratic classes" that received his implied censure in return for their vote.

We are servants all, and the only right that any of us may claim is to choose our master. Yet this construction would grant that right

*to none but those inclined to professional service, denying to those by
nature adapted for manual service the intelligent training that
dignifies labor and gives them choice of whom they will serve. . . .*

*Again, others said: "We vote against the industrial school bill
because we have already shown an extravagance in expending the
money of the people and because it is wrong to lay further burdens
upon the people until we are better able." This at least affords a
novel loophole of avoiding the payment of a just debt. Next time the
grocer presents his bill at an unlucky season, don't be afraid to
stand up boldly and say, "I can not pay your bill, because I have
already shown extravagance in my purchases for this month, and
it is wrong to impose further burdens upon my husband."*

*In the aggregate the present legislature appropriated $150,000
for "higher" education, not only for this year, but annually for
succeeding years, and the larger portion of it for higher "male"
education at that. Why not have proportioned the same fairly between youths who must earn it in the field of industry; between boys
and girls alike, instead of practically saying: "No, young woman,
if nature has not adapted you for the study of literature, you must
remain in the groove which circumstances has [sic] confined you.
We may lift your brother out, but we have already spent too much
money developing poets and lawyers, dredging creeks, creating new
offices and increasing the salaries of the official classes. If the hope-
lessness of your condition drives you crazy or to desperate deeds, we
will build you beautiful asylums and stout jails, but further than
that our pledge to public interests won't permit."*

Both houses of the Texas legislature rejected the 1899 Grubbs bill, but
Texas women were not to be denied. When the legislature convened in
1901, a similar bill was introduced and passed. The victory, however, came
only after tie-breaking votes by the presiding officers of both the House
and Senate. Signed into law by Governor Joseph D. Sayers in April, 1901,
the bill prompted a statewide search for a site, culminating in the selec-
tion of Denton.[9] The TFWC demonstrated their appreciation at their
May, 1901, state meeting with a "rising vote of thanks" to W. V. Grubbs,
whom they dubbed "the father of the State Industrial Schools for Girls."[10]

With a women's industrial arts college under way, Pauline Periwinkle
turned to the debate about marriage and the "College Woman" raging

in some education circles. Limited as her own educational opportunities had been, they had helped to develop not only her intellect but also the confidence that fueled her independence and assertiveness. She obviously wanted other women to seek higher education to reach their greatest potential. That higher education would make women more discerning in their choice of husbands was highly desirable in her opinion. Pauline Periwinkle's viewpoint suggests that although her first marriage had been a mismatch, her second marriage was based on an intellectual equality uncommon for the time. Her October 7, 1901, column illustrates her effective use of humor to counter arguments of those she found on the opposite side of an issue.

Every one interested in the schoolgirl has been scared most to death this summer by the assertion of Prof. G. Stanley Hall that she wasn't getting the kind of education that best fitted her for her prospective duties in life as wife and mother. On these high grounds alone (?) he was opposed to the so-called higher education of women—to the university-bred woman.

Now comes Prof. Edward L. Thorndike of Columbia University and calms our fears of impending calamity by statistics which prove conclusively that the large proportion of university-bred women don't marry at all! Then why all this mental perturbation on the part of male educators? If the university both unfits a woman for domesticity and inoculates her positively against the wiles of matrimony, where's the harm? Not only does it seem to be a case where the hair of the dog provides its own remedy, but if it be true—and who could doubt statistics compiled by university professors?—it would seem to forever solve the vexing old maid problem provided by the census in the shape of feminine preponderance.

The census, quite as crushing to the sex in the way of figures, dooms a goodly proportion of women to the single state for lack of material in the way of husbands. Now as there must be old maids, who is better fitted to disdain the poverty, homelessness, ennui or social odium supposed to be attached to old maid-ship than the college women, especially if, as Prof. Hall asserts, this fitness for the one has unfitted her for the other? By refusing to marry she would give her chance to the commonplace girl who wants to marry, while she would have resources at command, by reason of her superior education, that would lift her above the poverty and social ne-glect that has for so many generations been the conception of old maid-ship.

Of course, each of these learned assailants of woman's higher education had their same end in view, but it is unfortunate that they didn't get together and compare notes before giving their theo-retical conclusions to the world. Separately, the arguments of each might have had apparent value, but taken together they present a very encouraging outlook toward the end to which the friends of the college woman have been working. Prof. Thorndike very artlessly sums this up as one of his reasons why college women do not marry: in his own words, "They demand better husbands."

Yes, they demand better husbands, and they are in position to refuse the man who doesn't come up to their measure of what a man should be. The ban of old maid-ship has no terrors for them. Their lives are full to overflowing with resources and opportunities of which the half-educated can not know, and they can be quite as content and far happier than scores of girls who marry just to be a-marrying. They probably do not deny, even to themselves, that there is no life so complete and satisfying as that of the happily married, but they are also fully awake to the fact that there is nothing more sorrowful and humiliating than mismating in marriage, whether undertaken as a means of support, in conformity to the expecta-tions of friends and society, or in the mistaken impulsiveness of girlhood.

This article does not propose to go formally into a discussion of whether or not the higher education of woman unfits her for wife and motherhood, or of whether or not the university woman shuns matrimony. Not being a man or a university professor, the writer would probably be regarded as disqualified to express an opinion on these topics. Sometime, indeed, she may write an acceptable and conclusive article entitled: "The Higher Education of Man Unfits Him to Be a Husband and a Father" or "The College Bred Man Shuns Matrimony as He Would the Plague," in which event don't be alarmed; it will be bluff. More and more is the sensible indi-vidual, male or female, convinced that discussions of this sort are animated less by facts than by motives and that bluff and a D.D., Ph.D. attached to the signature pass for logic and argument.

The wise ones among us have been anticipating something ever since the issue of the annual post-graduation statistics showing that during the last year out of every twenty-five honors in co-educational institutions, sixteen were won by the young women. This injudicious activity on the part of college girls was bound to be heard from, even if it took the form of opposing any kind of education for women. Unless our girls learn discretion with their other studies our co-educational system is doomed. Opposition to woman's education is much the same caliber as opposition to woman's voting. Man would let her vote if she'd promise not to hold office, and he would acquiesce to her presence in college if she would agree not to win any of the honors. . . .

Prof. Thorndike pays a tribute to the modesty of his sex when he emphasizes the unwillingness of men to marry college women "because they feel themselves intellectually inferior." So far as a woman may judge of a man's feelings, the "modesty" referred to does not arise from any sense of inferiority on his part; his self-assurance simply evaporates before any woman whose reliance upon men is open to question. It is her independence that wilts him; the extent of her education has little to do with the case, but the mere fact that she is educated argues that she is independent, and that's enough. Take an uneducated man and an independent but uneducated woman, and the self-same "modesty" is in evidence to such an extent that her lack of education has no matrimonial allurements for him.

The truth is the educated woman, however independent, is far less superficial in her estimate of people than either the ignorant or the half-educated. Prof. Thorndike virtually makes this admission in the statement that college women demand that their husbands possess certain intellectual habits and interests. Nowhere does he specify that their demands go further; that they require a knowledge of all the certain parchments entitling them to the use of certain degrees, etc. Why shouldn't college women or any other women, demand certain intellectual habits and interests on the part of the men who aspire to life partnership with them? Why shouldn't all men demand the same of their wives? They certainly do of their business partners, or their intimate friends. It is only on this congeniality of ideas and tastes that lasting and agreeable associations

*can be built, whether in business, friendship or marriage. If college
education teaches young men and young women this one vital principle, then the more thorough and liberal that education is, the
better for the world. If it taught that and that alone, it would still
be a paying investment.*

Even with her spirited defense of a college education, Pauline Periwinkle
recognized that it was beyond the means of a great majority of women at
the turn of the century. Instead, many young women viewed their life's
mission as being a wife and mother while keeping house for their wage-
earning spouse. This romantic notion did not match the reality that countless women had to enter the workforce to support themselves and their
families.[11] She advised her readers that they were all vulnerable: "Do not
let your daughters have the bitter experience of many who have awakened from a rosy dream to the appallingly cold fact that they must go
out into the world for the first time in their lives and wrestle with the
problem of keeping body and soul together."[12] Women who worked
outside the home had a special place in the heart of Pauline Periwinkle
for obvious reasons. Her column of December 13, 1897, pointed out the
double burden borne by working women. The inequities she mentions
may seem familiar to many working women a century later.

*Comparing the state of the lorn woman of family [sic] with that
of the lorn man it is astonishing that even those who argue her as
the weaker vessel expect so much more of her. In those rare instances
where a man tries to keep his little flock together he is fairly overwhelmed with gratuitous advice and sympathy. Poor, dear man, to
have to work all day and come home to contend with children at
night! So the neighbors vie in scrubbing grimy fists and faces, smooth-
ing tangled locks, doing a bit of mending or contributing a tooth-
some dish to the dry fare. Whatever gets neglected from necessity or
ignorance furnishes reason for the exercise of more compassion, and
nothing is remembered but things to his praise. So virtuous is it for
a man to take care of his own family!*

*But if the woman is forced to win bread, that does not excuse her
for any domestic lapses. The fact that she keeps the children together
excites no commendation; it is expected of her. She must not keep
the oldest girl out of school, for that would occasion criticism. The*

neighbors are already talking about the reckless way in which the little ones roam the street during her absence. They are also taking note of rent clothing and soiled pinafores, and indignation is expressed because she has the girls' hair shingled to save her the time spent in reducing their braids to order. If the parlor goes undusted or the kitchen unscrubbed, the neighborhood is scandalized and views her with cold eyes and scant courtesy.

A woman toils all day in office or schoolroom and robs herself of needed rest at night on penalty of being called a sloven. A man works all day and retires at a reasonable hour, and is called a martyr. Yet the woman would be only too glad to housekeep according to the lights of her critics if the latter would provide the support.

The single woman wage-earner labors under similar disadvantages. A young man on the street car, with a ripped glove or frayed button-hole, is regarded warmly and sympathetically, while the shop girl, who gets a third his wages, and has not the means to repair her skirt braid or the time to do it herself, is eyed disapprovingly. Many a lonely "old maid" ekes out a scanty dole in office or store, comes home at night to a single back room, cooks a simple supper over the gas jet and spends the remainder of the evening fashioning and mending her wardrobe or doing as much of her weekly laundry as she can wash in the bowl and dry on the mirror.

This is not a matter of choice; it is dire necessity. Only by such pitiful economies she lives at all. Do you wonder she wishes she were a man?—the well-dressed bachelor at the next desk, for instance, who takes a small force of tailors, waiters, cooks, laundrymen, hotel landlords and distant relatives to keep him in his uniformly sleek and comfortable state. The firm for which they both work requires employees to make a respectable appearance. The girl is given a small salary, and out of her life makes good the deficit. The man must have sufficient to cover a liberal expense account and to provide entertainment for his idle, out-of-office hours.

This is what has been done for us by custom and a system of education that requires of man the assumption of no responsibilities except those of actual money. The yoke has been eased on his shoulders and made to double the burdens of those women who are thrown on their own resources. Financially and sympathetically the world refuses to pay the debt it owes the latter.

Pauline Periwinkle's defense of working women clearly grew out of her personal experiences, along with firsthand knowledge of the difficulties of women she had known. While acknowledging that some women had no choice but to enter the workforce, she recognized the downward pressure on wages created by their doing so. When public debate focused on passing legislation to prohibit women from competing with men in the labor market, she wrote of her opposition. She found the proposed action lacking in logic and explained why in her column of May 29, 1899. Yet her answer to the situation, laws compelling husbands to support their wives, would not help those women without spouses who had no other option than to work. Obviously, Pauline Periwinkle was not an economist. Her solution simply addressed the reason many women had to enter the workforce. The concept of paying women the same wage as men was not even suggested.

> The vexed problem of the day is the work and wage problem. Not long since the president of the general federation of women's clubs, Mrs. Rebecca D. Lowe, issued through the press an open letter to the club women of America, in which she expressed the conviction that the time had come for the thinking American woman to form a conscientious opinion concerning the industrial situation, and live up to it. She especially had reference to the problem of industry as it affected women, and her call was evidently the result of the recent agitation by various labor unions throughout the country to secure legislation against woman's competing with man in the labor market.
>
> It is questions like these that must be controlled by public sentiment, since it is obvious that no general legislation could be framed that would take cognizance of individual cases, and hence great wrongs might be perpetrated on a minority in the name of justice to the majority. Such legislation against women wage earners as demanded by these union agitators smacks of the inconsistency of our Puritan fathers, who fled to America for religious tolerance, and then persecuted with a vengeance any one on this new soil that dared differ with them in creed. It goes to show that very much the same spirit prompts oppressor and oppressed, the only difference being in the possession of power by the one and the lack of it by the

other. The labor union is self-proclaimed the bulwark that protects the weak from the strong; viewed in its new guise as a machine for crushing out still weaker competitors it must lose any sympathy it has gained from an ethical standpoint. . . .

Admitting the fact that woman's entrance into the labor market has increased the scramble for places and lowered the scale of wages, does not argue that the remedy lies in shutting her out from the various industries open to both sexes. Neither does that pet theory of man's (it can not be dignified with the name of argument): "Let the women marry and get men to support them," cover the case. In the first place, custom proscribes woman's asking a man to marry her or taking a club and going about compelling him to. In the second place, it is contrary to all that is best in the nature of both man and woman to found the institution of marriage primarily on the ground of woman's support. The census returns provide facts that would contradict this plan, even if the theory held good: Each decade shows a greater preponderance of women over men, and therefore a certain percent of the former must be self-supporting.

Taking a practical view of the situation, a few remedies do occur to the rational mind that would, if enforced, result in some relief, and positive benefit to both sexes. This department has frequently called attention to the injustice done the necessity-driven women by those of her sex who, not dependent on their own efforts for support, underbid her in wages in order to procure luxuries they otherwise could not afford. She is thus compelled to accept starvation wages, and the animosity of men competitors also falls more heavily upon her, since her necessity enables wages to be kept down. . . .

Probably those who are so fierce in demanding legislation against women workers would sanction every whit of the foregoing, yet it would never occur to one of them that a little legislation directed against their own sex for the home protection of women competitors might do as much as any other one thing to lessen the pressure in the labor market of which they complain. If they really want legislative relief, I would suggest they bring their influence to bear to secure the following and feel safe in saying that their efforts would receive the support and indorsement [sic] of women of every class: A law compelling under penalty every able-bodied man to support his wife.

Very few married women enter the labor market except when forced by necessity. If able-bodied men had to take choice between supporting their families or breaking stone for public highways, there would be fewer street loafers, fewer tramps, fewer broken-down women, less money spent at saloons, less cry of "cheap female labor," happier homes, better children and a brighter world generally.

Public sentiment should demand this of man, and where he has sunk below reach of sentiment, a sharp stick should be provided wherewith to prod him to duty. Much of the necessity of wage earning being thus removed from the married woman, public sentiment would go far toward restraining single women not in need of employment from competing either with men or with the less fortunate of their sex.

Pauline Periwinkle's opinions about husbands' responsibilities were shared by many at the time. More unconventional was a later column discussing her views on the ingredients for a successful marriage. As she pointed out on August 16, 1897:

Among recent petitions for advice on various momentous problems is one from the editor's ubiquitous friend, "Constant Reader," asking for rules for the management of husbands. . . .

While opinions vary slightly, I believe it is generally conceded that a husband is a creature of many good qualities, but that he must be tamed by his wife before the aforesaid qualities can develop or predominate over less desirable characteristics. Also that this taming process must be conducted with such artlessness that the subject shall not suspect that he is being tamed, otherwise his savage instincts will become alarmed and assertive and he may become wilder and more unmanageable than ever.

To be serious, did "Constant Reader" ever consider that husbands would often be not only better husbands, but better men if they received a little more affection and a little less management, a little more encouragement and a little less nagging? The husband may be a peculiar and sometimes fractious "critter," but take my word for it, he can't be successfully tamed. . . . No, "Constant Reader," you are mistaken; a man does not want managing, he wants consideration. He does not want taming, he wants respect. He does not want a boss, he wants a companion. And if you show him respect, affection and devotion, you find him quite docile and ready to give in return love, honor, and protection. If he does not, even taming would not repay your efforts.

Pauline Periwinkle addressed the matter of divorce in the same forthright fashion. It is unlikely, however, that her readers knew of her divorce, for no evidence has been found that she ever publicly acknowledged that part of her life. She did not find divorce nearly as disgraceful as those conditions in marriage that victimized women. And it is reasonable to assume that some of what she had to say in her January 9, 1905, column reflects her belief that the lack of a father and the inattention of her mother had affected her deeply. Someone, possibly her Aunt Rose or Ella Eaton Kellogg, had been a positive example to her, instilling a devotion to the idea of marriage as a committed relationship of trust, respect, and love between a man and a woman.

Since the frequency of divorce has resulted in public agitation of the subject, opportunity has been offered for the airing of many theories, both as to cause and remedy. Some are entirely superficial, some contain a modicum of truth; few get at the real issues. Preachers may exhort, the press may deplore, lawmakers may legislate, but unless there is right living in the home, the evils from which divorce springs go on.

Which is worse: Divorce or the conditions that produce divorce? Legislation and reform can go no further than checking the abuse of the divorce laws, unless that legislation and reform deals with the causes themselves. Where legislation gives right to existence to certain recognized evils that are generally held responsible for a large proportion of divorces it would be irrational to inflict further injustice on the innocent by revoking relief. So long as the drink and social evils have a legal status, so long as desertion, wife beating, infidelity, etc., go unpunished, though proven in court, it is useless to argue the inexpediency of divorce from the standpoint of the State or society.

We shall have to blot out those inspired words "life, liberty and the pursuit of happiness" before we can ask intelligent men and women to submit for the good of the public and the State to conditions for which the public and the State are chiefly responsible. While society and the State condone and legalize immorality and vice, we should have to find some higher motive on which to base the sacrifice of self in the most vital relation of life. The integrity of the home provides that higher motive, but divorce is merely legal recognition of an already accomplished fact, when home ceases to be a place of mutual love and forbearance; ceases to be a desirable place in which to beget and rear children.

It is folly to seek for causes of divorce outside the mutuality of home relations. Why blame it on poverty or other sociological conditions peculiar to the age when the fact remains that there are more divorces among the rich and well-to-do, among the idlers of society, than among the poor? . . . Where lies the cause and where the remedy for this grave condition? The cause lies in lax teaching in the home; the remedy with the parents who are allowing their children to grow up without proper regard for the sacredness of love and matrimony.

Nowadays, as soon as children arrive at the age of self-consciousness their elders begin to tease and joke them about "sweethearts." By the time they are grown their numerous boy-and-girl affairs have made sentiment a shopworn thing, cheap and commonplace and fickle as the season's change. The girl imagines she has not had all the good times coming to her, has not evidenced her popularity, unless she can exhibit a goodly string of proposals, and sport several engagement rings. The boy takes it a little more to heart, perhaps, because his self-conceit must suffer necessarily by the requirements of sex chivalry; but he, too, understands that it is all in the game. What have either of them left save the shreds and patches of sincerity to bring to the serious business of marriage and home-making? Perhaps neither the man nor the woman was ever addressed on the gravity of the marriage relation till they stood together before the altar. The injunction of the preacher came too late, if this be the case.

"Getting married is a serious matter," said an experienced woman to a young girl. "Yes," replied the latter, "but it's a good deal more serious not to get married at all." This is the spirit that prompts the final decision of many a girl whose beaux have been *legion. She has had her good time; she will soon be passé; the time has come when she must marry if she is ever going to, so she surveys the field as it is at the moment and selects the most eligible part, the best prospect from a worldly point of view. To more or less extent, in all walks of life, this spirit prevails—this playing with love, conquesting it to toss aside. Mothers are at fault for rearing their children without regard for the dignity of love as it relates to the sexes. Fathers and mothers are both at fault when their own attitude to each other proclaims to the inmates of the home that marriage means simply living together, not loving together. Lack of consideration and concession, stinginess, ragging, coldness and contempt between parents are enough to breed in the minds of the young the idea that love is not at all an essential in marriage.*

Fathers are peculiarly responsible for the most serious causes of unhappy marriages. They shield their daughters from even the knowledge of evil, and then turn them loose to fall prey to dangers of which they are unaware. The all important query: "Are you able to support a wife?" having been satisfactorily answered, fathers and brothers conspire to keep the girl in ignorance of the habits of the man she is going to marry. They excuse their conduct on the ground that certain vices are so prevalent that the girl has no option if she is to marry at all. Fathers neglect their duty to their sons in the matter of reasonable advice and warning. They neglect their duty to their daughters in the matter of investigating their courtships before affection is involved. . . . If those keenly alive to the perils of divorce could wake up the fathers and mothers to the necessity of maintaining a high ideal of matrimony in the home and of instilling respect for it in their children, the prime cause of divorce that never can be reached by legislation would be removed.

While Pauline Periwinkle wrote with great conviction about the necessity for women to secure better educational opportunities and higher wages, as well as to have a more realistic understanding of marriage, she was equally forthright in her belief that women should assume a significant role in determining public policies, particularly those dealing with women, children, and the family.[13] What could be more logical than a seat on the school board? She brought the idea before her readers in her August 11, 1902, column with a call for Texas women to serve on public school boards.

Women's clubs everywhere have crossed the Rubicon dividing self-seeking from the world's work. It would be hard to find a band of women nowadays content solely with filling up on literary pabulum whether represented by hardtack or syllabub—the classics or current fiction. Nowadays, when women meet and ask "what is your club doing?" the answer expected is not, "we're studying French history and literature" but, "we're establishing free kindergartens," or "we're working for civic improvement," etc. Even in States southernmost in feelings—and sentiment snaps its fingers at geographical lines—it is no longer considered unwomanly for women to take a good-sized dish in municipal affairs.

The justice of giving the woman taxpayer a voice in the expending of the money she contributes to the public fund can not be gainsaid. Woman's vote in matters relating to the public schools and municipal improvements would be especially desirable. The idea that woman should not vote because she doesn't pay a poll tax is an exploded one in Texas at least, where the school fund loses $70,000 annually because male voters evade the tax. And why if the Governor can legally appoint women to serve on the board of the Girls' Industrial School, which is supported by public funds, can not the people legally elect women to serve on the boards of public schools—a much-needed innovation?

When conditions in Dallas public schools had grown so bad that crowding caused double sessions, truancy was rampant, and buildings were in need of improvements, Pauline Periwinkle took up her pen to rally support for improving public schools. Her opening salvo, fired in her July 9, 1906, column, reiterated her call for the election of women to school boards.

The thought of leading sociologists, men and women, is turning to the public schools as never before, in the conviction that the free educational system offers the only solution to the problem of how to reach the masses with those ideas that make for the uplift of the race. Every where the call is for women to assist in this great work. Still, only in rare instances have their services been asked in positions where their intelligence and influence will have direct effect. . . . In this respect America is way behind England and Scotland in using the intelligence of women to further educational causes. . . .

It is pertinent to ask "What can the women of Texas do to aid their public schools?" First, they can organize a good live mothers' club in every school district or ward. Agitate the sentiment for clean attractive schoolrooms and grounds. Agitate the employment of the best teachers and the payment of such salaries as will attract and hold the best teaching talent. Get in touch with all parents and children and secure their patronage and support. Get in touch with the teacher, find out the local needs and try to supply them through the medium of the club. Agitate raising the tax for school improvements and the issuing of bonds. Nothing will prove so helpful to the community from a business point of view as to have the report go out that here is a town alive to the value of good schools. . . .

The time is ripe, too, to begin making public sentiment for women on school boards. Unlike the situation in many other states, there is nothing in the statutes of Texas to prevent women from qualifying for such a position. . . . While only four American states have given suffrage to women, more than twenty American states have special provisions by which women can vote in school matters. . . .

Of the more than a half million teachers in the United States, nearly four-fifths are women, hence it should not be looked upon as an alarming innovation to ask that the sex be represented in advisory and official capacity, especially when it is everywhere granted that women not only understand children better than they do, but understand each other in an intuitive manner in which no man, however penetrating, can hope to aspire.

The columnist offered encouragement to women who felt reluctant to become involved in political matters outside the home. She reinforced the growing confidence of active clubwomen that municipal housekeeping was a logical extension of their concern for their own families and therefore an entirely appropriate activity.[14] Her heartfelt commitment to the general welfare of children was apparent as she wrote on March 9, 1908: "Do not let your better impulses be paralyzed by the fear that some one may criticise your actions as unwomanly, on the ground that everything outside the home should be left for men to do. . . . No woman need fear the stigma 'unwomanly' for any undertaking that seeks to better conditions for children. Wherever civics touch child life no woman should shrink from entering. The cause will dignify her every service. The man, absorbed in business concerns, may be forgiven, perhaps, for being self-centeredly—thinking little beyond his own family, his own children. But the mother-heart is all-embracing."

Mothers' clubs in Dallas were already active in the schools when Pauline Periwinkle wrote her column promoting school improvement. In fact, they had made numerous appearances at Dallas Board of Education meetings before she began her efforts to influence public opinion in favor of measures to improve public schools.[15] Her April 1, 1907, column describes conditions she found on an "inspection tour" made with one of the mothers' club presidents:

> *There is no more important subject to which intelligent men and women can turn their attention than our public schools and their problems. Rabbi Hirsch of Chicago wasn't half wrong when he told a big convention of club women that if they were really aching to do something worth while, to thoroughly inform themselves on school conditions in their communities, then focus their efforts for a year on two aims: Securing the absolutely needful things, and doing away with the absolutely obnoxious things. But this is too great an undertaking for club women to handle alone. The men, not only because they represent half the citizenship, but because in their vote rests the final decision, should be stirred to take an early and active interest. As a rule, people adopt two viewpoints on matters of public welfare—the schools included: they are either pessimists, inclined to the belief that everything is headed toward the bow-wows, or so rosily optimistic that they are perfectly satisfied with conditions as they are. . . . Until the organization of mothers' clubs became popular, few parents ever thrust noses in a school house door except to sniff.*
>
> *In company with a mothers' club president, I have been doing the rounds of the public schools, and after a visit to seven schools in less than a week, we have both confessed to the dissipation of much ignorance, the accumulations of much information, and strange as it may seem, an unslaked desire to continue the quest. There are fourteen white and five colored schools in Dallas. Conditions here may be taken as representative of conditions in every rapidly growing city of Texas, and as there are few Texas towns that are not*

either affected with rapid growth or hoping to be so affected, there are some problems relating to growth whose discussion may happily prove suggestive. For everywhere in answer to the query, "What most do you need?" came the chorus from principals and teachers: "Room, more room!"

The cry is not alone from the smaller buildings of from eight to ten rooms. It is even more clamorous from buildings of sixteen rooms. Some of these latter have temporary structures—portable rooms— taking up space on the already overcrowded grounds, and yet these schools are compelled to have double sessions in as many as six of the grades. More rooms, more grounds! . . . And they keep right on coming: an army of little tots a thousand strong descends on these unprepared school houses each fall. They are as inevitable as taxes, and a great deal more to be depended upon than school bond issues. What is going to be done about it?

It is in no spirit of criticism of past shortsightedness that the suggestion is made to school boards everywhere to buy plenty of land while it is available. Lots adjacent to school grounds that could have been bought for a few hundred dollars a while back are now priced at as many thousands. Adjacent properties to other schools are out of the question entirely because they have been built upon. . . .

In spite of crowded school rooms, every principal so far interviewed declared in favor of a compulsory education law that should enforce attendance of all children of scholastic age, unless engaged in some more profitable pursuit than loafing on the streets. Truancy is the most [sic] disciplinary problem with which teachers have to deal. It is largely augmented by the street gangs who loiter about school grounds and allure with their apparent enjoyment of freedom the pupil who feels a strong "call of the wild." One principal reported a gang of eleven boys in one ward whose delight it was to hover around the building, "cat-calling" during school hours, and at recess enticing the hooky-loving pupil away. . . .

Every time school opens in the fall a number of the gang show up for enrollment, partly out of curiosity, partly to "size up" the teacher. If they think they stand a chance of having things their own way, and making an enjoyable lot of trouble in the school, they stay on for a while; otherwise they drop out at once. Very few come for legitimate purposes. Little is gained by appealing to the par-

ents. Their sense of citizenship is very poorly developed, if at all. In fact, most cases of truancy are traceable to the ignorant or foolish parent. The latter class includes many of the so-called respectable and intelligent. They fail in refusing to co-operate with the teacher in the management and discipline of the child. . . .

Asked if the new juvenile court law could be made of assistance in correcting truancy, all the principals thought it possible, by vesting the probation officers with truant officer rights. A wholesome regard for the majesty of the law might be helpful to delinquent parents and pupils, and of course could deal effectively with street gangs. . . .

Of physical lacks in our schools, other than this overwhelming demand for more room, and of some other matters that have a direct bearing on their efficiency, but of which the general public may be unconscious, I shall speak further, as the data now in my possession is rendered more complete.

Pauline Periwinkle did speak further on the subject the very next week, on April 8, describing the lack of basic necessities such as heating and decent sanitary facilities in Dallas schools. She used graphic descriptions designed to raise eyebrows and, she hoped, an outcry for improvements.

This may not be the proper kind of weather in which to inject interest in the discussion of stoves, but speaking on a warm subject, why is it that residences, hotels and public buildings, no matter the size, can be properly and economically heated by various "plants" while our school houses fall back on the antiquated stove?

I do not believe that the majority of our taxpayers object to increasing the levy for public school purposes if they can have the assurance that the funds will be wisely expended; that they will get good value for their money. . . .

The majority of the school buildings of Dallas were fitted out with furnaces of some sort, not one of which is in use or is usable. In one respect, at least, the children of today have no advantage over the children of half a century ago. They still enjoy the alternating sensations of grilling and chilling in rooms where the piece de resistance is a stove of generous proportions. In severe weather lessons come practically to a standstill while "teacher" engages in the pleasant diversion of changing, every few minutes, children who are too hot with children who are too cold. In the present crowded condition of the schools this little game of "flower basket" fills up the day quite adequately especially when ventilation languishes, and a mental fog settles dully over the school room. Odors of asafetida "witch bags" and garlic occasionally smite the drowsing senses, and the initiated know that certain aspiring and perspiring young candidates for American citizenship are within the heated zone. . . .

In a prime essential, that of sanitation, the schools are almost wholly dependent upon the janitor. Only in one building has there been installed an automatic flushing device; in all the others that service is performed by the janitor under circumstances at times adverse. As we entered the main hall of one of our largest school buildings a most obnoxious odor became manifest. It was not difficult to trace the source. . . . As some 850 students attend this school, the inadequacy of the present system of sewerage employed is apparent.

The same unholy sanitary methods are in vogue in most of the schools, the drains remaining unflushed except for the few times during school hours that the janitor can attend to it. . . .

One marked neglect we found everywhere—lack of any provision for teachers. It is a reflection on our school system to find it so far behind office and store buildings, and even factories, in this respect. Before another scholastic year begins, every building should be equipped with an indoor lavatory for the teachers. There are no conveniences for the ladies employed in our schools that are not exceeded by the humblest washerwoman in the land. . . .

Another very pressing need of a rest room with toilet facilities is for children suddenly taken ill or injured in any way. One principal spoke of a very recent case, a little girl whose mother was the bread winner of the family. She could not send the child home, the mother had the key to the house and was working in some factory down town. There were no conveniences to make the child comfortable, and yet it would be a matter of small expense compared to the constant service it would render if every school building was thus properly equipped. . . .

■ ■ ■

The Dallas mothers' clubs recognized that making improvements in the public schools would require more than simply publicizing the problems. Pauline Periwinkle announced their tactics in her March 23, 1908, column, writing, "The Mothers' Clubs of the various ward schools in Dallas have taken the initiative in a campaign that has for its object the placing of two women—mothers and patrons of the public schools—on the Board of Education." The idea was by no means a new one, for Pauline Periwinkle had devoted an entire column to "reasons why women would make good members of school boards" ten years earlier.[16] It had taken a decade for the necessary circumstances to develop.

The activities of the next two weeks demonstrated the extent of Dallas clubwomen's organizational skills. The two candidates, Adella Kelsey Turner and Ella Stephenson Tucker, were active clubwomen. Mrs. Turner, the wife of a Texas & Pacific Railroad official, had served as president of the TFWC from 1903 to 1905 and had resigned her position as president of the Dallas Woman's Forum to run for the school board. Mrs. Tucker, married to insurance man Pascal P. Tucker, had helped organize several mothers' clubs. In a politically astute move, they named as their campaign manager a woman who could command public attention in the community better than almost anyone: the woman's editor of the *News*. Although she was still writing her weekly Pauline Periwinkle column in 1908, Isadore Callaway was also heavily involved in club work, serving as president of the Dallas Federation of Women's Clubs. She was the ideal person for the job.

Accordingly, Mrs. Callaway began meeting with representatives of mothers' clubs and women's clubs to muster support for the candidates. At these meetings campaign plans were mapped out and club endorsements given "enthusiastically." Members reported success with petitions for placing the names of the women on the regular ballots, along with "assurances from prominent business men of the city that the women candidates shall have active support." The candidates' platform, summed up simply as "The welfare of the children," was announced. Finally, the city federation decided to print and issue ten thousand cards with a "concise statement of the aims of the movement and results hoped for." Club members took charge of card distribution throughout the city.[17] On March 26 the two women candidates were the first to file their petitions for places on the ballot. The petitions, gathered so energetically, turned out to be unnecessary. The candidates were informed that, according to the attorney general's office, "where there are no other officers than members of the Board of Education to be elected, it is unnecessary."[18]

As the campaign moved to its final week, Mrs. Callaway hosted a kindergarten tea at her home to allow "ladies whose minds are in doubt as to the desirability of women for School Board members. . . . to come laden with all the obstacles they can bring up against this representation."[19] Her association with the newspaper seemed to have helped her candidates: a news story containing endorsements from several prominent men in the community appeared in the *News* four days before the election.[20] Willing to use every option available, the campaign manager took to her desk and produced a Pauline Periwinkle column titled "Women Make Good on School Boards," which arrived on city doorsteps April 6, 1908, three days before the election.

Contrary to the accepted belief that to give women a place on school boards is a movement foreign to Southern conceptions of woman's "sphere," looms the fact that Kentucky was the very first State in the Union to recognize woman's fitness to have voice in educational affairs. . . . Louisiana grants the same right to all taxpaying women. Twenty-eight other States—East, North and West —do the same. . . .

The State Orphans' Home and the College of Industrial Arts have women on their boards. A woman served on the present State textbook board. True, they hold these offices by appointment of the Governor. But since there are women County Treasurers and women Country Clerks elected by the voters, and since these positions involve the question of salaries, which school board membership does not, the logic of the comparison counts for the women. . . . As for women notaries public, they are thick as blackberries in June.

School boards are not political boards in the same sense that other governing bodies are. The question of education should never become a partisan issue. It is menacing enough to the public welfare that so much of the business of government is conducted upon other than business principles. As educational interests develop, and more and more funds pass into the hands of school trustees for expenditure, making it of grave financial concern to the citizenship that politics are excluded, nothing will do more to avert the danger than active participation in school management by women, whose interests will be solely for the best possible educational returns without regard to the success of any existing faction. . . .

Texas women are as intelligent, as capable, as self-sacrificing and as devoted to the welfare of their children and the community as the women of Kentucky, Mississippi, Louisiana, Florida, Georgia or Tennessee can possibly be, or the women from every other section of the United States or, from the other civilized Nations that have recognized woman's fitness for school management.

The day before the election found the campaign manager and her assistants canvassing for the two women candidates. Isadore informed a *News* reporter that she had "thoroughly worked the South Dallas district of factories, all the Tenth Ward, the district of Exposition and Fair Park. . . . distributed 2,000 cards, visiting small drug stores, grocery stores and spots wherever men were assembled. Personally . . . talked to several hundred men and found cordial support from every person. Only one man stated that he did not approve of women running for office and two others were undecided about the casting of their votes."[21]

When the vote was tabulated, Mrs. Turner and Mrs. Tucker had been elected, although Mrs. Tucker had been only seven votes ahead of the next candidate for the sixth and final seat before the last box was counted.[22] A special ten-cent tax to fund local school maintenance and extensive improvements failed when it did not receive the required two-thirds vote.[23] Although Mrs. Turner and Mrs. Tucker had run on a platform that promised to put children first, the loss of the special tax fund would make their task more difficult.

The initial efforts of the two women on the school board addressed problems the mothers' clubs had brought to the board earlier: fire escapes, toilet facilities, and sidewalks. Then they turned to the food service available at the various schools and ultimately recommended the installation of a lunch system for the high school.[24] But the biggest problem was the dearth of classrooms. The finance committee, which included Mrs. Turner, identified $150,000 in needed repairs and expansion.[25]

Pauline Periwinkle could write about the specific problems existing in the Dallas schools, but the underlying solution—an increase in the amount of money available for schools—would require more than special local tax levies. Funding for education came partly from the state of

Texas and partly from local taxpayers. The existence of the state's permanent school fund, dating from 1852, lulled many into assuming that public schools were well provided for. The truth was that Texas school funding was woefully inadequate. Any significant improvement in education would require an amendment to the state constitution permitting local school districts to tax themselves at a higher rate than currently allowed and reduce the percentage of voters needed to approve local tax increases from two-thirds to one-half. Efforts to amend the constitution had begun even before the two clubwomen ran for spots on the school board.

In 1907 various factions in the state began a campaign to improve the quality of education. The Conference for Education organized by R. B. Cousins, the state superintendent of education, and other educators began the grassroots effort to publicize the need for improvements.[26] The TFWC took part, making education the theme of their program at their November, 1907, meeting.[27] Pauline Periwinkle provided facts and figures to her readers supporting the need for additional school funding and a compulsory education law. To promote passage of a proposed amendment for increasing local school tax limits, she urged clubwomen to devote a program to education in their communities and make certain the local press published the proceedings.[28]

The constitutional amendment passed statewide in November, 1908, with Dallas citizens approving it by a nearly three to one vote.[29] During the two-year tenure of Mrs. Turner and Mrs. Tucker, the Dallas school system added more than fifty new school rooms and made repairs in older buildings. A significant increase in board of education expenditures for buildings had taken place, from $4,800 for school houses in the 1907–1908 school year to $88,844.52 in 1908–1909 and $142,506.08 in 1909–1910.[30] The election of two women to the school board was the result of the combined efforts of the mothers' clubs and other clubwomen. Their campaign activities reflected the growing political sophistication among women throughout Texas that would fuel other projects in the next decade.

Pauline Periwinkle would continue to support their efforts until her death six years later. Each time she took up her pen, her observations—informed and matter-of-fact in tone, yet often displaying flashes of indignation or humorous sarcasm—would help lead the way. She understood her role as a journalist and the broader significance of the newspaper page she edited. She had explained the importance of the Woman's

Century page nearly a decade earlier: "[It] exists for no other purpose than to exploit the doings of Texas women in the way of advancement and good work. It could be made specially valuable as a medium for preserving the record of woman's work in Texas, and specially helpful by suggesting that what women have done, other women can do. . . . Yet fifty and a hundred years from now, the events of today that strike us as perhaps too trifling to record will have their own value as commentaries on existing social and ethical conditions."[31]

For twenty years Pauline Periwinkle's columns preserved a record of women's work in Texas. When she died, the women of Texas lost a valuable ally in their efforts to improve their lives. One of the many tributes at her death reveals the perception shared by those who mourned her: "She had initiative and ambition for the improvement of womankind and with it sufficient brains and perseverance to achieve whatever she began."[32] It is a fitting epitaph for one whose life's work affected so many.

Notes

PREFACE

1. Doris Kearns [Goodwin], "Angles of Vision," in *Telling Lives: The Biographer's Art,* ed. Mark Pachter (Washington, D.C.: New Republic Books/National Portrait Gallery, 1979), p. 91.
2. Mrs. LaMoreaux also maintained that her daughter's will stipulated money be provided to educate her brother Daniel Sutherland's daughter, Charlotte, to whom the letter containing these claims is addressed. Maria LaMoreaux to "My dear children Francis and Charlotte" April 21, 1931, copy supplied to author by Mrs. Joel Sutherland Rhoads.

INTRODUCTION

1. Elizabeth Brooks, *Prominent Women of Texas,* pp. 127–28; Ferdinand B. Baillio, *A History of the Texas Press Association, from Its Organization in Houston in 1880 . . .,* p. 170.
2. Kate Friend served as official editor of the Texas Federation of Women's Clubs news for ten years. Kate Harrison Friend Papers, 4Al04, files 8 and 9, Texas Collection, Baylor University. Flint wrote a column, "Of Interest To Women," from 1912 until 1920. Hallie Flint Papers, Woodson Research Center, Rice University.
3. *Dallas Morning News* (hereafter *DMN*), Oct. 14, 1896.
4. *DMN,* June 4, 1900.
5. Letters in Texas Federation of Women's Clubs Collection (hereafter TFWC Collection), Blagg-Huey Library, Texas Woman's University, Denton, Tex. (Uncataloged at time of finding by Dr. Judith N. McArthur.)
6. Genevieve G. McBride has noted that the press supplied many leaders in the women's movement across the nation, and their writings contain a detailed record of the activities of women engaged in reform activities. Genevieve M. McBride, *On Wisconsin Women: Working for Their Rights from Settlement to Suffrage,* p. xvii. For the work of Texas women, see Judith N. McArthur, *Creating the New Woman: The Rise of the Southern Women's Progressive Movement in Texas.*
7. TFWC, *Who's Who of the Womanhood of Texas,* vol. 1, *1923–1924,* p. 33.

8. *DMN,* Aug. 21, 1916.

9. S. Isadore Miner to Probate Judge of Calhoun County, Mich., Oct. 8, 1877, Calhoun County Probate files. Copy in author's possession.

10. *DMN,* Nov. 13, 1899; Oct. 14, Nov. 18, 1901; Apr. 11, 1904; Jan. 20, 1908; Nov. 22, 1909.

11. *DMN,* Sept. 18, 1899; May 19, 1902.

CHAPTER 1. WOMEN JOURNALISTS AND REFORM MOVEMENTS

1. While debate continues about the definition of feminism, in this instance I use the term "feminist" to denote a woman who was aware of the institutional injustices women experienced as a group and who would openly challenge those injustices. Given the conservatism and traditional attitudes evident in Dallas at the time of her arrival, Isadore Miner would qualify as a feminist, for she had strong convictions and appeared impervious to the restraints against speaking one's mind that were commonly placed on women. For evidence of others who shared Miner's sentiments, see Sylvia Hunt, "'Throw Aside the Veil of Helplessness': A Southern Feminist at the 1893 World's Fair," *Southwestern Historical Quarterly* 100 (1996): 49. For a broader discussion of the term "feminism," see Karen Offen, "Defining Feminism: A Comparative Historical Approach," *Signs: A Journal of Women in Culture and Society* XIV (Autumn, 1988): 152.

2. Alonzo Wasson's observations are not surprising, for such women were just becoming active in conservative Dallas. Alonzo Wasson, "The Good Old Days of the Dallas News," reprinted from the Texas Unlimited Edition of the *Dallas Morning News,* May 22, 1949. Copy in author's possession.

3. Elizabeth Bancroft Schlesinger, "The Nineteenth-Century Woman's Dilemma and Jennie June," *New York History* (Oct., 1961): 3.

4. Susan E. Dickinson, "Women in Journalism," in *Woman's Work in America,* ed. Annie Nathan Meyer, p. 128; Maurine H. Beasley and Shelia J. Gibbons, *Taking Their Place: A Documentary History of Women and Journalism,* pp. 8–9.

5. Glenna Matthews, *The Rise of Public Woman: Woman's Power and Woman's Place in the United States, 1630–1970,* pp. 31, 93. Matthews notes that in the earliest years of the American Revolution, women did express their opinions with consumer boycotts and fund-raisers for Washington's troops. See also Nancy Woloch, ed., *Women and the American Experience,* pp. 64, 72.

6. The earliest reform periodicals were usually single-issue oriented. See E. Claire Jerry, "The Role of Newspapers in the Nineteenth-Century Woman's Movement," in *A Voice of Their Own: The Woman Suffrage Press, 1840–1910,* ed. Martha M. Solomon, pp. 17–29.

7. Bertha-Monica Stearns, "Reform Periodicals and Female Reformers, 1830–1860," *American Historical Quarterly* 37 (July, 1932): 679–85; Marion Marzolf, *Up from the Footnote: A History of Women Journalists,* p. 219.

8. Quotes from Stearns, "Reform Periodicals," p. 690; see also pp. 686, 689–94. Dickinson, "Women in Journalism," pp. 128–29; Beasley and Gibbons, *Taking Their Place,* pp. 9, 67–68; Marzolf, *Up from the Footnote,* pp. 14–15; "Jane Grey Swisshelm," in *Notable American Women, 1607–1950: A Biographical Dictionary,* ed. Edward T. James, pp. 416–17.

9. Excerpts from an 1859 speech cited in *Crusader and Feminist: Letters of Jane Grey Swisshelm, 1858–1865,* ed. Arthur J. Larsen, pp. 38–39.

10. *DMN,* Dec. 13, 1897.

11. In her groundbreaking article, "The Cult of True Womanhood: 1820–1860," in *Dimity Convictions: The American Woman in the Nineteenth Century,* ed. Barbara Welter, Welter describes in detail the expectations of women, including piety, purity, submissiveness, and domesticity, and notes that women's magazines of the period constantly reinforced these ideals. See also Woloch, *Women and the American Experience,* pp. 101–17.

12. Stearns, "Reform Periodicals," pp. 680–81; Beasley and Gibbons, *Taking Their Place,* pp. 77–78.

13. Stearns, "Reform Periodicals," p. 697; Matthews, *Rise of Public Woman,* p. 98.

14. Margaret Fuller's life and work continue to be of interest to scholars. See Catherine C. Mitchell, ed., *Margaret Fuller's New York Journalism: A Biographical Essay and Key Writings;* Joan von Mehren, *Minerva and the Muse: A Life of Margaret Fuller;* Marie Mitchell Olesen Urbanski, ed., *Margaret Fuller: Visionary of the New Age;* and Jeffrey Steele, ed., *The Essential Margaret Fuller.* Other women whose work appeared in large city newspapers in the 1840s include Miss Cornelia Wells Walter of the *Boston Transcript* and Sara Jane Clarke, whose letters signed "Grace Greenwood" appeared in several East Coast papers in 1845 and 1846.

15. Dickinson, "Women in Journalism," pp. 128–31; Marzolf, *Up from the Footnote,* pp. 16–17; Beasley and Gibbons, *Taking Their Place,* p. 90. See also Donald A. Ritchie, *Press Gallery: Congress and the Washington Correspondents,* for the place of women correspondents, especially pp. 43–46, 85, 145–62.

16. Beasley and Gibbons, *Taking Their Place,* pp. 11, 87; Schlesinger, "Nineteenth-Century Woman's Dilemma," p. 3.

17. Jane Grey Swisshelm, *Letters to Country Girls,* quoted in Marzolf, *Up from the Footnote,* p. 15.

18. Matthews, *Rise of Public Woman,* p. 95; quote from *Home-Maker,* May, 1892, as cited in Schlesinger, "Nineteenth-Century Woman's Dilemma," pp. 5, 8–9; Ishbel Ross, *Ladies of the Press: The Story of Women in Journalism by an Insider,* Ishbel Ross, pp. 44–45; James, *Notable American Women,* pp. 409–11.

19. Jennie June, *Jennie Juneiana: Talks of Women's Topics,* p. 186.

20. Schlesinger, "Nineteenth-Century Woman's Dilemma," pp. 5, 13; See also Jane Cunningham Croly, *Memories of Jane Cunningham Croly: "Jenny June";* Marzolf, *Up from the Footnote;* Dickinson, "Women in Journalism."

21. Jane Cunningham Croly, *Memories of Jane Cunningham Croly,* p. 126; *DMN,* June 12, 1899.

22. *DMN,* May 31, 1909.
23. Nancy A. Walker, *Fanny Fern,* pp. 5–14; Elizabeth Bancroft Schlesinger, "Sara Payson Willis Parton," in *Notable American Women,* vol. 3, p. 24; Beasley and Gibbons, *Taking Their Place,* pp. 11, 87; Joyce W. Warren, *Fanny Fern: An Independent Woman,* p. 215; Ann D. Wood, "The 'Scribbling Women' and Fanny Fern: Why Women Wrote," *American Quarterly* 23 (Spring, 1971): 14–15, 17. According to Wood, the nom de plume chosen by Sara Willis came from her childhood memories of her mother's love of a sweet-smelling fern they would pick when walking together in the woods.
24. *New York Ledger,* Nov. 17, 1860, as quoted in Warren, *Fanny Fern,* p. 1.
25. Boston *True Flag,* Apr. 23, 1853, as quoted in Warren, *Fanny Fern,* p. 3.
26. *New York Ledger,* July 16, 1870, as quoted in Warren, *Fanny Fern,* p. 299; also pp. 2, 291–94. Walker, *Fanny Fern,* p. 105. See also Elizabeth Bancroft Schlesinger, "Fanny Fern: Our Grandmothers' Mentor," *New York Historical Society Quarterly* 38 (Oct., 1954).
27. *DMN,* May 15, 1911.
28. Warren, *Fanny Fern,* p. 299; *DMN,* Nov. 27, 1897.
29. Warren, *Fanny Fern,* pp. 2–4, 266–67, 291–93, 296, 298, 308–309. Warren's biography illuminates the methods Fanny Fern used to point out the inequities in society. Walker, *Fanny Fern,* pp. 101, 105, 116–19; Beasley and Gibbons, *Taking Their Place,* p. 87; Ross, *Ladies of the Press,* pp. 42–43; Marzolf, *Up from the Footnote,* p. 22. Wood, "'Scribbling Women' and Fanny Fern," pp. 3, 14–15. This article contains a thoughtful analysis of what motivated many of the women writers of the day.
30. Marzolf, *Up from the Footnote,* p. 18; Dickinson, "Women in Journalism," pp. 132–35; Beasley and Gibbons, *Taking Their Place,* pp. 81–93. For a detailed examination of the suffrage press, see Martha M. Solomon, "The Role of the Suffrage Press in the Woman's Rights Movement," in *A Voice of Their Own.*
31. The *Independent,* Mar. 7, 1878, quoted in Beasley and Gibbons, *Taking Their Place,* p. 91.
32. Grace Greenwood, "The New Order of Things," *New York Times,* July 3, 1877, as quoted in Beasley and Gibbons, *Taking Their Place,* p. 98.
33. This understanding of early restraints upon women's public involvement is being challenged by new research, which suggests that before the Civil War in some areas of the South women were encouraged to assert a public presence in the political arena. See Elizabeth R. Varon, "Tippecanoe and the Ladies, Too: White Women and Party Politics in Antebellum Virginia," *Journal of American History* 82 (Sept., 1995). For a discussion of the "southern lady" role and those women who defied opposition to become reformers, see Marjorie Spruill Wheeler, *New Women of the New South: The Leaders of the Woman Suffrage Movement in the Southern States.*
34. Matthews, *Rise of Public Woman,* pp. 72–92, 116, 131. Matthews also argues that the nineteenth-century "domestic" novels played a significant role in expanding reading women's notions of their own self-worth and justification

for their anger with male privilege. The novels also encouraged them to imagine new activities and behaviors for themselves. See also Woloch, *Women and the American Experience*, pp. 222–35.

35. Matthews, *Rise of Public Woman*, pp. 131, 157; Eleanor Flexner, *Century of Struggle: The Woman's Rights Movement in the United States*, rev. ed., pp. 147–49. See also Ruth Bordin, *Woman and Temperance: The Quest for Power and Liberty, 1873–1900*, and Barbara Leslie Epstein, *The Politics of Domesticity: Women, Evangelism, and Temperance in Nineteenth-Century America*.

36. Glenda Riley, *Inventing the American Woman: An Inclusive History*, 2nd ed., p. 181. Riley attributes the success of Progressive Era reform efforts to the "municipal housekeeping" efforts of clubwomen. Clubwomen's activities have been documented in numerous works, including Ann Firor Scott, *Natural Allies: Women's Associations in American History;* Matthews, *Rise of Public Woman;* Marsha Wedell, *Elite Women and the Reform Impulse in Memphis, 1875–1915;* and Karen Blair, *The Clubwoman as Feminist: True Womanhood Redefined, 1868–1914*. For an early view of the workings of the General Federation of Women's Clubs, see Mary I. Wood, *History of the General Federation of Women's Clubs*.

37. Pre–Civil War suffragists and temperance advocates had recognized the need for newspaper coverage, although press reaction was uniformly negative when and if suffrage activities were acknowledged. Suffragists solved the problem by producing their own newspapers. The late-nineteenth-century wave of reformers viewed the general circulation press as a means of reaching a broader constituency. Jerry, "Role of Newspapers," pp. 17–29; Matthews, *Rise of Public Woman*, pp. 156–60; Marzolf, *Up from the Footnote*, pp. 9–11, 234; Beasley and Gibbons, *Taking Their Place*, p. 11. For a study of how women's groups at the turn of the century accomplished their aims, see Elisabeth S. Clemens, "Organizational Repertoires and Institutional Change: Women's Groups and the Transformation of U.S. Politics, 1890–1920," *American Journal of Sociology* 98 (Jan., 1993): 783–84. For a discussion of the particular constraints southern women faced, see Wheeler, *New Women*, pp. xv, 4–13.

38. Mary Kavanaugh Oldham Eagle, ed., *The Congress of Women*, p. 437; Mary P. Ryan, *Women in Public: Between Banner and Ballots, 1825–1880*, pp. 131–32, 166–68.

39. The increase could be attributed to a number of factors: recognition of the growing number of women readers, the increase in the number of women seeking employment following school, or changing attitudes toward women in the workplace. Barbara Miller Solomon, *In the Company of Educated Women: A History of Women and Higher Education in America*, p. 129; U.S. Bureau of the Census, *Statistics of Population of the United States at the Tenth Census, 1880* (hereafter U.S. Census, *Statistics of Population, 1880*), p. 829; Joseph Hill, *Women in Gainful Occupations, 1870–1920*, p. 42; Ritchie, *Press Gallery*, pp. 151–53.

40. Allan Forman, "By-the-By," *The Journalist* 8 (Jan. 26, 1889): 12. Forman fo-

cused his attention on the work of Anglo and African American women in the East and Midwest.

41. Note the difference in attitude toward women journalists expressed by Forman and Alonzo Wasson of the *Dallas Morning News*. Eagle, *Congress of Women,* p. 435; Ritchie, *Press Gallery,* p. 151; *The Journalist,* 1894, as quoted in Marzolf, *Up from the Footnote,* p. 33.

42. Marzolf, *Up from the Footnote,* pp. 205–207.

43. McBride, *On Wisconsin Women,* pp. xvi, 7. McBride demonstrates the way the reformers in the press and women's groups worked in tandem to accomplish their aims in Wisconsin. Pauline Periwinkle and the TFWC closely parallel the Wisconsin experience. Ritchie, *Press Gallery,* pp. 151–52.

44. McBride, *On Wisconsin Women,* pp.134–50.

45. Ross, *Ladies of the Press,* pp. 553, 594–95.

46. James, *Notable American Women,* pp. 416–17, 503.

47. G. B. Dealey, notes from unpublished manuscript (n.d.), A. H. Belo Corporation archives. By 1900, the census counted eight female journalists in Dallas. U.S. Census, *Twelfth Census of the United States,* vol. 2, pt. 2, pp. 558–59.

48. The most extensive society news was reported in *Beau Monde,* a sixteen-page Dallas weekly edited by Alice Fitzgerald from 1895 to 1910. *Beau Monde* featured lengthy descriptions of parties and utilized French phrases to give the accounts a more elegant note. John William Rogers, *The Lusty Texans of Dallas,* pp. 179–89.

CHAPTER 2. "TIE A KNOT IN YOUR THREAD"

1. Mrs. Joel Sutherland Rhoads, telephone interview with author, Fairfax, Va., Jan. 15, 1990, and May 27, 1992; Sutherland family records, including copies of marriage registration; Office of the Commissioner of Pensions, Adjutant General's Office, Washington, D.C. Annette Igra, ed., *Battle Creek: The Place behind the Products,* p. 30. Salisbury prison was deemed the "worst southern prison," with a mortality rate of 34 percent. James McPherson, *Battle Cry of Freedom,* p. 797, n. 48; Baltimore National Cemetery office.

2. Isadore Callaway to D. W. Sutherland, July 14, 1900. Sutherland family letters in possession of Joel Sutherland Rhoads, Fairfax, Va. Isadore was incorrect in recalling her father's age at his death. He was twenty-nine. *The Review and Herald,* June 6, 1865.

3. Sutherland family records, including copy of marriage registration, provided by Mrs. Joel Sutherland Rhoads, Fairfax, Va. Location of Oneida and Grand Ledge found in *Michigan State Gazetter and Business Directory, 1875* and Walter Romig, *Michigan Place Names,* pp. 232, 416; both sources located in the Local History Division, Willard Library, Battle Creek, Mich. *Albion Evening Recorder,* Albion, Mich., Feb. 19, 1936.

4. 1880 U.S. Census, State of Michigan, Supervisor's District #3, Enumeration District #57, p. 44, 1. 36.

5. Maria listed her occupation as "teacher" on the 1860 manuscript census (township of Oneida, Eaton County, Mich., p. 663). Ronald L. Numbers, *Prophetess of Health: A Study of Ellen C. White*, p. 86. The LaMoreauxs' marriage certificate indicates that the official performing the ceremony was Elder John Byington, the first Conference President of the Seventh Day Adventists. Maria testified to her faith in a letter to the *Review and Herald*, July 12, 1864.
6. Petition for the Appointment of Guardian to the Judge of Probate for the County of Calhoun in the State of Michigan, dated July 26, 1866. Copy in author's possession. Declaration of Guardian of Minor Children for Pension—Act of July 26, 1866. My thanks to Mrs. Jean Davis of Battle Creek, Michigan, who searched court records and libraries for information which proved enormously helpful in reconstructing Isadore Sutherland's early years.
7. U.S. Statutes at Large, vol. 12, Thirty-Seventh Congress, Session II, 1862, p. 566; Vol. 13, Thirty-Eighth Congress, Session I, 1864, p. 388; Vol. 14, Thirty-Ninth Congress, Session I, 1866, p. 230.
8. Isadore Sutherland Miner to attorney "Mr. Ingersol," Feb. 20, 1885, from probate file #2867, Calhoun County Probate Court records (hereafter CCPC).
9. Volume in possession of Anne Tyler Rawlins, a great niece of Isadore and William Allen Callaway.
10. *Calhoun County, Michigan Marriages, 1836–1870,* compiled by the Daughters of the American Republic, family records; Isadore Sutherland to Probate Judge of Calhoun County, Oct. 8, 1877; Isadore Sutherland Miner to attorney "Mr. Ingersol," Feb. 20, 1885; *DMN,* Oct. 14, 1917; *Dallas Times Herald* (hereafter *DTH*), Nov. 22, 1925; U.S. Census, *Statistics of Population, 1880*, pp. 212–13. Daniel Sutherland worked in Battle Creek as a travel agent and as a salesman in Dallas, and later lived in Albion, Mich. *Battle Creek City Directory,* 1886; *Charlotte (Michigan) Tribune,* Feb. 9, 1898; *Gratiot County Herald,* Ithaca, Mich., Feb. 3, 1898; *Albion Evening Recorder,* Feb. 3, 1936.
11. In a letter resigning his guardianship of the Sutherland children, F. F. LaMoreaux claimed that "although he has not been careful to keep in detail an account of his expenditure in the management of the estate of said minors, that the entire account on their behalf has been expended in the management and care of said minors." Guardian's Bond, CCPC, May 24, 1869. Letter to Ingersoll, Feb. 20, 1885, file #2867, CCPC. Transcribed copy in author's possession.
12. Letter to CCPC, Oct. 9, 1877, file #2867, CCPC. Copy in author's possession.
13. Letter to Probate Judge of Calhoun County, Mich., Oct. 8, 1877. Transcribed copy in author's possession.
14. Official court documents signed by Probate Judge Charles Dickey, Mar. 6, 1878. Copy in author's possession.
15. Letter to Mr. Ingersoll, Feb. 20, 1885. Copy in author's possession.
16. *Battle Creek College Record Book,* pp. 71, 79, in Adventist Heritage Center, Andrews University, Berrien Springs, Mich. Battle Creek College was, in effect, a high school, but it called itself a college like many similar schools of the period.

17. Letters of Sept. 23, 1862, from Rose Worden, and July 12, 1964, from Maria Sutherland, to the *Review and Herald;* obituary, Aug. 11, 1903, the *Review and Herald.*

18. Among the early visions received by Ellen White, the founder of the faith, was that of eating two meals a day and avoiding meat. Emmett K. Vande Vere, *The Wisdom Seekers,* p. 36.

19. The denomination was a product of the millennialism and adventism movements of the 1840s. Notable among its leaders was William Miller, a New York farmer who prophesized the coming of Christ in 1844 to his followers, the Millerites. When the appearance did not take place, many followers returned to their denominations. Others, however, joined the Seventh Day Adventists. Russell Blaine Nye, *Society and Culture in America, 1830–1860,* pp. 314–15. See also Arthur Whitefield Spalding, *Origin and History of Seventh-day Adventists,* vol. 2.

20. Amy South, "How Jeff's Bridge Divided B.C.," *Scene Magazine* (Apr., 1987): 25; Vande Vere, *Wisdom Seekers,* pp. 11, 14, 23, 35, 36; Leigh Johnsen, "Brownsberger and Battle Creek: The Beginning of Adventist Higher Education," *Adventist Herald* (Winter, 1976): 36, 37.

21. *The Republican,* St. Clair, Mich., July 13, 1881.

22. Ibid., July 6, 1881.

23. U.S. Census, *Statistics of Population, 1880.* Among all occupations, domestic servants were the most numerous, with 26,746 counted, but the number of high school graduates among them was probably insignificant.

24. Ibid., pp. 212–13.

25. When Michigan voted to give blacks the vote as part of a new state constitution in 1868, Battle Creek residents favored the move, although it was defeated statewide. Carlton Mabee with Susan Mabel Newhouse, *Sojourner Truth: Slave, Prophet, Legend,* pp. xiv, 95, 97.

26. *Battle Creek Daily Journal,* Nov. 11, 1887. Given her job and interests, it is quite possible that Isadore Sutherland Miner attended this gathering.

27. Maxine Atteberry, "Seventh Day Adventist Nurses: A Century of Service, 1883–1983," *Adventist Heritage* 8 (Fall, 1983): 4; unidentified newspaper clipping, Mar. 31, 1923, Ross Coller Collection.

28. Igra, *Battle Creek,* pp. 7, 8, 39, 44; Gerald G. Herdman, "Early Battle Creek," *Adventist Heritage* (Jan., 1974): 17–18.

29. *Battle Creek City Directory,* 1889; *Good Health* (hereafter *GH*), Apr., 1889, p. 128.

30. In 1880 the Michigan census counted 84 women as printers and 9 as journalists. In the entire United States, there were only 288 women journalists counted, 320 women "authors, lecturers and literary persons," and 36 women "publishers of books, maps and newspapers." U.S. Census, *Statistics of Population, 1880,* pp. 745, 829.

31. Obituary, unidentified Battle Creek newspaper, Feb. 27, 1931, Ross Coller Collection, Willard Library, Battle Creek, Mich.

32. Unidentified news clippings, June 24, 1913, and Mar. 31, 1923, Ross Coller Collection.

33. In the 1850s Amelia Bloomer was the first editor of the temperance and suffrage newspaper, *Lily*. She supported the adoption of a radical new dress style of full flowing trousers under a shorter skirt. Although the costume allowed freedom of movement, public ridicule made the "Bloomers" a short-lived fashion statement. Harman and Shaw's choice of bloomers suggests an independence from fashion dictates and a practical approach to comfort while at their work. Marzolf, *Up From the Footnote*, pp. 221–23.

34. Berenice Bryant Lowe, *Tales of Battle Creek*, pp. 262–63; deposition given by Emma Shaw, June 17, 1895, for case #6-495, Sara I. Miner vs. James W. Miner, Circuit Court file, Calhoun County; *DMN*, Aug. 21, 1916. No examples of Isadore's published poetry in *Wide Awake* have been found, but her obituary noted that her work had appeared there.

35. The social purity movement sought to reform the sexual customs of America by abolishing prostitution, reforming prostitutes and prosecuting their customers, censoring pornography, and establishing sex education and the right of women to refuse to have marital sex. See Linda Gordon, *Woman's Body, Woman's Rights;* David J. Pivar, *Purity Crusade: Sexual Morality and Social Control, 1868–1900.*

36. Washington Gardner, *History of Calhoun County, Michigan,* p. 1350.

37. Miner file, Ross Coller Collection.

38. Ibid.; *Battle Creek City Directory,* 1884, pp. 148, 149, 213; deposition given by Anna Miller, June 17, 1895, for case #6-495, Sarah [*sic*] I. Miner vs. James W. Miner, Circuit Court file, Calhoun County.

39. "How Careless Kate Became Careful Kate," *GH,* Oct., 1888, pp. 394–96.

40. "Aids in Early Training," *GH,* May, 1890, pp. 146–47.

41. "A Dear Experience," Nov., 1888, to Mar., 1889; "The Wiser Choice," Jan., 1890; "A 'Commonplace' Girl," Feb.–Mar., 1890, all in *GH*. Nina Baym, *Woman's Fiction: A Guide to Novels by and about Women in America, 1820–1870,* pp. 1, 17. More recently, scholars have been examining these novels as a form of muted social criticism that gave rise to changes in women's attitudes and behavior. Matthews, *Rise of Public Woman,* pp. 80–83.

42. *GH,* Feb.–Nov., 1890. See Shelia M. Rothman, *Woman's Proper Place: A History of Changing Ideals and Practices, 1870 to the Present,* pp. 21–33; and Delores Hayden, *The Grand Domestic Revolution: A History of Feminist Designs for American Homes, Neighborhoods, and Cities,* pp. 67–89.

43. Clipping file, Ross Coller Collection.

44. Letter from Myrta Castle to her parents, Feb. 20, 1897. Wanda Johnson's personal collection, Rockwall, Tex.

45. Proofs and Report of Commissioner, Calhoun County, June 17, 1895; Bill for Divorce, Circuit Court for Calhoun County, filed July 24, 1894.

46. Isadore Sutherland is listed in Sarah Ramsey Foley, *Toledo Women Writers of Yesterday,* as one "whose specialty was the children, hygiene and kindred sub-

jects" (p. 24). The only other record of her stay is found in the 1891 *Toledo City Directory,* which lists her as a reporter, while in the 1892 *Toledo City Directory* she is listed as a proofreader.

47. *Toledo Blade,* Dec. 26, 1906; Women Alive! Coalition, Rules and Achievements Committee, YWCA, *In Search of Our Past: Women of Northwest Ohio,* vol. 1, pp. 38–39.

48. John A. Killits, ed., *Toledo and Lucas County, Ohio, 1623–1923,* vol. 1, pp. 484–85.

49. The watch is now owned by Joel Sutherland Rhoads, a descendant of Isadore's brother, Daniel Sutherland. Joel Sutherland Rhoads, telephone interview with author, Dallas, Tex., Mar. 29, 1997.

CHAPTER 3. "AN ALL-AROUND WOMAN"

1. U.S. Census, *Compendium of the Eleventh Census: Population, 1890; DMN,* Feb. 19, 1893. Dallas city government was established as a mayor/council form soon after its 1856 charter. There were no machine politics headed by a "boss" like those found in other nineteenth-century cities. A ward system in which aldermen were elected from each ward, and a smaller number was elected at large, provided the leadership with the support of elected administrators for such departments as water, streets, and taxes. Aldermen usually served single terms and then returned to private life, resulting in a lack of experience among elected officials. This led to repeated management mistakes, which culminated in a severe cash-flow problem in the late 1890s. The political fallout from such a poorly run city led to the change to a commission form of government in 1907. One positive byproduct of the city's inaction was the increased activity of women's clubs to address the city's problems. Harry Jebsen, Robert Newton, and Patricia R. Hogan, "Centennial History of the Dallas, Texas Park System, 1876–1976," pp. 889–904. Darwin Payne, *Big D: Triumphs and Troubles of an American Supercity in the 20th Century,* pp. 8–9.

2. C. D. Morrison and J. V. Fourmy, comps., *Morrison and Fourmy's General Directory of the City of Dallas,* 1894–1895.

3. Ibid.; Marriage license division, birth certificate division, Dallas County Records Building.

4. Elaine Tyler May has pointed out that, despite the rapidly expanding job opportunities for women at the turn of the century, it was rare to find a working woman whose earnings allowed her true economic independence. Elaine Tyler May, *Great Expectations: Marriage and Divorce in Post-Victorian America,* p. 117.

5. Morrison and Fourmy, *Directory of the City of Dallas,* 1891–1892.

6. *DMN,* Oct. 30, 1913; *DTH,* Oct. 14, 1917.

7. Isadore Callaway to D. M. Sutherland, July 14, 1900. Sutherland family letters, in possession of Mrs. Joel Sutherland Rhoads.

8. Ibid.

9. *Dallas Daily Times Herald* (hereafter *DDTH*), Apr. 11, 1893; *DMN,* July 3, 1893, Aug. 21, 1916.

10. *The History of the Texas Women's Press Association* makes no mention of this involvement, but in her tribute to Isadore in the *DMN*, Aug. 21, 1916, Virginia Goffe McNealus confirmed that the constitution and bylaws were "the work of her hand." Also confirmed in TFWC, *Who's Who*, vol. 1, p. 33. Elizabeth Brooks, *Prominent Women*, pp. 127–29.

11. *DMN*, Aug. 8, Aug. 21, 1893.

12. The originator of the idea for a Woman's Day was Dr. Ellen Lawson Dabbs of Fort Worth, who had been a founder of the Dallas chapter of the Texas Equal Rights Association. *DMN*, July 7, 1893; *DDTH*, Aug. 12, 1893. Dr. Dabbs attended the World's Congress of Representative Women, at the World's Columbian Exposition, in the summer of 1893. She is most likely responsible for the name of the meeting being changed. McArthur, *Creating the New Woman*.

13. *DMN*, Oct. 25, 1893.

14. *Fort Worth Gazette*, Oct. 29, 1893.

15. *DMN*, Oct. 30, 1893. This was the beginning of a long-term reliance on the *DMN* as the source of information for women's activities that were not entirely "social" in nature.

16. Ibid., Oct. 27, 1893.

17. Ibid., Nov. 27, 1893.

18. Their given names have not been found, only their husbands' occupations. Morrison and Fourmy, *Directory of the City of Dallas, 1891–1892, 1893–1894*.

19. The Woman's Home was established in 1886 as a "refuge for poor and unfortunate women and children." *DDTH*, Feb. 6, 1889. The Woman's Home was limited in its capacity and depended on donations to keep it running. Elizabeth York Enstam, "Virginia K. Johnson: A Second Chance for the 'Wayward,'" *Heritage News* 10 (1985): 7.

20. *DDTH*, Oct. 6, Oct. 8, Nov. 21, 1891; June 14, 1892; Feb. 2, Mar. 28, 1894. *DMN*, Feb. 19, Feb. 26, Mar. 5, Apr. 2, Apr. 9, 1894; Jan. 21, 1895.

21. *DMN*, Mar. 14, 1894.

22. Ibid.; meeting program, Texas Equal Rights Association, June 6, 7, 8, 1894, found in the McCallum Family Papers, Austin History Center, Austin, Tex.

23. Lowe, *Tales of Battle Creek*, pp. 256–57.

24. *DMN*, Apr. 30, 1894.

25. Ibid., Oct. 6, 1894.

26. Ibid.; Catherine Clinton, *The Other Civil War*, p. 168; Scott, *Natural Allies*, p. 142. See also Barbara Kuhn Campbell, *The "Liberated" Woman of 1914: Prominent Women in the Progressive Era*, p. 95.

27. *DMN*, Nov. 2, 1894.

28. Marilyn Ferris Motz, *True Sisterhood: Michigan Women and Their Kin, 1820–1920*, pp. 29, 123, 124; *Battle Creek Daily Moon*, Oct. 3, 1894.

29. Bordin, *Woman and Temperance*, p. 114; William L. O'Neill, *Divorce in the Progressive Era*, pp. 170–71, 206; Elizabeth Cady Stanton, "Divorce vs. Domestic Warfare," *Arena* 1 (1890): 568; Aileen Kraditor, *The Ideas of the Woman*

Suffrage Movement, 1890–1920, pp. 115–17. See also Glenda Riley, *Divorce: An American Tradition,* pp. 73–79; May, *Great Expectations;* Epstein, *Politics of Domesticity.*

30. Unlike most working women in the late nineteenth century, women journalists in cities could command similar wages to those of their male counterparts, according to an 1891 report. Their salaries could range from eight to ten dollars a week to as much as fifty or sixty dollars a week. Assuming Isadore's salary fell somewhere in the middle, she might take home more than one hundred dollars a month. Meyer, *Woman's Work in America,* p. 138.

31. *DMN,* Jan. 9, 1895.

32. Bill for Divorce, Divorce Decree, file #6-495, Circuit Court for Calhoun County, July 24, 1894.

33. *DMN,* Jan. 28, 1895.

34. S. Isadore Miner, "The Woman's Department," *National Printer-Journalist* 11, no. 11 (Nov., 1894): pp. 513–15; no. 12 (Dec., 1894): pp. 584–85.

35. *DMN,* Apr. 15, 1896.

36. Miner, "Woman's Department," *National Printer-Journalist.*

37. *Houston Daily Post,* Apr. 12, 1896.

38. *Fort Worth Gazette,* Mar. 15, 1896. Three years earlier Mrs. M. R. Walton did offer an occasional observation in her Ladies' Department, but she had disappeared from the newspaper by 1896. *Fort Worth Gazette,* Oct. 1, Dec. 3, 1893.

39. *El Paso Daily Times,* Sept. 11, 1895; Mar. 1, 1896.

40. *DMN,* Sept. 29, July 21, Oct. 6, 1895; Mar. 1, Apr. 12, 1896; Oct. 6, 1900. The *Houston Daily Post* had a children's column, "Happy Hammers," which offered some of the same sorts of articles and letters from children. *Houston Daily Post,* Apr. 12, Apr. 19, 1896.

41. Wasson, "The Good Old Days." Many young women in the workforce in major cities, free from parental restraint and in control of their own finances, enjoyed an active social life. See Rothman, *Woman's Proper Place;* Riley, *Inventing the American Woman.*

42. *DMN,* Dec. 13, 1896; Jan. 1, Feb. 1, Feb. 15, Aug. 30, Sept. 13, 1897.

43. Alfred P. Wozencraft, the thirty-seven-year-old city attorney, had run for mayor of Dallas in 1895, losing to W. C. Conner. Wozencraft was named adjutant general of Texas in 1898, at the beginning of the Spanish-American War. His wife of two years had died in 1893, leaving him with a young son, Frank, who became the "Boy Mayor" of Dallas at age twenty-six. Myrta Castle to her parents, Dec., 1896, in Rockwall County Historical Foundation Collection (hereafter RCHF).

44. Myrta had been hired by the *DMN* to write poetry and book reviews. (An early poem appears in the Mar. 15, 1897, edition.) The railroad trip was paid for by the "Central Mexicano Railroad," according to Myrta, who reported that they had "traveled nearly 8,000 miles in the nearly three weeks we were gone." Myrta Castle to her parents, Mar. 9, 1897, in RCHF. Isadore wrote about her impressions of Mexico in her Mar. 15, 1897, column.

45. Myrta Castle to her parents, Mar. 9, 1897.

46. Ibid.

47. Ibid.

48. Isadore Miner to Jesse Castle, Mar. 4, 1897, in RCHF.

49. *DMN*, Nov. 15, 1930; 1900 Manuscript Census for Dallas, vol. 27, E.D. 112, sheet 5.

50. *DMN*, Nov. 15, 1930.

51. *Beau Monde*, July 7, 1900. Copy in Texas/Dallas Division, Dallas Public Library (hereafter T/D, DPL). Pauline Periwinkle's columns between Sept. 10, 1900, and June 3, 1901, chronicle her European experiences. Her determination to continue working was not surprising, considering her background, although in 1900 only 5.6 percent of all married women worked. Traditionalists, however, still expressed grave reservations at the prospect of married women remaining in the workforce. May, *Great Expectations*, pp. 115–16; William H. Chafe, *The American Woman: Her Changing Social, Economic, and Political Roles*, p. 56.

52. Mrs. Pennybacker, an active clubwoman in Texas since 1892, went on to hold the offices of treasurer and auditor in the national General Federation of Women's Clubs and became its president in 1912. Isadore, who had become a friend and adviser, served as the publicity chairman for her national campaign.

53. Mineral Wells was a popular destination for many Texans with medical problems. The mineral waters were believed to be helpful in curing a variety of ailments. A thorough account of Mineral Wells and other Texas health spas can be found in Janet Valenza, "'Taking the Waters' at Texas's Health Spas," *Southwestern Historical Quarterly* 98 (Jan., 1995). H. N. Fitzgerald, managing editor, *DMN*, to Mrs. Percy Pennybacker, May 29, 1901. Isadore Callaway to Mrs. Pennybacker, June 18, 1901. Correspondence to Mrs. A. J. H. Pennybacker for 1901, TFWC Collection. Isadore Callaway knew both Mrs. Clark and Mrs. Charlton well, as they were all members of the Quaero Club of Oak Cliff (later a part of Dallas). *Dallas Democrat*, Sept., 1901. Mrs. Pennybacker subsequently appointed Mrs. Clark as chairman of the art committee. Isadore was true to her promise, as Mrs. Clark wrote Mrs. Pennybacker "what a great help she has been." Mrs. Luther Clark to Mrs. A. J. H. Pennybacker, Nov. 11, 1901, TFWC Collection.

54. *DMN*, Jan. 22, 1902. Club affiliations found in *Red Book of Dallas*, 1895–96.

55. Newspaper reporters were not welcomed in clubs in the early days, nor were many working women invited to join early clubs. Wood, *History of the GFWC*, p. 293.

56. The papers of the Quaero Club have not been found in local archives. Isadore entertained the Quaero Club for its meeting on May 15, 1902, just after returning from a tour of Texas and Mexico with her Aunt Rose Worden. Her "Auntie Rose" remained in Dallas and lived with her for a time. *DMN*, May 15, 1902.

57. *DMN*, Nov. 22, 1903.

58. *DDTH,* Feb. 20, 1903.

59. Isadore Callaway is acknowledged as the "applier for copyright" of the volume on the inside front page.

60. Isadore Callaway to Mrs. A. J. H. Pennybacker, Apr. 7, 1903, TFWC Collection.

61. *Dayton (Ohio) Daily Journal,* Sept. 11, 1903.

62. *DMN,* Jan. 11, Jan. 25, 1904. Women had made significant strides in the decade separating the 1893 Chicago World's Fair and the 1904 Louisiana Purchase Exposition in St. Louis. See Hunt, "'Throw Aside the Veil,'" pp. 48–62.

63. Kathleen Mayne, the daughter of Alberta Fetterly, in an interview with the author, Dallas, Tex., Aug. 8, 1992. The two nieces, Isadore and Alberta Fetterly, lived with the Callaways until their marriages. Both attended St. Mary's College, a Dallas private preparatory school for girls, and Alberta made her debut at the Idelwild Ball in Nov., 1912.

64. *DMN,* Mar. 5, 1906; Stella L. Christian, ed., *History of the Texas Federation of Women's Clubs,* pp. 112–13; Wood, *History of the GFWC,* p. 186.

65. *History of the Dallas Federation of Women's Clubs, 1898–1936,* p. 45.

66. Martha Lavinia Hunter, *A Quarter of a Century History of the Dallas Woman's Forum, 1906–1931,* p. 1; *DMN,* Apr. 15, 1907.

67. Mrs. Dealey's husband was George Bannerman Dealey, general manager of the *DMN* at the time.

68. *DMN,* Aug. 21, 1916; Oct. 1, 1935.

69. *History of the DFWC,* pp. 41–46; letterhead of TFWC., Box 2M33, TFWC Collection; Library Association Minutes, Book 1, T/D, DPL.

70. Mrs. W. A. Callaway to Mrs. S. J. Wright, Dec. 13, 1909, TFWC Collection.

71. Mrs. W. A. Callaway to Mrs. S. J. Wright, Jan. 2, 1910, TFWC Collection.

72. *DMN,* Mar. 21, 1908. See Michael V. Hazel, "A Mother's Touch: The First Two Women Elected to the Dallas School Board," *Heritage News* 12 (Spring, 1987): 9–10; *Dallas Clubwoman,* Jan. 8, 1909.

73. William L. McDonald, *Dallas Rediscovered: A Photographic Chronicle of Urban Expansion, 1870–1925,* pp. 205, 208.

74. *DMN,* June 19, 1911; Jan. 1, 1913. J. R. Babcock, "The Campaign for a City Plan in Dallas," *The American City,* Oct., 1910. Typed copy in George Bannerman Dealey Papers, Dallas Historical Society.

75. Christian, *History of the TFWC,* p. 273; "Pauline" [Isadore Callaway] to "My Dear" and "Dear Friend" [Pennybacker], undated, Pennybacker Papers, Center for American History, University of Texas, Austin. My thanks to Dr. Judith McArthur who found these letters while doing research for her own project.

76. Isadore is not listed as a founding member of the 1894 group. Her involvement can be inferred, however, from her previous relationship with several women on the Woman's Council who were founders of the Dallas club, and from her attendance and speech before the Texas Equal Rights Association state meeting that year. Her support for suffrage in numerous columns dating from 1893 was acknowledged by Minnie Fisher Cunningham, who wrote of

"Remembering that you were fighting the good fight for Suffrage when the Texas Woman Suffrage Association was in it's [*sic*] infancy . . ." in a 1915 letter to her. Minnie Fisher Cunningham Papers, Box 5, Folder 68, Houston Metropolitan Research Center, Houston Public Library. My thanks to Dr. Elizabeth Enstam who found this letter while doing research for her own project. For a report of activities in Dallas and other Texas locales, see Ruthe Winegarten and Judith N. McArthur, eds., *Citizens At Last: The Woman Suffrage Movement in Texas,* p. 23.

77. Flexner, *Century of Struggle,* p. 256.
78. Winegarten and McArthur, *Citizens At Last,* p. 26; *DMN,* Mar. 16, 1913. Isadore remained committed to suffrage throughout this period.
79. Isadore was elected a member of the Board of Directors of the Dallas Humane Society in 1915, but appears not to have been active. Letter in the Minnie Fisher Cunningham Papers, Box 5, Folder 68.
80. *DMN,* Aug. 11, Aug. 21, 1916.
81. Death certificate, City of Dallas, number 1075. *DMN,* Aug. 11, 1916.
82. *DMN,* Aug. 21, 1916.
83. Ibid., Oct. 1, 1935.
84. Dallas Woman's Forum, *Yearbook, 1917–1918.* The fund was maintained as a scholarship fund at least until 1949, after which records were unavailable. Archives of the Dallas Woman's Forum.
85. Christian, *History of the TFWC,* pp. 348, 351.
86. *DMN,* Aug. 21, 1916.

CHAPTER 4. "VERILY, WE ARE COMING ON"

1. Blair, *Clubwoman as Feminist,* pp. 106–107. See also Paula Baker, "The Domestication of Politics: Women and American Political Society, 1780–1920," in *Women, the State, and Welfare,* ed. Linda Gordon; Noralee Frankel and Nancy S. Dye, eds., *Gender, Class, Race, and Reform in the Progressive Era,* pp. 1–9.
2. We don't know if Isadore would have called herself a feminist, but she appeared impervious to the restraints against speaking one's mind that had been traditionally placed on women. Her behavior is consistent with the criteria I have used to define the term "feminist." This view is also taken by Sylvia Hunt in "'Throw Aside the Veil,'" p. 9. For a fuller discussion of the term, see Karen Offen, "Defining Feminism," p. 152.
3. *DMN,* Apr. 19, 1896.
4. Mrs. J. C. Terrell, "Succinct History of the Women's Club Movement," *DMN,* Nov. 22, 1903. According to Mrs. Terrell, twenty women's clubs had been formed in Texas by the late 1880s, with at least three clubs sending delegates to the 1892 General Federation of Women's Clubs conference in Chicago.
5. See Megan Seaholm, "Earnest Women: The White Woman's Club Movement in Progressive Era Texas, 1880–1920" (Ph.D. diss., Rice University, 1988), for a comprehensive treatment of the birth and growth of the club movement in Texas.

6. Precise figures for pre-1900 membership in most Texas women's organizations have proved elusive. The papers of many early women's clubs have not been placed in archival institutions. Most club members, however, would have been middle-class women who were not working outside the home.

7. The Woman's Council renewed earlier efforts by other groups to establish an industrial school for girls, as well as to construct a Woman's Building at the state fairgrounds. Neither effort had made much headway by 1896. The Woman's Council joined the WCTU in supporting efforts to raise the age of consent for girls to above age twelve. See McArthur, *Creating the New Woman*.

8. *DDTH*, Aug. 12, 1893. *DMN*, Oct. 24, 25, 27, 29, and 30, 1893; Nov. 27, 1893; Feb. 19, Feb. 26, Mar. 5, Apr. 2, Oct. 6, Nov. 2, 1894; Jan. 14, 1895; Oct. 13, Oct. 25, 1896.

9. Scott, *Natural Allies*, pp. 142–43; Clinton, *Other Civil War*, pp. 166–74.

10. Christian, *History of the TFWC*, pp. 4–5. For further discussion of this attitude, see Clinton, *Other Civil War*; Scott, *Natural Allies*; Rothman, *Woman's Proper Place*; and Jean E. Friedman, *The Enclosed Garden: Women and Community in the Evangelical South, 1830–1900*.

11. McArthur, *Creating the New Woman*.

12. *DMN*, Apr. 10, June 8, 1887; Dec. 21, 1888. *DDTH*, Feb. 6, 1889. My thanks to Dr. Elizabeth Enstam for identifying the membership of the two groups as almost identical.

13. Anne Firor Scott has pointed out that, in many places in the South, women were beginning to use the study of literature as a springboard to discussions for improving the community. Anne Firor Scott, "The 'New Woman' in the New South," *South Atlantic Quarterly* 61 (Autumn, 1962): 478.

14. Scott, *Natural Allies*, pp. 80–81; Blair, *Clubwoman as Feminist*, pp. 98–99.

15. *DMN*, Sept. 26, 1896.

16. Ibid., June 7, 1896.

17. Ibid., July 5, 1896.

18. Ibid.

19. Ibid., Nov. 1, 1896.

20. The official minutes acknowledged the Wednesday Club of Fort Worth as the originator of the movement by suggesting a federation in 1895. Eighteen clubs sent delegates to the meeting, but twenty-one clubs were named charter members. While the original constitution gives the official name as the Texas Federation of Women's Literary Clubs, the minutes of the first meeting refer to the organization as the State Federation of Woman's [*sic*] Literary Clubs. The two names appear interchangeably in material concerning the first two years of the organization. In 1899, the name was shortened to the Texas Federation of Women's Clubs when the new constitution was adopted. Christian, *History of the TFWC*, pp. 8–15; Terrell, "Succinct History." The Woman's Council appears to have ceased functioning after its 1896 meeting. Judith

McArthur has suggested several reasons: the new state federation's appeal to more conservative women, the death of the Texas Equal Rights Association, and the deaths or retirement of several leaders. *DMN*, May 24, 1897; McArthur, *Creating the New Woman.*

21. While serving as secretary of the Woman's Congress, Isadore Miner's fellow board members included Mrs. J. C. Terrell of the Woman's Wednesday Club of Fort Worth, who is credited with being the first to suggest the creation of a statewide federation of women's literary clubs in 1895. Mrs. Terrell was named the first vice president of the state federation in 1897. Another Woman's Council board member, Mrs. C. S. Cobb of the XXI Club in Gainesville, was named fifth vice president at the 1897 meeting. Christian, *History of the TFWC,* pp. 8–9, 15, 37.

22. *DMN,* Nov. 8, 1897.

23. As secretary of the State Council of Women of Texas, she had helped develop their constitution. This group's leadership figured prominently in the establishment of the TFWC. Christian, *History of the TFWC,* pp. 5, 9.

24. "Things Done by a Woman's Club," in the *Woman's Journal* (reprinted in *DMN,* Nov. 22, 1897), notes that the Chicago Woman's Club has supplied 50,000 people with work during the depression which followed the closing of the world's fair; introduced a kindergarten system into the public schools; established the Children's Aid society which distributes garments to poor school children; raised $35,000 to aid the Kenwood Industrial school for boys; secured the appointment of a woman physician in the insane asylum at Dunning; supported school for boys in the city jail; inaugurated the movement for raising funds for the woman's dormitory at the Chicago university [sic]; raised an endowment fund scholarship for the art institute; organized the following associations: The Protective Agency for Women and Children, the Physiological Institute, the Society of Physical Culture and Correct Dress, the Public School Art association and the Chicago Political Economy League.

25. *DMN,* May 9, 1898.

26. For a variety of explanations, see Mrs. A. O. Granger, "The Effects of Club Work in the South," *American Academy of Political and Social Science Annals* 28 (Sept., 1906): 248–56; Patricia Marks, *Bicycles, Bangs and Bloomers: The New Woman in the Popular Press,* preface; Scott, "'New Woman'"; Rothman, *Woman's Proper Place,* introduction.

27. Isadore Callaway to Anna A. H. Pennybacker, June 18, 1901, Section I: 1901–1904, Correspondence to Anna J. H. Pennybacker, TFWC Collection.

28. Terrell, "Succinct History."

29. *DMN,* Apr. 30, 1900, contains a "resume" of the work of the TFWC as reported at its third annual meeting. The *DMN* underwrote the postage and stationery cost for the TFWC representative to gather club news. H. N. Fitzgerald managing editor, *DMN,* to Mrs. Percy V. Pennybacker, Sept. 11, 1901, TFWC Collection, Ms. 32, Sec. I, 1901.

CHAPTER 5. "THE CITY THAT HAS NOT DOFFED ITS VILLAGE SWADDLING CLOTHES"

1. Frankel and Dye, *Gender, Class, Race, and Reform,* introduction.
2. Wood, *History of the GFWC,* p. 72.
3. Martin V. Melosi, *Garbage in the Cities: Refuse, Reform, and the Environment, 1880–1980,* pp. 34–36; Martin V. Melosi, ed., *Pollution and Reform in American Cities, 1870–1930,* p. 22. Blair, *Clubwoman as Feminist,* pp. 100–101; Baker, "The Domestication of Politics," in Gordon, *Women, the State, and Welfare,* pp. 71–72.
4. Jebsen et al., "Centennial History," pp. 889–904.
5. *DMN,* Nov. 8, 1897.
6. Ibid., Oct. 25, 1897.
7. Christian, *History of the TFWC,* pp. 21, 25. The General Federation of Women's Clubs encouraged women's clubs to become active in the establishment of libraries during this period. Wood, *History of the GFWC,* p. 103.
8. *DMN,* Nov. 29, 1897.
9. Ibid., Mar. 28, 1898. U.S. Census, *Twelfth Census;* 1900 Manuscript Census, Grayson County, vol. 48, Enumeration District 88, sheet 11, line 61.
10. *DMN,* Apr. 11, 1898. U.S. Census, *Twelfth Census;* 1900 Manuscript Census, Dallas County, vol. 26, Enumeration District 109, sheet 26, line 71.
11. *DMN,* Mar. 28, 1898.
12. Ibid., May 9, 1898.
13. Ibid.
14. Ibid., June 6, 1898.
15. Ibid., June 13, 1898.
16. While designated City Federation of Women's Clubs at its founding, the organization was known more commonly as the Dallas Federation of Women's Clubs within a few years.
17. The men included Jules Schneider, president of the Dallas Gas & Fuel Company; the Reverend W. M. Anderson, pastor of First Presbyterian Church; Rabbi George A. Kohut of Temple Emanu-el; John M. Howell, president of the school board; and School Superintendent J. L. Long.
18. *History of the DFWC,* pp. 15–16; *DMN,* Mar. 7, Mar. 31, 1899.
19. Dallas Public Library Association, Board of Trustees Minutes from secretary's book; Official Minutes of Organizational Meeting of Dallas Public Library Association, Mar. 30, 1899. T/D, DPL.
20. *DMN,* Apr. 3, 4, 5, 6, 7, 11, 1899.
21. Ibid., May 11, 1899.
22. Carnegie had built numerous libraries for towns and cities, with the requirement that the community provide the land and ongoing support once the building was completed. For Dallas, Carnegie agreed to provide up to $50,000 for the building if the city would provide the lot and commit $4,000 a year for support. *History of the DFWC,* p. 19; *DMN,* Sept. 19, 1899; *DTH,* Sept. 22, 1899.
23. Blair, *Clubwoman as Feminist,* pp. 100–101. Blair notes that in 1933 the Ameri-

can Library Association acknowledged women's clubs as responsible for starting 75 percent of the public libraries in existence at the time.

24. For a study of how four early women's organizations in Dallas became involved in political activity, see Elizabeth York Enstam, "They Called It 'Motherhood': Dallas Women and Public Life, 1895–1918," in *Hidden Histories of Women in the New South,* ed. Virginia Bernhard, et al., pp. 71–95.

25. *DMN,* Feb. 14, Feb. 22, 1899. M. E. Bolding and Eric H. Bolding, *Origin and Growth of the Dallas Water Utilities,* pp. 37, 45. *DDTH,* May 4, 1894.

26. *DDTH,* Aug. 26, 1895; Department of Public Health, City of Dallas, *Ninety Years of Public Health,* pp. 40–41.

27. Sam Bass Warner, Jr., *The Urban Wilderness: A History of the American City,* pp. 202–203. Judith W. Leavitt and Ronald L. Numbers, eds., *Sickness and Health in America: Readings in the History of Medicine and Public Health,* p. 9. G. T. Ferris, "Cleansing of Great Cities," *Harper's Weekly,* Jan. 10, 1891, p. 33, quoted in Melosi, *Garbage in the Cities,* p. 34. See also Susan Strasser, *Never Done: A History of Housework in America,* pp. 93–99.

28. Melosi, *Pollution and Reform,* pp. 20–21, and *Garbage in the Cities,* pp. 34–35, 110–11. See also Strasser, *Never Done,* pp. 99–103.

29. *DMN,* Mar. 5, 27, 1899.

30. Jebsen, et al., "Centennial History," pp. 903–904.

31. *DMN,* Feb. 22, 1899.

32. Ibid., Mar. 24, 26, 1899. Undated clipping from Cleaner Dallas League scrapbook. Dallas Historical Society, A44110, Box 5.

33. *DMN,* May 7, 1899.

34. Suellen M. Hoy, "'Municipal Housekeeping': The Role of Women in Improving Urban Sanitation Practices, 1880–1917," in Melosi, *Pollution and Reform,* pp. 193–94; Wood, *History of the GFWC,* p. 134. In the first years after the turn of the century, the nationwide work of women's clubs in cleaning up and beautifying their communities was directed by the Civic Committee of the General Federation of Women's Clubs, led by Dallasite Adella Kelsey Turner. She had headed the cleanup campaign in Oak Cliff, a suburb that joined Dallas in 1903, before she was named to the national post.

35. Among those named were Mrs. T. L. Lauve, Kate Cabell Currie, Mrs. C. A. Bill, Mrs. Mary Louise Christian Shelmire, Mrs. A. F. Pittman, Mrs. H. L. McCorkle, Mrs. A. T. Obenchain, Mary Hill Davis, Grace Simpson Allen, and Mrs. John H. Shelley. *DMN,* May 14, May 16, 1899.

36. *DMN,* May 14, 1899.

37. Ibid., May 26, 1899.

38. Ibid., May 26, 1899; June 14, 15, 1899.

39. Dallas City Council Minutes, Apr. 22, 1901, Book 26; *DMN,* June 14, 1899.

40. Dallas City Council Minutes, May 13, 1901, Book 27. Other statistics suggest this was actually less than the national norm. The total death rate per thousand in 1900 was found to be 17.2. *Historical Statistics of the U.S., Colonial Times to 1970,* pt. 1, p. 60.

41. Dallas City Council Minutes, Oct. 27, 1902, Book 28, and Apr. 22, 1901, Book 26.
42. *DTH*, May 21, 1899.
43. Isadore Callaway was one of the leaders of the effort. *DMN*, Mar. 10, 1908. The 150,000 Club had been established in 1906 with the goal of pushing the city's population to 150,000 by 1910 or as soon as possible. This figure was said to have come from the 1887 prediction by visiting railroad magnet Jay Gould that Dallas would reach 150,000 in his lifetime. He died in 1892; Dallas reached 158,000 in the 1920 census. Rogers, *Lusty Texans*, p. 199; Payne, *Big D*, p. 4.
44. *DMN*, Mar. 10, 1908.
45. Ibid., Apr. 3, 1912.
46. Bolding and Bolding, *Dallas Water Utilities*, pp. 7, 18, 49, 58–67.
47. *DMN*, Mar. 21, 1909.
48. *History of the DFWC*, pp. 56–67; *DMN*, Mar. 21, 1909; Bolding and Bolding, *Dallas Water Utilities*, pp. 68, 72, 74.
49. The 1904 General Federation of Women's Clubs biennial meeting at St. Louis included among its resolutions one requesting members to "do all we can to secure national and state legislation that will stop the fraudulent manufacture of food products." Wood, *History of the GFWC*, pp. 169–70, 183.
50. George W. Cox, *History of Public Health in Texas*, p. 18.
51. Department clubs were so called because they were made up of several departments, each of which was devoted to one area of interest. Early departments of the Woman's Forum included music, current events, household economics, philosophy and science, the bible, and art. *DMN*, Feb. 7, Apr. 15, 1907.
52. *DMN*, June 8, 1907. My thanks to Dr. Judith McArthur for finding the given name of Mrs. Johnson.
53. Ibid., Dec, 9, 1907. Dallas Mayor Curtis P. Smith stated publicly that it was "through the efforts of the Woman's Forum that the ordinance was enacted." In his opinion "a pure food law would not have been passed by the Legislature if the Woman's Forum of Dallas had not smoothed the way for it." *DMN*, Apr. 15, 1907.
54. *DMN*, Feb. 7, 1907.
55. The club was organized Mar. 20, 1906. It aimed "to study and correct wrongs and abuses wherever woman's influence is needed." *DMN*, Apr. 15, 1907; Hunter, *Dallas Woman's Forum*, pp. 1–6.
56. *DMN*, May 11, Nov. 30, 1908.
57. Ibid., June 7, 1909.

CHAPTER 6. "THE CHILDREN OF THE PRESENT—THEY ARE THE FUTURE"

1. Isadore Callaway to D. M. Sutherland, July 14, 1900. Sutherland family letters.

2. Throughout the country many women who worked to improve or profes-
sionalize social work were never married or were divorced. Despite their
marital status, their credentials were seldom questioned, for men ceded without question the care of children to women. See Robyn Muncy, *Creating a
Female Dominion in American Reform, 1890–1935;* Kathryn Kish Sklar, *Florence
Kelley and the Nation's Work: The Rise of Women's Political Culture, 1830–1900.*

3. *DMN,* Dec, 12, 1899; *DDTH,* Aug, 26, 1899; Frederick Eby, *The Development
of Education in Texas,* pp. 127, 219; U.S. Census, *Twelfth Census,* pp. 127, 400.

4. E. G. Dexter, *History of Education in the United States,* pp. 174–76; *Dallas City
Directory, 1897–1898,* p. 25; *DTH,* Apr. 11, 1899.

5. School attendance was affected by a number of social and economic factors.
See Priscilla Ferguson Clement, "The City and the Child, 1860–1885," in
Joseph M. Hawes and N. Ray Hiner, eds., *American Childhood: A Research
Guide and Historical Handbook,* pp. 247–50. The Dallas city school system
graduated 28 white and 3 black students in 1896, when there were 4,900 students in the system; and 31 white and 5 black students in 1897, when the system had 5,700 students. *DTH,* Oct. 20, 1896; Apr. 2, May 23, 1897; Dec. 12,
1899.

6. Clement, "City and the Child," pp. 245–47. For early objectives of kindergartens, see also Richard W. Gilder, "The Kindergarten: An Uplifting Social
Influence in the Home and the District," *National Education Association Proceedings, 1903,* pp. 390–91; William T. Harris, "Report from a Department Sub-
Committee on Kindergartens," *Journal of Social Science* XII (1880): 8–11. Both
quoted in *Children and Youth in America: A Documentary History, Volume II,
1866–1932,* ed. Robert H. Bremner, pp. 1457–60.

7. *DDTH,* Mar. 28, 1894.

8. Jackie McElhaney, "The Only Clean, Bright Spot They Know," *Heritage News*
11 (Fall, 1986): 19–22; "Clubdom in Dallas" section, *Dallas Democrat,* Sept.,
1901.

9. A petition to the school board in 1895 had not been successful, in part due to
their financial problems. *DDTH,* Mar. 14, 1895.

10. *DMN,* Jan. 5, 1903; July 18, 1904; Oct. 16, 1905; Dec. 17, 1906.

11. Ibid., Jan. 5, Oct. 10, 1903. For a comprehensive description of Hull House
activities, see Sklar, *Florence Kelley.*

12. Dallas Free Kindergarten and Industrial Association, *Report, 1903–1904;* Dallas
Free Kindergarten Training School and Industrial Association, *Report, 1909–
1910,* T/D, DPL.

13. *DMN,* Feb. 4, 1907.

14. Ibid., Feb. 27, 1905; May 4, 1908.

15. Walter J. Schiebel, *Education in Dallas: Ninety-Two Years of History,* pp. 155–56.

16. In 1896 the grand jury returned eighty-three indictments, most against boys
between the age of nine and fifteen. *DDTH,* Oct. 3, 1896.

17. Rothman, *Woman's Proper Place,* pp. 4–5.

18. Gerald K. Marsden, "Philanthropy and the Boston Playground Movement, 1885–1907," *Social Service Review* 35 (Mar., 1961); Joseph F. Kett, *Rites of Passage: Adolescence in America, 1790 to the Present,* pp. 224–25.

19. McDonald, *Dallas Rediscovered,* p. 91.

20. Jacquelyn M. McElhaney, "Another Time, Another Place . . . A History of Old City Park," *Heritage News* (Fall, 1982): 6–7.

21. Jebsen, et al., "Centennial History," pp. 80–81. *Dallas City Ordinance Book,* vol. 9, p. 317.

22. *DTH,* June 12, 1897.

23. *DDTH,* Aug. 18, 1896.

24. Jacquelyn M. McElhaney, "Childhood in Dallas, 1870–1900" (M.A. thesis, Southern Methodist University, 1982), pp. 45–59.

25. *DMN,* June 19, 1911. Kansas City had hired landscape designer George E. Kessler in 1890 to develop a park system. Dallas was to engage Kessler twenty years later to develop a plan for the city. Paul Boyer, *Urban Masses and Moral Order in America, 1820–1920,* p. 236.

26. Jacob A. Riis, *How the Other Half Lives.* Boyer, *Urban Masses,* pp. 233–51. Some historians have argued that while parks did provide a better site for play than the streets, those who pressed for parks had another motive: to socialize the children of newly arrived immigrants whose behavior threatened the social order. Dominick Cavallo, *Muscles and Morals: Organized Playgrounds and Urban Reform, 1880–1920,* pp. 1–8, 105.

27. See *DMN,* July 16, 1906; July 29, Aug. 26, 1907; May 10, Nov. 1, Dec. 6, 1909; Feb. 14, 1910; Mar. 6, 1911; May 5, 1913; Mar. 20, 1916.

28. *DMN,* Feb. 17, 29, 1908; *History of the DFWC,* pp. 48–50; *DMN,* Nov. 26, 1909.

29. For a comprehensive treatment of juvenile courts and Progressive Era child saving, see Joseph M. Hawes, *Children in Urban Society: Juvenile Delinquency in Nineteenth-Century America;* Steven L. Schlossman, *Love and the American Delinquent: The Theory and Practice of "Progressive" Juvenile Justice, 1825–1920;* and Robert M. Mennell, *Thorns and Thistles: Juvenile Delinquents in the United States, 1825–1940.*

30. Mrs. Turner was named president of the city federation for the 1903–1905 term, and she was then elected to a two-year term as head of the TFWC in Nov., 1903. *History of the DFWC,* p. 26. Christian, *History of the TFWC,* pp. 93–108.

31. Hawes, *Children in Urban Society,* pp. 163–70.

32. *DMN,* May 16, 1904.

33. *History of the DFWC,* p. 33.

34. Ibid., p. 27; Christian, *History of the TFWC,* pp. 103–18.

35. *DMN,* Jan. 4, 1904.

36. *DMN,* June 19, 1911; Lindsey's court was preceded by the Chicago Juvenile Court, which had been created in 1899. D'Ann Campbell, "Judge Ben Lindsey

and the Juvenile Court Movement, 1901–1904," in *Growing Up in America: Children in Historical Perspective*, ed. N. Ray Hiner and Joseph M. Hawes, pp. 149–60; Susan Tiffin, *In Whose Best Interest? Child Welfare Reform in the Progressive Era*, pp. 52–53.

37. Christian, *History of the TFWC*, p. 125.
38. Tiffin, *In Whose Best Interest?*, pp. 7–8.
39. *DMN*, Apr. 12, 16, 1905.
40. Christian, *History of the TFWC*, pp. 130–31.
41. *History of the DFWC*, p. 11; *DMN*, Nov. 26, 1909; June 19, 1911.
42. The active support for the projects of the Dallas federation by Olivia Allen Dealey, wife of the publisher of the *DMN*, no doubt helped cement the newspaper's commitment.
43. *DMN*, Feb. 14, 1910.

CHAPTER 7. "AN ENLIGHTENED WOMANHOOD MEANS MORE FOR THE FUTURE"

1. "Story of the *News*," unpublished manuscript by G. B. Dealey, n.d., Archives of the A. H. Belo Corporation.
2. *DMN*, Oct. 4, 1896. The Woman's Council was following the lead of the State Grange and Patrons of Husbandry, which had recommended a state industrial college for women at its 1889 annual meeting. The Texas WCTU added its voice to the campaign in 1893. Joyce Thompson, *Marking a Trail: A History of the Texas Woman's University*, pp. 1–2.
3. Only five institutions admitted women before the Civil War: Oberlin, Hillsdale, and Antioch Colleges in Ohio, and the state universities of Utah and Iowa. Joyce Antler, *The Educated Woman and Professionalization: The Struggle for a New Feminine Identity 1890–1920*, pp. 26–29. See also Lynn D. Gordon, *Gender and Higher Education in the Progressive Era*, pp. 8–19.
4. Gordon, *Gender and Higher Education*, pp. 8–30; Antler, *Educated Woman and Professionalization*, pp. 25, 49. See also Flexner, *Century of Struggle*, pp. 124–28; Riley, *Inventing the American Woman*, pp. 183–86.
5. *DMN*, Oct. 11, 1896.
6. Ibid., Oct. 25, 1896.
7. Thompson, *Marking a Trail*, pp. 1–2.
8. The curriculum included dressmaking, scientific and practical cooking, practical housekeeping, trained nursing care for the sick, and a study of the "care and culture of children." Thompson, *Marking a Trail*, p. 2. *DMN*, Feb. 20, 1899.
9. The victory was due in part to the fact that V. W. Grubbs had convinced the Democratic Party in 1900 to adopt a platform plank favoring the establishment of a women's college. Among the sponsors of the 1901 legislation was Senator Barry Miller from Dallas. Thompson, *Marking a Trail*, p. 2.

10. Christian, *History of the TFWC,* p. 74.

11. Riley, *Inventing the American Woman,* pp. 192–94; Rothman, *Woman's Proper Place,* pp. 42–56.

12. *DMN,* May 15, 1911.

13. For an examination of nationwide efforts, see Ronald D. Cohen, "Child-Saving and Progressivism, 1885–1915," in Hawes and Hiner, *American Childhood,* pp. 273–99.

14. Karen Blair points to the creation of the General Federation of Women's Clubs in 1890 and the subsequent local federations as formalizing "the right of women to turn their attention to civic work." Blair, *Clubwoman as Feminist,* p. 119. A contemporary account of club work from a southern perspective notes, "Without neglecting their homes, without becoming mannish or losing one charm of their womanhood, the club women of the South have become broadened and their work has made them a recognized force wherever they dwell." Granger, "Effects of Club Work," p. 255. Recent evaluations of the work of child saving in the Progressive Era have cast their activities in a less positive light. Cohen, "Child-Saving and Progressivism," pp. 291–99.

15. Mothers' clubs, the forerunners of the P.T.A., had been formed to address problems with school facilities. The first mothers' club had been formed in 1895 at the William B. Travis School. *History of the Dallas P.T.A.,* n.d., n.a. Other clubs organized at the San Jacinto, McKinney Avenue, Stephen F. Austin, William B. Travis, Cedar Lawn, and Colonial Hill schools during the period. Members' appearances before the Dallas Board of Education are recorded in Board of Education Minutes, Book 4: Apr. 8, Nov. 11, 1901; Jan. 13, Mar. 10, Nov. 17, 1902. Board of Education Minutes, Book 5: Feb. 16, Apr. 30, Aug. 22, Oct. 16, Oct. 19, Dec. 14, 1903; Jan. 18, 1904; Jan. 16, June 5, Nov. 13, 1905; Jan. 15, Feb. 12, 1906.

16. *DMN,* Sept. 12, 1898. Pauline Periwinkle repeated the call again in her Nov. 8, 1902, July 9, 1906, and Feb. 25, 1907, columns.

17. Ibid., Mar. 24, Mar. 25, 1908.

18. Ibid., Mar. 26, 1908.

19. Ibid., Mar. 31, 1908.

20. Ibid., Apr. 5, 1908.

21. Ibid., Apr. 7, 1908.

22. Ibid., Apr. 8, Apr. 10, 1908. Isadore Callaway reported that $39.56 had been spent on the campaign for the two women.

23. Ibid., Apr. 8, Apr. 10, 1908.

24. Dallas Board of Education Minutes, Book 6: May 4, Dec. 14, 1908.

25. Dallas Board of Education Minutes, Book 6: Jan. 18, 1909.

26. Rupert N. Richardson, *Texas: The Lone Star State,* 2nd ed., p. 291.

27. Christian, *History of the TFWC,* pp. 187–88.

28. *DMN,* Dec. 16, 1907; Oct. 12, 1908.

29. The actual tally in the city of Dallas was 1,783 for and 521 against; the vote in Dallas County was 3,019 for and 1,078 against. *DMN,* Nov. 5, 1908.

30. Dallas Board of Education Minutes, Book 7: Mar. 28, 1910. J. S. Kendall, State Superintendent, *Sixteenth Biennial Report of the State Superintendent of Public Instruction for 1907–1908,* p. 473 (hereafter RSSPI). *Seventeenth RSSPI for 1908–1909,* p. 370. *Eighteenth RSSPI for 1909–1910,* p. 719. T/D, DPL.

31. *DMN,* Dec. 4, 1899. Isadore Callaway's awareness that the events reported on the Woman's Century page would be of future value was fortunate, for it has provided the most detailed record we have of the issues and debates that surrounded the Texas women's clubs during that period.

32. DMN, Aug. 21, 1916.

Bibliography

Acheson, Sam. *35,000 Days in Texas*. New York: Macmillan Company, 1987.

Antler, Joyce. *The Educated Woman and Professionalization: The Struggle for a New Feminine Identity, 1890–1920*. New York: Garland Publishing Company, 1987.

Atteberry, Maxine. "Seventh Day Adventist Nurses: A Century of Service, 1883–1983." *Adventist Heritage* 12 (Fall, 1983): 4–10.

Babcock, J. R. "The Campaign for a City Plan for Dallas." *The American City* (October, 1910). Typed copy in George Bannerman Dealey Papers, Dallas Historical Society.

Baillio, Ferdinand B. *A History of the Texas Press Association, from Its Organization in Houston in 1880* . . . Dallas: Southwestern Printing Company, 1916.

Battle Creek (Michigan) City Directory, 1884, 1886, 1889.

Battle Creek (Michigan) College Record Book.

Baym, Nina. *Woman's Fiction: A Guide to Novels by and about Women in America, 1820–1870*. Ithaca, N.Y.: Cornell University Press, 1978.

Beasley, Maurine H., and Shelia J. Gibbons. *Taking Their Place: A Documentary History of Women and Journalism*. Washington, D.C.: American University Press, 1993.

Bernhard, Virginia, et al. *Hidden Histories of Women in the New South*. Columbia: University of Missouri Press, 1994.

Blair, Karen. *The Clubwoman as Feminist: True Womanhood Redefined, 1868–1914*. New York: Holmes and Meier, 1980.

Bolding, M. E., and Eric Bolding. *Origin and Growth of the Dallas Water Utilities*. Temple, Tex.: Gresham's Graphics, 1981.

Bordin, Ruth. *Woman and Temperance: The Quest for Power and Liberty, 1873–1900*. New Brunswick, N.J.: Rutgers University Press, 1981.

Boyer, Paul. *Urban Masses and Moral Order in America, 1820–1920*. Cambridge, Mass.: Harvard University Press, 1978.

Bremner, Robert H., ed. *Children and Youth in America: A Documentary History*. Vol. 2. *1866–1932*, pts. 7–8. Cambridge, Mass.: Harvard University Press, 1978.

Brooks, Elizabeth. *Prominent Women of Texas*. Akron, Ohio: Werner Co., 1896.

Campbell, Barbara Kuhn. *The "Liberated Woman" of 1914: Prominent Women in the Progressive Era*. Ann Arbor, Mich.: UMI Research Press, 1978.

Cavallo, Dominick. *Muscles and Morals: Organized Playgrounds and Urban Reform, 1880–1920*. Philadelphia: University of Pennsylvania Press, 1981.

Chafe, William H. *The American Woman: Her Changing Social, Economic, and Political Roles.* London: Oxford University Press, 1972.

Christian, Stella, ed. *History of the Texas Federation of Women's Clubs.* Houston, Tex.: Dealey-Adey-Elgin Co., 1919.

Cleaner Dallas League. Scrapbook. Dallas Historical Society.

Clemens, Elisabeth S. "Organizational Repertoires and Institutional Change: Women's Groups and the Transformation of U.S. Politics, 1890–1920." *American Journal of Sociology* 98 (January, 1993): 755–98.

Clinton, Catherine. *The Other Civil War.* New York: Hill and Wang, 1984.

Coller, Ross. Collection. Willard Library, Battle Creek, Mich.

Cousins, R. B., State Superintendent of Public Instruction. *Biennial Report, 1907–08.* Austin, Tex.: Von Boeckmann, Moore and Schutze, 1908.

———. *Biennial Report, 1908–09.* Austin, Tex.: Von Boeckmann, Moore and Schutze, 1909.

———. *Biennial Report, 1909–10.* Austin, Tex.: Von Boeckmann, Moore and Schutze, 1910.

Cox, George W. *History of Public Health in Texas.* Austin: Texas State Department of Health, 1950.

Croly, Jane Cunningham. *Memories of Jane Cunningham Croly: "Jenny June."* New York: G. P. Putnam, 1904.

Cunningham, Minnie Fisher. Papers. Houston Metropolitan Research Center, Houston Public Library, Houston, Tex.

Dallas City Council. Minutes, 1899–1902.

Dallas City Directory, 1897, 1898.

Dallas City Ordinance Book. Vol. 9.

Dallas Free Kindergarten and Industrial Association. *Report, 1903–1904.* Texas/Dallas Division, Dallas Public Library.

Dallas Free Kindergarten Training School and Industrial Association. *Report, 1909–1910.* Texas/Dallas Division, Dallas Public Library.

Dallas Public Library Association. Official Minutes of the Organizational Meeting, 1899. Texas/Dallas Division, Dallas Public Library.

Dallas Woman's Forum. *Yearbook, 1917–1918.*

Daughters of the American Republic, compiler. "Calhoun County, Michigan Marriages, 1836–1870." Undated, typed notebook.

Dealey, George Bannerman. "Story of the *News.*" Undated, unpublished manuscript, A. H. Belo Archives, Dallas, Tex.

———. Undated, unpublished notes, A. H. Belo Archives, Dallas, Tex.

Department of Public Health, City of Dallas. *Ninety Years of Public Health.* Dallas: City of Dallas, 1963.

Dexter, E. G. *History of Education in the United States.* London: Macmillan Company, 1914.

Eagle, Mary Kavanaugh Oldham, ed. *The Congress of Women.* Chicago: American Publishing House, 1894.

Eby, Frederick. *The Development of Education in Texas*. New York: Macmillan Company, 1925.

Enstam, Elizabeth York. "Virginia K. Johnson: A Second Chance for the 'Wayward.'" *Heritage News* 10 (1985): 6–8, 14.

Epstein, Barbara Leslie. *The Politics of Domesticity: Women, Evangelism, and Temperance in the Nineteenth Century*. Middletown, Conn: Wesleyan University Press, 1981.

Fleming, Anne Tyler. Interview with author. Dallas, Tex., July 14, 1994.

Flexner, Eleanor. *Century of Struggle: The Woman's Rights Movement in the United States*. Rev. ed. Cambridge, Mass.: Harvard University Press, Belknap Press, 1975.

Flint, Hallie. Papers. Woodson Research Center, Rice University, Houston, Tex.

Foley, Sara Ramsey. *Toledo Women Writers of Yesterday*. Toledo, Ohio: Kraus Publishers, 1924.

Forman, Allan. "By-the-By." *The Journalist* 8 (January 26, 1889): 1–25.

Frankel, Noralee, and Nancy Dye, eds. *Gender, Class, Race, and Reform in the Progressive Era*. Lexington: University of Kentucky Press, 1991.

Friedman, Jean E. *The Enclosed Garden: Women and Community in the Evangelical South, 1830–1900*. Chapel Hill: University of North Carolina Press, 1985.

Friend, Kate Harrison. Papers. Texas Collection, Baylor University.

Gardner, Washington. *History of Calhoun County, Michigan*. Chicago: Lewis Publishing Company, 1913.

Gordon, Linda. *Woman's Body, Woman's Rights*. New York: Penguin, 1977.

———. ed. *Women, the State, and Welfare*. Madison: University of Wisconsin Press, 1990.

Gordon, Lynn D. *Gender and Higher Education in the Progressive Era*. New Haven, Conn.: Yale University Press, 1990.

Granger, Mrs. A. O. "The Effects of Club Work in the South." *American Academy of Political and Social Science Annals* 28 (September, 1906): 248–56.

Hawes, Joseph M. *Children in Urban Society: Juvenile Delinquency in Nineteenth-Century America*. New York: Oxford University Press, 1971.

———, and N. Ray Hiner, eds. *American Childhood: A Research Guide and Historical Handbook*. Westport, Conn.: Greenwood Press, 1985.

Hayden, Delores. *The Grand Domestic Revolution: A History of Feminist Designs for American Homes, Neighborhoods, and Cities*. Cambridge, Mass.: MIT Press, 1981.

Hazel, Michael V. "A Mother's Touch: The First Two Women Elected to the Dallas School Board." *Heritage News* 12 (Spring, 1987): 9–12.

Herdman, Gerald G. "Glimpses of Early Battle Creek." *Adventist Heritage* (January, 1974): 17–22.

Hiner, N. Ray, and Joseph M. Hawes, eds. *Growing Up in America: Children in Historical Perspective*. Urbana: University of Illinois Press, 1985.

History of the Dallas Federation of Women's Clubs, 1898–1936. Dallas: Clyde C. Cockrell & Sons, 1936.

Hunt, Sylvia. "'Throw Aside the Veil of Helplessness': A Southern Feminist at the 1893 World's Fair." *Southwestern Historical Quarterly* 100 (1996): 49–62.

Hunter, Martha Lavinia. *A Quarter of a Century History of the Dallas Woman's Forum, 1906–1931.* Dallas, Tex.: Clyde Cockrell, 1932.

Igra, Annette, ed. *Battle Creek: The Place behind the Products.* Battle Creek, Mich.: Windsor Publications, 1984.

James, Edward T., ed. *Notable American Women, 1607–1950: A Biographical Dictionary.* Cambridge, Mass.: Harvard University Press, Belknap Press, 1971.

Jebsen, Harry, Robert Newton, and Patricia R. Hogan. "Centennial History of the Dallas, Texas, Park System, 1876–1976." Unpublished report prepared for the City of Dallas Department of Park Administration, Landscape, Architecture, and Horticulture; in cooperation with the Department of History, Texas Tech University, 1976. Texas/Dallas Division, Dallas Public Library.

Johnsen, Leigh. "Brownsberger and Battle Creek: The Beginning of Adventist Higher Education." *Adventist Herald* (Winter, 1976): 30–39.

Johnson, Wanda. Personal Collection, Rockwall, Tex.

June, Jennie [Jane Cunningham Croly]. *Jennie Juneiana: Talks on Women's Topics.* Boston: Lee and Shepherd, 1869.

Kett, Joseph. *Rites of Passage: Adolescence in America, 1790 to the Present.* New York: Basic Books, 1977.

Killits, John A., ed. *Toledo and Lucas County, Ohio, 1623–1923.* Vol 1. Chicago: S. J. Clarke Publishing Company, 1923.

Kraditor, Aileen. *The Ideas of the Woman Suffrage Movement, 1890–1920.* New York: Columbia University Press, 1965.

Larsen, Arthur J., ed. *Crusader and Feminist: Letters of Jane Grey Swisshelm, 1858–1865.* Saint Paul: Minnesota Historical Society, 1934.

Leavitt, Judith W., and Ronald L. Numbers. *Sickness and Health in America: Readings in the History of Medicine and Public Health.* Madison: University of Wisconsin Press, 1978.

Lowe, Berenice Bryant. *Tales of Battle Creek.* Battle Creek, Mich.: Albert L. and Louise B. Miller Foundation, 1976.

Mabee, Carlton, and Susan Mabee Newhouse. *Sojourner Truth: Slave, Prophet, Legend.* New York: New York University Press, 1993.

Marks, Patricia. *Bicycles, Bangs, and Bloomers: The New Woman in the Popular Press.* Lexington: University of Kentucky Press, 1990.

Marsden, Gerald K. "Philanthropy and the Boston Playground Movement, 1885–1907." *Social Science Review* 35 (March, 1961): 48–58.

Marzolf, Marion. *Up from the Footnote: A History of Women Journalists.* New York: Hastings House, 1977.

Matthews, Glenna. *The Rise of Public Woman: Woman's Power and Woman's Place in the United States, 1630–1970.* New York: Oxford University Press, 1992.

May, Elaine Tyler. *Great Expectations: Marriage and Divorce in Post-Victorian America.* Chicago: University of Chicago Press, 1980.

Mayne, Kathleen Crawford. Interview with author. Dallas, Tex., August 8, 1992.

McArthur, Judith N. *Creating the New Woman: The Rise of the Southern Women's Progressive Movement in Texas*. Urbana: University of Illinois Press, forthcoming.

McBride, Genevieve G. *On Wisconsin Women: Working for Their Rights from Settlement to Suffrage*. Madison: University of Wisconsin Press, 1993.

McCallum Family Papers. Austin History Center, Austin, Tex.

McDonald, William L. *Dallas Rediscovered: A Photographic Chronicle of Urban Expansion, 1870–1925*. Dallas, Tex.: Dallas Historical Society, 1978.

McElhaney, Jacquelyn M. "The Only Clean, Bright Spot They Know." *Heritage News* 11 (Fall, 1986): 19–22.

———. "Another Time, Another Place . . . A History of Old City Park." *Heritage News* 7 (Fall, 1982): 6–7.

———. "Childhood in Dallas, 1870–1900." Master's thesis, Southern Methodist University, Dallas, Tex., 1982.

McPherson, James M. *Battle Cry of Freedom*. New York: Oxford University Press, 1988.

Melosi, Martin V. *Garbage in the Cities: Refuse, Reform, and the Environment, 1880–1980*. College Station: Texas A&M University Press, 1981.

———, ed. *Pollution and Reform in American Cities, 1870–1930*. Austin: University of Texas Press, 1980.

Mennell, Robert M. *Thorns and Thistles: Juvenile Delinquents in the United States, 1825–1940*. Hanover, N.H.: The University Press of New England, 1973.

Meyer, Annie Nathan, ed. *Woman's Work in America*. New York: Henry Holt and Company, 1891.

Michigan State Gazetteer and Business Directory. 1875.

Miner, Isadore Sutherland. Vertical File. Ross Coller Collection, Willard Library, Battle Creek, Mich.

———. "The Woman's Department." *National Printer-Journalist* 11, no. 11 (Nov., 1894): 513–15; no. 12 (Dec., 1894): 584–85.

Mitchell, Catherine C., ed. *Margaret Fuller's New York Journalism: A Biographical Essay and Key Writings*. Knoxville: University of Tennessee Press, 1995.

Morrison, C. D., and J. V. Fourmy, comps. *Morrison and Fourmy's General Directory of the City of Dallas, 1891–1892*. Galveston, Tex.: Morrison and Fourmy, 1890.

———. *Morrison and Fourmy's General Directory of the City of Dallas, 1894–1895*. Galveston, Tex.: Morrison and Fourmy, 1893.

Motz, Marilyn Ferris. *True Sisterhood: Michigan Women and Their Kin, 1820–1920*. Albany: State University of New York Press, 1983.

Muncy, Robyn. *Creating a Female Dominion in American Reform, 1890–1935*. London: Oxford University Press, 1991.

Numbers, Ronald L. *Prophetess of Health: A Study of Ellen C. White*. New York: Harper and Row, 1976.

Nye, Russell Blaine. *Society and Culture in America, 1830–1860*. New York: Harper and Row, 1974.

Offen, Karen. "Defining Feminism: A Comparative Historical Approach." *Signs: A Journal of Women in Culture and Society* 14 (Autumn, 1988): 119–57.

O'Neill, William L. *Divorce in the Progressive Era*. New Haven: Yale University Press, 1967.

Payne, Darwin. *Big D: Triumph and Troubles of an American Supercity in the 20th Century*. Dallas, Tex.: Three Forks Press, 1994.

Pivar, David J. *Purity Crusade: Sexual Morality and Social Control, 1868–1900*. Westport, Conn.: Greenwood Press, 1973.

Red Book of Dallas. 1895–96. 1895. Reprint, Dallas, Tex.: A. H. Belo Corporation, 1966.

Rhoads, Mrs. Joel Sutherland. Telephone interviews with author, Jan. 15, 1990, May 27, 1992, and March 29, 1997.

Richardson, Rupert N. *Texas: The Lone Star State*. 2nd ed. Englewood Cliffs, N.J.: Prentice Hall, 1958.

Riis, Jacob A. *How the Other Half Lives*. New York: The Macmillan Company, 1904.

Riley, Glenda. *Inventing the American Woman: An Inclusive History*. 2nd ed. Vol. 2. *Since 1877*. Wheeling, Ill.: Harland Davidson, 1995.

———. *Divorce: An American Tradition*. New York: Oxford University Press, 1991.

Ritchie, Donald A. *Press Gallery: Congress and the Washington Correspondents*. Cambridge, Mass.: Harvard University Press, 1991.

Rockwall County Historical Foundation Collection. Rockwall, Tex.

Rogers, John William. *The Lusty Texans of Dallas*. New York: E. P. Dutton, 1951.

Romig, Walter. *Michigan Place Names*. Grosse Pointe, Mich.: Walter Romig, n.d.

Ross, Ishbel. *Ladies of the Press: The Story of Women in Journalism by an Insider, Ishbel Ross*. New York: Harper Brothers, 1936.

Rothman, Shelia M. *Woman's Proper Place: A History of Changing Ideals and Practices, 1870 to the Present*. New York: Basic Books, 1978.

Ryan, Mary P. *Women in Public: Between Banner and Ballots, 1825–1880*. Baltimore, Md.: The Johns Hopkins University Press, 1990.

Schiebel, Walter J. *Education in Dallas: Ninety-Two Years of History*. Dallas, Tex.: Taylor Publishing Company, 1966.

Schlesinger, Elizabeth Bancroft. "The Nineteenth-Century Woman's Dilemma and Jennie June." *New York History* (October, 1961): 3–17.

———. "Fanny Fern: Our Grandmother's Mentor." *New York Historical Society Quarterly* 38 (October, 1954): 501–19.

Schlossman, Steven L. *Love and the American Delinquent: The Theory and Practice of "Progressive" Juvenile Justice, 1825–1920*. Chicago: University of Chicago Press, 1977.

Scott, Ann Firor. *Natural Allies: Women's Associations in American History*. Urbana: University of Illinois Press, 1991.

———. "The 'New Woman' in the New South." *South Atlantic Quarterly* 61 (Autumn, 1962): 473–83.

Seaholm, Megan. "Ernest Women: The White Woman's Club Movement in Progressive Era Texas, 1880–1920." Ph.D. diss., Rice University, Houston, Tex., 1988.

Sklar, Kathryn Kish. *Florence Kelley and the Nation's Work: The Rise of Women's Political Culture, 1830–1900.* New Haven, Conn.: Yale University Press, 1995.

Solomon, Barbara Miller. *In the Company of Educated Women: A History of Women and Higher Education in America.* New Haven, Conn.: Yale University Press, 1985.

Solomon, Martha M., ed. *A Voice of Their Own: The Woman Suffrage Press, 1840–1910.* Tuscaloosa: University of Alabama Press, 1991.

South, Amy. "How Jeff's Bridge Divided B.C." *Scene Magazine* (April, 1987): 25–26.

Spalding, Arthur Whitefield. *Origin and History of Seventh-day Adventists.* Vol. 2. Washington, D.C.: Review and Herald Publishing Association, n.d.

Stanton, Elizabeth Cady. "Divorce vs. Domestic Warfare." *Arena* 1 (1890): 560–69.

Stearns, Bertha-Monica. "Reform Periodicals and Female Reforms, 1830–1860." *American Historical Quarterly* 37 (July, 1932): 678–99.

Steele, Jeffrey, ed. *The Essential Margaret Fuller.* New Brunswick, N.J.: Rutgers University Press, 1992.

Strasser, Susan. *Never Done: A History of Housework in America.* New York: Pantheon Books, 1982.

Terrell, Mrs. J. C. "Succinct History of the Women's Club Movement." *Dallas Morning News,* November 22, 1903.

Texas Federation of Women's Clubs, ed. *Who's Who of the Womanhood of Texas.* Vol. 1. *1923–1924.* Fort Worth: The Federation, 1924.

Thompson, Joyce. *Marking a Trail: A History of the Texas Woman's University.* Denton: Texas Woman's University Press, 1982.

Tiffin, Susan. *In Whose Best Interest? Child Welfare Reforms in the Progressive Era.* Westport, Conn.: Greenwood Press, 1982.

Toledo City Directory. Toledo, Ohio: R. L. Polk and Co., 1891, 1892.

Urbanski, Marie Mitchell Olesen, ed. *Margaret Fuller: Visionary of the New Age.* Orono, Maine: Northern Lights, 1994.

U.S. Bureau of the Census. *Population of the United States in 1860.* Washington, D.C.: Government Printing Office, 1864.

———. *Statistics of Population of the United States at the Tenth Census, 1880.* Washington, D.C.: Government Printing Office, 1887.

———. *Compendium of the Eleventh Census: Population, 1890.* Washington, D.C.: Government Printing Office, 1892.

———. 1900 Manuscript Census, Dallas County.

———. 1900 Manuscript Census, Grayson County.

———. *Twelfth Census of the United States.* Vol. 2. *Population.* Pt. 2, *1900.* Washington, D.C.: Government Printing Office, 1902.

———. *Women in Gainful Occupations, 1870–1920.* Compiled by Joseph Hill. Census Monograph 9. Washington D.C.: Government Printing Office, 1929.

U.S. Department of Commerce, Bureau of the Census. *Historical Statistics of the U.S., Colonial Times to 1970.* Pt. 1. Washington, D.C.: Government Printing Office, 1975.

U.S. Statutes at Large. Vol. 12. Thirty-Seventh Congress, Session II, 1862.

———. Vol. 13. Thirty-Eighth Congress, Session I, 1864.

———. Vol. 14. Thirty-Ninth Congress, Session I, 1866.

Valenza, Janet. "'Taking the Waters' at Texas's Health Spas." *Southwestern Historical Quarterly* 98 (January, 1995): 426–56.

Vande Vere, Emmett K. *The Wisdom Seekers.* Nashville: Southern Publishing Company, n.d.

Varon, Elizabeth R. "Tippecanoe and the Ladies, Too: White Women and Party Politics in Antebellum Virginia." *Journal of American History* 82 (September, 1995): 494–521.

Von Mehren, Joan. *Minerva and the Muse: A Life of Margaret Fuller.* Amherst: University of Massachusetts Press, 1994.

Walker, Nancy A. *Fanny Fern.* New York: Twayne Publishers, 1993.

Warner, Sam Bass, Jr. *The Urban Wilderness: A History of the American City.* New York: Harper and Row, 1973.

Warren, Joyce W. *Fanny Fern: An Independent Woman.* New Brunswick, N.J.: Rutgers University Press, 1992.

Wasson, Alonzo. "The Good Old Days of the Dallas News: And Some of the Stalwarts Who Made It." Reprint from the Texas Unlimited Edition of the *Dallas Morning News*, May 22, 1949.

Wedell, Marsha. *Elite Women and the Reform Impulse in Memphis, 1875–1915.* Knoxville: University of Tennessee Press, 1991.

Welter, Barbara, ed. *Dimity Convictions: The American Woman in the Nineteenth Century.* Athens: University of Ohio Press, 1976.

Wheeler, Marjorie Spruill. *New Women of the New South: The Leaders of the Woman Suffrage Movement in the Southern States.* New York: Oxford University Press, 1993.

Winegarten, Ruthe, and Judith N. McArthur, eds. *Citizens At Last: The Woman Suffrage Movement in Texas.* Austin, Tex.: Ellen C. Temple, 1987.

Woloch, Nancy, ed. *Women and the American Experience.* New York: McGraw Hill, 1994.

Women Alive! Coalition, Rules, and Achievements Committee, YWCA. *In Search of Our Past: Women of Northeast Ohio.* Vol. 1. Toledo, Ohio: YWCA, 1987.

Wood, Ann D. "The 'Scribbling Women' and Fanny Fern: Why Women Wrote." *American Quarterly* 23 (Spring, 1971): 3–24.

Wood, Mary I. *History of the General Federation of Women's Clubs.* New York: History Department, General Federation of Women's Clubs, 1912.

Index

Note: Pages with illustrations are indicated by italic type.